REVIEW AND ASSESSMENT OF THE INDONESIA–MALAYSIA–THAILAND GROWTH TRIANGLE ECONOMIC CORRIDORS

INDONESIA COUNTRY REPORT

Sandy Nur Ikfal Raharjo

MARCH 2023

ASIAN DEVELOPMENT BANK

ADB

CONTENTS

Tables, Figures, and Maps iv
Acknowledgments vii
Abbreviations ix

CHAPTER 1: INTRODUCTION **1**
    Overview 2
    Study Objectives 2
    Methodology 2
    Structure of the Report 3
    Existing Economic Corridors 4

CHAPTER 2: DEVELOPMENT CONTEXT **7**

CHAPTER 3: REVIEW OF THE ECONOMIC CORRIDORS IN INDONESIA **14**
    Economic Corridor 1. The Extended Songkhla–Penang–Medan Economic Corridor 15
    Economic Corridor 3. The Banda Aceh–Medan–Pekanbaru–Palembang Economic Corridor 32
    Economic Corridor 4. The Melaka–Dumai Economic Corridor 56
    Economic Corridor 5. The Ranong–Phuket–Aceh Economic Corridor 71

CHAPTER 4: PROPOSED ROUTE FOR ECONOMIC CORRIDOR 6 .... **86**

CHAPTER 5: THE NETWORK OF IMT-GT ECONOMIC CORRIDORS **106**

CHAPTER 6: ECONOMIC CORRIDORS FROM A VALUE CHAIN PERSPECTIVE **111**

CHAPTER 7: ADDRESSING GAPS IN INSTITUTIONAL MECHANISMS FOR ECONOMIC CORRIDOR DEVELOPMENT **132**

CHAPTER 8: SUMMARY OF FINDINGS AND RECOMMENDATIONS **139**

REFERENCES **147**

APPENDIXES **154**
    Appendix 1: Physical Connectivity Projects of the IMT-GT Implementation Blueprint 2017–2021 155
    Appendix 2: Ministries and Agencies Involved During the Country Consultations 159

TABLES, FIGURES, AND MAPS

Tables

1	IMT-GT Provinces and States	9
2	Growth Areas in Sumatera Region Development Plan	11
3	Economic Corridor 1: Socioeconomic Profile of North Sumatera	18
4	Economic Corridor 1: Maritime Connectivity in Indonesia	19
5	Economic Corridor 1: Flight Routes in Kualanamu International Airport, North Sumatera	20
6	Economic Corridor 1: North Sumatera's Foreign Trade Volume	21
7	Economic Corridor 1: North Sumatera's Foreign Trade Value	21
8	Economic Corridor 1: Foreign Trade Volume Handled by International Gateways in North Sumatera, 2014–2018	22
9	Economic Corridor 1: Top Three Commodities Traded through Belawan Port, 2018	23
10	Economic Corridor 1: North Sumatera's Trade Volume with Malaysia	23
11	Economic Corridor 1: North Sumatera's Trade Volume with Thailand	24
12	Economic Corridor 1: Foreign Visitor Arrivals in North Sumatera	25
13	Economic Corridor 1: Existing and Additional Provinces and Nodes, by Type	29
14	Economic Corridor 3: Basic Information on Existing Corridor Nodes	32
15	Economic Corridor 3: Population and Population Density in Aceh, North Sumatera, Riau, and South Sumatera	34
16	Economic Corridor 3: GRDP and GRDP per Capita of Aceh, North Sumatera, Riau, and South Sumatera	35
17	Economic Corridor 3: Status of Land Connectivity	36
18	Economic Corridor 3: Maritime Links of Ports in Aceh, North Sumatera, Riau, and South Sumatera	39
19	Economic Corridor 3: Flight Routes Served by Airports in Aceh, North Sumatera, Riau, and South Sumatera	40
20	Economic Corridor 3: Foreign Trade Volume of Aceh, North Sumatera, Riau, and South Sumatera, 2018	42
21	Economic Corridor 3: Foreign Trade Volume and Value of Economic Corridor 3 Provinces with Malaysia and Thailand, 2018	43
22	Economic Corridor 3: Domestic Trade of Provinces in Sumatera, 2018	43
23	Economic Corridor 3: Domestic Trade among Economic Corridor 3 Provinces in Sumatera and with Java, 2018	44
24	Economic Corridor 3: Transportation Usage for Domestic Trade Activities, 2018	45
25	Economic Corridor 3: Foreign Visitor Arrivals in Aceh, North Sumatera, Riau, and South Sumatera, 2018	46
26	Economic Corridor 3: Special Economic Zones	48
27	Economic Corridor 3: Existing and Additional Provinces and Nodes, by Type	50
28	Economic Corridor 4: Socioeconomic Profile of Riau Province	56
29	Economic Corridor 4: Maritime Connectivity of Dumai Port	60
30	Economic Corridor 4: Main Services in Dumai Port	61
31	Economic Corridor 4: Flight Routes Served by Airports in Riau Province	61
32	Economic Corridor 4: Riau Province's Foreign Trade Volume	62
33	Economic Corridor 4: Riau Province's Foreign Trade Value	62
34	Economic Corridor 4: Main Trading Ports in Riau Province, 2018	63
35	Economic Corridor 4: Riau's Trade Volume with Malaysia	63
36	Economic Corridor 4: Riau's Trade Value with Malaysia	64

37 Economic Corridor 4: Foreign Visitor Arrivals in Riau's Sultan Syarif Kasim II   64
    International Airport, 2015–2018
38 Economic Corridor 4: Existing and Additional Provinces and Nodes, by Type   70
39 Economic Corridor 5: Existing Nodes in Aceh Province by Type   71
40 Economic Corridor 5: Socioeconomic Profile of Aceh Province   74
41 Economic Corridor 5: Status of Maritime Connectivity of Ports in Aceh   77
42 Economic Corridor 5: Flight Routes in Sultan Iskandar Muda International Airport, Aceh   77
43 Economic Corridor 5: Aceh's Foreign Trade Volume, 2007, 2014–2018   78
44 Economic Corridor 5: Aceh's Foreign Trade Value, 2007, 2018–2018   78
45 Economic Corridor 5: Major Trade Gateways in Aceh, 2018   79
46 Economic Corridor 5: Aceh Trade with Thailand (million tons)   80
47 Economic Corridor 5: Aceh Trade with Thailand ($ million)   80
48 Economic Corridor 5: Top Exports and Imports of Aceh with Thailand, 2018   81
49 Economic Corridor 5: Foreign Visitor Arrivals in Aceh, 2017–2018   81
50 Economic Corridor 5: Number of Visitor Arrivals to Sabang, 2013–2017   82
51 Economic Corridor 5: Number of Cruise Ships and Yacht Arrivals to Sabang   82
52 Economic Corridor 5: Existing and Additional Provinces and Nodes, by Type   84
53 Provinces, States, and Nodes in the Proposed Economic Corridor 6, by Type   95
54 Economic Corridor 6: Socioeconomic Profile of the Provinces in Southern Sumatera   96
55 Economic Corridor 6: Port Links in Sumatera   98
56 Economic Corridor 6: Domestic and International Destinations Served by Airports in Sumatera   99
57 Economic Corridor 6: Trade between Riau Islands Province and Malaysia 2014–2018   100
58 Economic Corridor 6: Major Export–Import Commodities Traded   100
    by Riau Islands Province with Malaysia, 2018
59 Economic Corridor 6: Trade between Riau Islands Province and Thailand 2014–2018   101
60 Economic Corridor 6: Major Export–Import Commodities of Riau Islands Province with Thailand, 2018   101
61 Economic Corridor 6: Trade between Bangka Belitung Islands Province and Malaysia, 2015–2018   102
62 Economic Corridor 6: Trade between Bangka Belitung Islands Province and Thailand, 2014–2018   103
63 Economic Corridor 6: Trade of Four Mainland Sumatera Provinces with Malaysia and Thailand, 2018   104
64 Economic Corridor 6: Major Commodities Traded between the Four Mainland Sumatera Provinces   104
    and Malaysia and Thailand, 2018
65 Economic Corridors Involved in Major Commodities Traded in Sumatera   112
66 Palm Oil Plantations and Production in Sumatera, 2018   114
67 Palm Oil Mills by Province in Sumatera, 2017   115
68 Volume of Crude Palm Oil Exports by Port of Loading, 2018   116
69 Value of Crude Palm Oil Exports by Port of Loading, 2018   116
70 Top Destination Countries of Indonesia's Palm Oil Exports, 2018   117
71 Production of Capture Fisheries and Horticulture in Sumatera, 2017   122
72 Number of LPPOM Halal-Certified Products, 2012–2017   124
73 Rubber Plantations and Production in Sumatera, 2018   126
74 Natural Rubber Factories by Province in Sumatera, 2020   128
75 Volume of Rubber Exports by Port of Loading, 2018   129
76 Top Destination Countries of Indonesia's Rubber Exports, 2018   130
A1.1   Economic Corridor 1   155
A1.2   Economic Corridor 3   156
A1.3   Economic Corridor 4   158
A1.4   Economic Corridor 5   158

Figures

1   Palm Oil Supply Chain   113
2   Palm Oil Exports by Products, 2015–2019   118
3   Halal Food and Beverage Value Chain in Indonesia   121
4   Procedure for Halal Product Certification in BPJPH   123
5   IMT-GT Institutional Coordination Mechanism Structure   134

Maps

1   Five Indonesia–Malaysia–Thailand Growth Triangle Economic Corridors   5
2   Growth Corridor and Equalization Corridor in Sumatera   10
3   Indicative Plan for Sumatera   12
4   Extended Songkhla–Penang–Medan Economic Corridor (Economic Corridor 1)   16
5   Extended Songkhla–Penang–Medan Economic Corridor (Economic Corridor 1) - Indonesia   17
6   Southern Thailand–Northern Malaysia–North Sumatera Economic Corridor   30
    (Reconfigured Economic Corridor 1) - Indonesia
7   Southern Thailand–Northern Malaysia–North Sumatera Economic Corridor   31
    (Reconfigured Economic Corridor 1)
8   Banda Aceh–Medan–Pekanbaru–Palembang Economic Corridor (Economic Corridor 3)   33
9   Trans-Sumatera Toll Road   37
10 Trans-Sumatera Economic Corridor (Reconfigured Economic Corridor 3)   51
11 Melaka–Dumai Economic Corridor (Economic Corridor 4)   57
12 Melaka–Dumai Economic Corridor (Economic Corridor 4) - Indonesia   58
13 Central Sumatera–Southern Malaysia Economic Corridor   67
    (Reconfigured Economic Corridor 4) - Indonesia
14 Central Sumatera–Southern Malaysia Economic Corridor   68
    (Reconfigured Economic Corridor 4)
15 Ranong–Phuket–Aceh Economic Corridor (Economic Corridor 5)   72
16 Ranong–Phuket–Aceh Economic Corridor (Economic Corridor 5) - Indonesia   73
17 Southwestern Thailand–Northern Sumatera–Northwestern Malaysia Economic Corridor   85
    (Reconfigured Economic Corridor 5)
18 Southeastern Thailand–Eastern Malaysia–Southern Sumatera Economic Corridor   91
    (Proposed Route for Economic Corridor 6)
19   Southeastern Thailand–Eastern Malaysia–Southern Sumatera Economic Corridor   92
    (Proposed Route for Economic Corridor 6) - Indonesia
20 Interlink Corridors in Indonesia   109
21 Six Indonesia–Malaysia–Thailand Growth Triangle Economic Corridors   141

ACKNOWLEDGMENTS

This technical study was coordinated by a team in the Regional Cooperation and Operations Division (SERC), Southeast Asia Department of the Asian Development Bank (ADB). The technical study forms part of the analytical work produced under the ADB Technical Assistance 9572: Enhancing Effectiveness of Subregional Programs to Advance Regional Cooperation and Integration in Southeast Asia, which has funding support from the People's Republic of China Regional Cooperation and Poverty Reduction Fund, and the Republic of Korea e-Asia and Knowledge Partnership Fund.

The study was conducted by a team of consultants led by Carolina S. Guina, regional cooperation expert and team leader who provided specific guidance in carrying out the study and wrote the integrative report. A team of national consultants conducted the research on economic corridors in Indonesia, Malaysia, and Thailand and wrote the individual country reports. They are Sandy Nur Ikfal Raharjo (Indonesia), Abdul Rahim Anuar (Malaysia), and Pawat Tangtrongjita (Thailand).

Alfredo Perdiguero, director of SERC, and Gary Krishnan, senior country specialist, supervised the study team. Maria Theresa Bugayong, senior operations officer (Resource Planning), and Jordana Queddeng-Cosme, consultant, provided technical and logistic support and coordinated the field visits where they also participated.

The Indonesia–Malaysia–Thailand Growth Triangle (IMT-GT) ministers Agus Suparmanto, minister of trade, Republic of Indonesia; Dato' Sri Mustapa Mohamed, minister in Prime Minister's Department (Economy), Malaysia; and Arkhom Termpittayapaisith, minister of finance, the Kingdom of Thailand, at the 26th IMT-GT Ministerial Meeting held in November 2020, provided overall strategic guidance in the course of reviewing the report.

The study benefited from the valuable inputs and insights of the following senior officials: Rizal Affandi Lukman and Raldi Hendro Koestoer, Coordinating Ministry for Economic Affairs of Indonesia; Saiful Anuar Bin Lebai Hussen, Noor Zari Bin Hamat, Mohd Shafiee B. Mohd Shah, and Sarimah Binti Amran, Economic Planning Unit, Prime Minister's Office of Malaysia; and Danucha Pitchayanan, Pattama Teanravisitsagool, and Wanchat Suwankitti, Office of the National Economic and Social Development Council of Thailand. The national secretariats worked closely with the team, especially the national consultants, in facilitating access to information and data, arranging and participating in consultations with various stakeholders and meticulously reviewing the many drafts of the report. They are Netty Muharni, Tri Hidayatno, Sonny Ameriansah Soekoer of the Coordinating Ministry of Economic Affairs in Indonesia; Suhana Binti Md Saleh, Ahmad Zamri Bin Khairuddin, Balamurugan Ratha Krishnan, Nurul Ezzah Binti Md Zin, Mohammad Akhir Abdul Rahman, and Mattias Murphy Lai of the Economic Planning Unit, Prime Minister's Office in Malaysia; and Thuttai Keeratipongpaiboon, Chiraphat Chotipimai, Orachat Sungkhamanee, Potcharapol Prommatat, and Puntasith Charoenpanichpun of the Office of the National Economic and Social Development Council of Thailand. The Centre for IMT-GT Subregional Cooperation headed by Firdaus Dahlan and relevant IMT-GT working groups also provided insights.

The integrative report and country reports were copyedited by Maria Theresa Mercado and proofread by Maria Guia de Guzman and Jess Alfonso Macasaet. Michael Cortes handled typesetting, graphics generation, and designed the cover artwork. Pamela Asis-Layugan, Alona Mae Agustin, Raquel Tabanao, Nicole Marie Afable, Marian Macabingkil, Cira Rudas, and Camille Genevieve Salvador provided overall assistance in the publications process. Angel Villarez and Rienzi Niccolo Velasco prepared the maps under the supervision of Abraham Villanueva and Carmela Fernando-Villamar. The ADB Department of Communications team provided invaluable assistance in design and publishing.

ABBREVIATIONS

ADB	Asian Development Bank
ASEAN	Association of Southeast Asian Nations
BCP	border crossing point
BPKS	Badan Pengusahaan Kawasan Sabang (Sabang Free Trade Zone and Free Port Authority)
BPS	Badan Pusat Statistik (Central Bureau of Statistics)
CMEA	Coordinating Ministry of Economic Affairs
CMGF	Chief Ministers and Governors Forum
CPKO	crude palm kernel oil
CPO	crude palm oil
DWT	dead weight ton
EC	economic corridor
ECRL	East Coast Rail Link
GDP	gross domestic product
GRDP	gross regional domestic product
GT	gross ton
ha	hectare
HS	harmonized system
IB	Implementation Blueprint
IMT-GT	Indonesia–Malaysia–Thailand Growth Triangle
JBC	Joint Business Council
LNG	liquefied natural gas
LPPOM	Lembaga Pengkajian Pangan, Obat-obatan, dan Kosmetika Majelis Ulama Indonesia (Assessment Institute for Foods, Drugs, and Cosmetics)
PRC	People's Republic of China
PT	Perseroan Terbatas (Limited Company)
Ro-Ro	roll on, roll off
RPJMN	Rencana Pembangunan Jangka Menengah Nasional (National Medium-Term Development Plan)
RPJPN	Rencana Pembangunan Jangka Panjang Nasional (National Long-Term Development Plan)
SAPULA	Sabang–Phuket–Langkawi
SEC	Southern Economic Corridor
SEZ	special economic zone
SIR	Standard Indonesian Rubber
TEU	20-foot equivalent unit
US	United States

CHAPTER

1

INTRODUCTION

Overview

On 1 October 2018 in Melaka, Malaysia, the 24th Indonesia–Malaysia–Thailand Growth Triangle (IMT-GT) Ministerial Meeting directed a review of existing IMT-GT economic corridors (ECs), and a study of the proposed sixth corridor linking Pattani–Yala–Narathiwat in Thailand with Perak and Kelantan in Malaysia, and with southern Sumatera in Indonesia. The countries requested technical assistance from the Asian Development Bank (ADB) in conducting this review.

The economic corridor (EC) approach to development was first emphasized in the IMT-GT Road Map 2007–2011 as a key anchor for clustering major economic activities in the subregion. The IMT-GT Implementation Blueprint 2012–2016 (IB 2012–2016)—the successor to the road map—included economic corridor development programs and projects among the flagship initiatives in the transport and energy sector. The importance of economic corridors was carried over to the IB 2017–2021, which reaffirmed economic corridor development as a spatial framework to help achieve the IMT-GT 2036 Vision.

The IMT-GT strategic framework documents over the past years indicate the absence of a definitive framework for economic corridor development at a subregional level. The progress achieved so far has resulted from independent national initiatives vetted through the IMT-GT platform rather than from deliberate, evidence-based, corridor-wide planning at the subregional level. This review is the first endeavor that looks at economic corridors from a broader perspective since it became a focus of IMT-GT economic cooperation in 2007.[1]

Study Objectives

In assessing the IMT-GT economic corridors, this review aims to:

(i) analyze the corridors' connections by road, rail, sea, and air;

(ii) identify gaps in such connections, and recommend new routes for expansion of economic opportunities;

(iii) review the proposed sixth EC, and recommend its configuration;

(iv) review links between ECs and the emerging subregional corridor network;

(v) review ECs from a value chain perspective;

(vi) recommend ways to improve EC development.

Methodology

As an initial activity, the study identified specific nodes in each corridor to establish the role of different economic units in relation to the major transport backbone and gateways. The nodes provided the reference points for assessing connectivity in the corridor. It also provided the basis for identifying linkages with potential nodes by expanding the corridor configuration based on emerging national strategies and economic opportunities. The nodes were classified according to the roles they perform: capital cities and urban areas, commercial nodes, border crossing points (BCPs), maritime gateway ports, tourism nodes, and interlink nodes.

---

[1]   C. S. Guina. 2023. *Review and Assessment of the Indonesia–Malaysia–Thailand Growth Triangle Economic Corridors: Integrative Report*. Manila: Asian Development Bank. The introduction was based on the integrative report, which is published as a separate publication.

The study considered possibilities for expanding existing corridors to other provinces and states. The motivation was to loop strategically positioned areas in the government's spatial strategy into the regional economic corridors to derive additional benefits from continuity and scale effects. The expanded corridor would optimize regional spatial use by taking advantage of new production, growth, and logistics centers located in a wider area; enhance supply chain opportunities; and contribute to a more equitable distribution of benefits. The additional provinces or states can upgrade to the main logistics routes that connect to other corridor networks, thus diversifying economic and social outcomes.

The study also looked at the value chain[2] of three major products in IMT-GT—palm oil, rubber, and halal foods—to get a broad perspective on the geography of their production, processing, and distribution components in the economic corridors. The geography of value chain components is a basis for determining the appropriate interventions to make the chain more efficient and their products more competitive.

The study is qualitative in nature and draws its observations and findings from inferences and interpretation of data collected from official and other sources. Desk research was conducted on IMT-GT documents, reports of meetings, references, and research materials. Fieldwork in Indonesia was conducted with the team leader during 21–26 October 2019 and 3–7 December 2019. In addition, the national consultant also participated in the IMT-GT Cruise Business Forum in Sabang, 15–17 October 2021. The ministries and agencies involved in providing relevant information during the fieldwork are listed in Appendix 2.

The fieldwork covered many of the corridor provinces and involved meetings with the National Secretariat of Indonesia, relevant line ministries, bodies responsible for spatial development programs or national corridors, provincial and state planning units, ports authorities, customs houses at border crossing points (BCPs), and the private sector (including representatives from the IMT-GT Joint Business Council [JBC]).

Several consultations with the national secretariat were also conducted in the course of the study. The representatives from various ministries and agencies that participated during the consultations with the national secretariat are also listed in Appendix 2.

Structure of the Report

The Indonesia Country Report, which has been incorporated into the integrative report, is divided into eight chapters as follows:

(i)   Introduction (Chapter 1),

(ii)   Development Context (Chapter 2),

(iii)   Review of Economic Corridors in Indonesia (Chapter 3),

(iv)   Proposed Route for Economic Corridor 6 (Chapter 4),

(v)   The Network of IMT-GT Economic Corridors (Chapter 5),

(vi)   Economic Corridors from a Value Chain Perspective (Chapter 6),

---

[2]   In this study, the distinction between the terms **value chain** and **supply chain** is not strictly applied. It is noted that a value chain is a process by which a company adds value to its raw materials to produce products eventually sold to consumers, while the supply chain represents all the steps required to get the product to the customer. https://www.investopedia.com/ask/answers/043015/what-difference-between-value-chain-and-supply-chain.asp#:~:text=The%20value%20chain%20is%20a,the%20product%20to%20the%20customer.

(vii)   Addressing Gaps in Institutional Mechanisms for Economic Corridor Development (Chapter 7), and

(viii) Summary of Findings and Recommendations (Chapter 8).

The study comes in four separate publications—the integrative report, which presents the overall findings from a subregional perspective, and individual county reports for Indonesia, Malaysia, and Thailand, which reflect the national perspectives.

Existing Economic Corridors

There are five existing IMT-GT economic corridors (Map 1). The new EC6 corridor was proposed by Thailand at the 24th IMT-GT Ministerial Meeting in Melaka in October 2018. Provinces in Sumatera are participating in four of the five economic corridors. EC1 includes North Sumatera; EC3 includes North Sumatera, South Sumatera, Riau, and Aceh; EC4 includes Riau across Melaka State in Malaysia, and EC5 includes Aceh. The reconfiguration of the existing corridors and the proposed route for EC6 have included the remaining eight provinces, thus bringing all 10 provinces in Sumatera as part of the IMT-GT network of economic corridors.

The five existing ECs are described briefly below:

(i)   **Extended Songkhla–Penang–Medan Economic Corridor (EC1)**. EC1 consists of three main sections: two overland routes and a maritime route. The two overland routes connect (i) the Southern Thailand provinces of Nakhon Si Thammarat, Phatthalung, and Pattani with the international gateway port in Songkhla, Yala, and Narathiwat; (ii) an overland route from Songkhla to Penang; and (iii) the maritime route that links Penang to Medan, the capital of North Sumatera, across the Strait of Malacca. Within North Sumatera, the important land connectivity is between Medan City and Belawan Port. Belawan Port in Medan is currently the main international port that supports this maritime connectivity segment. EC1 hosts some of the most agriculture-rich provinces in Southern Thailand that trade with Malaysia, Sumatera, and Singapore and plays a vital role in the supply chain of traded goods outside the subregion. EC1 covers several provinces in the border areas of Malaysia and Thailand and serves as the anchor for clustering major economic activities through the development of industrial hubs and special economic zones.

(ii) **Strait of Malacca Economic Corridor (EC2)**. EC2 is a coastal corridor connecting Thailand's southern provinces of Trang and Satun with Malaysia's states of Perlis, and on to Port Klang, Penang, and Melaka along the western coast. The maritime gateways in EC2 under the existing configuration are Tammalang Port (Satun), Port Klang (Selangor), Penang Port (Penang), and Tanjung Bruas Port (Melaka). The approach to corridor connectivity is multimodal, with land and coastal linkages. Due to the proximity of this corridor to Sumatera, there is considerable potential to complement the various stages of the production chain with the island, especially if a series of economic and industrial zones are established at strategic points along the corridor. This corridor has the potential to serve as a food hub, especially for halal, since a number of food terminals and integrated food centers are being planned within the corridor.

(iii) **Banda Aceh–Medan–Pekanbaru–Palembang Economic Corridor (EC3)**. EC3 is a national corridor in Sumatera. Connectivity among these provinces is envisaged to build traffic volume leading to Sumatera's international ports along its eastern coast—Banda Aceh, Medan, Pekanbaru, Dumai, and Jambi—complementing coastal connectivity with ports in Penang and Melaka. This corridor, which is part of the Association of Southeast Asian Nations (ASEAN) Highway Network, is critical for developing Sumatera, as well as an important building block for further enhancing connectivity within the IMT-GT subregion. Its development is closely linked with that of the other three corridors.

Map 1: Five Indonesia–Malaysia–Thailand Growth Triangle Economic Corridors

INDONESIA–MALAYSIA–THAILAND
GROWTH TRIANGLE

Ranong–Phuket–Aceh
Economic Corridor (EC5)

Extended Songkhla–
Penang–Medan
Economic Corridor (EC1)

Strait of Malacca
Economic Corridor (EC2)

Melaka–Dumai
Economic Corridor (EC4)

Banda Aceh–Medan–
Pekanbaru–Palembang
Economic Corridor (EC3)

Legend:
- ⊛ National Capital
- ◉ Provincial/State Capital
- ● City/Town
- ⊕ Airport
- —— National Road
- —— Other Road
- ·········· Provincial Boundary
- –··–··– International Boundary
- **EC** = economic corridor

Boundaries are not necessarily authoritative.

This map was produced by the cartography unit of the Asian Development Bank. The boundaries, colors, denominations, and any other information shown on this map do not imply, on the part of the Asian Development Bank, any judgment on the legal status of any territory, or any endorsement or acceptance of such boundaries, colors, denominations, or information.

Source: Asian Development Bank.

(iv) **Melaka–Dumai Economic Corridor (EC4)**. EC4 is a maritime corridor linking Riau Province in Sumatera to the state of Melaka in Peninsular Malaysia. The underpinning economic rationale for this link is based on the strategic location of Dumai Port and Tanjung Bruas Port located opposite each other in one of the narrowest stretches of the Strait of Malacca, thus having the shortest distance between them across the Strait. The corridor includes the development of land connectivity to Dumai Port and the development of Tanjung Bruas Port. EC4 has a long tradition of freight and passenger traffic between Sumatera and Malaysia. Dumai is the gateway port of Riau Province, one of the richest provinces of Indonesia with abundant palm oil plantations and on–shore oil and gas resources. Dumai is principally a palm oil-related export port with general cargo, fertilizer, cement, and rice being the primary import traffic.

(v) **Ranong–Phuket–Aceh Economic Corridor (EC5)**. EC5 is mainly a maritime corridor linking ports in the northern part of Sumatera (mainly Ulee Lheue and Malahayati in Aceh Province) with Southern Thailand along its western coast facing the Andaman Sea, intending to exploit tourism potentials. In Sumatera, Aceh Province is part of the corridor and Banda Aceh, the capital, and Sabang (located in the adjacent We Island) are the gateway and tourism nodes, respectively. EC5 is envisaged to enhance the connectivity between Sumatera and Southern Thailand primarily through the maritime mode. Connectivity was envisaged to be established through the development of facilities in key ports in Sumatera.

In Indonesia, there are 10 provinces in Sumatera participating in the IMT-GT, four of which are involved in four existing corridors—EC1, EC3, EC4, and EC5. These provinces are Aceh, North Sumatera, South Sumatera, and Riau. EC3, a national corridor, was expanded to include four additional provinces: West Sumatera, Jambi, Bengkulu, and Lampung. The two archipelagic provinces of Riau Islands and Bangka Belitung Islands were included in EC6. Thus, all 10 provinces in Sumatera are now part of the IMT-GT economic corridor network.

CHAPTER

2

DEVELOPMENT CONTEXT

As a nation-state, Indonesia aspires to be an independent, united, sovereign, just, and prosperous nation (Preamble of the 1945 Constitution). These ideals were reaffirmed in the National Long-Term Development Plan (RPJPN) 2005–2025 which set the vision of "an Independent, Advanced, Fair, and Prosperous Indonesia."[3] To realize this vision, eight development missions have been established, one of which is "to realize equitable development and justice."[4] The mission mandates the state to support linkages of economic activities in underdeveloped and remote areas with fast-growing and strategic areas by developing "regional economic development systems."[5] The development orientation in border areas would also need to be changed from "inward-looking" to "outward-looking" to serve as gateways for economic and trade activities with neighboring countries.[6]

The mission to develop disadvantaged areas and borders above also inspired the development of subregional economic cooperation. The Indonesia–Malaysia–Thailand Growth Triangle (IMT-GT) was formed in 1993 to accelerate the economic transformation of underdeveloped provinces or states in the three member countries. The objective is to narrow the development gap between regions in the three countries near or adjacent to each other.[7]

The IMT-GT is a subregional cooperation program that aims to accelerate economic cooperation and integration between Indonesia, Malaysia, and Thailand. The program involves 32 provinces or states with a combined population of around 70 million people, consisting of 10 provinces of Indonesia, 8 states of Malaysia, and 14 provinces of Thailand. The IMT-GT promotes private sector-led economic growth and facilitates subregional development by exploiting member countries' complementary and comparative advantages.[8]

All participating provinces of Indonesia in IMT-GT are located on the island of Sumatera. Sumatera plays a vital role in Indonesia's national development. The island's land area of 480,793.3 square kilometers (km^2) is 25.08% of Indonesia's total land area. In 2018, 57.74 million people live in Sumatera, or about 22% of Indonesia's total population. The cumulative gross regional domestic product (GRDP) of the 10 Sumatera provinces was Rp2.23 quadrillion in 2018 (equivalent to $153.96 billion), contributing 21.39% of Indonesia's gross domestic product (GDP).

Sumatera is envisaged to maintain its strategic role in the future development of Indonesia. The National Medium-Term Development Plan (RPJMN) 2020–2024, issued through Presidential Regulation No.18/2020, is the last in a series of four medium-term plans that form part of Indonesia's RPJPN 2005–2025. It is the starting point for achieving Indonesia's vision in the next 20 years—Vision 2045—which aspires for "A Developed Indonesia" to rank 5th in the list of the world's largest economies. Under this scenario, Indonesia's per capita income will have entered the middle-income group. The country will have better infrastructure, quality human resources, public services, and improved people's welfare. To achieve this goal, eight development agendas have been set: (i) strengthening economic resilience for quality and equitable growth; (ii) developing regions to reduce inequality and ensure equity; (iii) increasing qualified and competitive human resources; (iv) mental revolution[9] and cultural development; (v) strengthening infrastructure to support

---

3   Appendix of Law No.17, 2007 on 2005–2025 National Long-Term Development Plan, p. 36.

4   Appendix of Law No.17, 2007, p. 40.

5   Appendix Law No.17, 2007, pp. 65–66.

6   Appendix Law No.17, 2007, pp. 66.

7   IMT-GT. 2017. IMT-GT Vision 2036. Adopted in Manila, 29 April. p. 4.

8   IMT-GT, "About IMT-GT," accessed from https://imtgt.org/about-imt-gt/ on 11 October 2019.

9   "Mental revolution" is the official English translation used for the term "revolusi mental." https://www.ksi-indonesia.org/file_upload/KSI-Knowledge-Sharing-Session-How-do-you-Evalu-01Feb2017112147.pdf.

economic development and basic services; (vi) building the environment, enhancing resilience to disasters and climate change; and (vii) strengthening political, legal, defense, security and stability; and (viii) transforming public services.

Table 1: IMT-GT Provinces and States

No.	Indonesia (Province)	Malaysia (State)	Thailand (Province)
1	Aceh	Perlis	Surat Thani
2	North Sumatera	Kedah	Chumphon
3	West Sumatera	Pulau Pinang	Krabi
4	Riau	Perak	Nakhon Si Thammarat
5	Riau Islands	Selangor	Narathiwat
6	Jambi	Kelantan	Pattani
7	South Sumatera	Melaka	Phangnga
8	Bengkulu	Negeri Sembilan	Phatthalung
9	Bangka Belitung Islands		Phuket
10	Lampung		Ranong
11			Satun
12			Songkhla
13			Trang
14			Yala

IMT-GT = Indonesia–Malaysia–Thailand Growth Triangle, No. = number.
Source: www.imtgt.org.

Agenda No. 2—developing regions to reduce inequality and ensure equity—will address the following objectives: (i) increasing interregional equity (e.g., between western and eastern regions, between Java and outside Java); (ii) increasing the competitive advantage of regional growth centers; (iii) increasing the quality of, and access to, basic services, competitiveness, and regional independence; and (iv) increased synergy in regional spatial use. Regional development will be carried out through two main approaches: (i) the growth approach, and (ii) the equity approach. These two approaches are reflected in the designation of two main corridors in Sumatera—the growth corridor and the equalization corridor. The growth corridor is oriented toward spurring national economic growth by accelerating the development of growth areas. The growth areas include national activity centers, regional activity centers, special economic zones (SEZs), industrial zones, national strategic tourism zones, as well as cities and urban agglomeration areas in districts or cities located in the growth corridor. Meanwhile, the equalization corridor is oriented toward the provision of more equitable access to basic services through the development of regional activity centers and local activity centers, which will serve as new basic service centers to reach more expansive service areas in districts or cities in the equalization corridor.

Agenda No. 6—building the environment, enhancing resilience to disasters and climate change—will be an equally important dimension in developing infrastructure and industries along the corridors. Sumatera is rich in agriculture, forests, and minerals on which majority of the people depend for their livelihoods. Disruption of ecosystems risks impacting the water and food security of rural communities, and ultimately, social equity in growth. The RPJMN 2005–2025 has recognized that the management of natural resources in Indonesia has not yet been sustainable and still neglects the conservation of functions of the natural environment, so that the carrying capacity of the environment and the availability of natural resources have been reduced. Strategies for the development of sustainable and resilient economic corridors would need to ensure that ecosystems are sustained through a resource-efficient, low-carbon economy that reduces poverty and increases social equity. For the transport sector in particular, the challenge is how to develop intermodal and intramodal transport systems (i.e., systems that link freeways, railways, ports, as well as secondary roads to rural and remote areas) that takes into account the carrying capacity of the environment, and vulnerability to disasters given the constant risk of volcanic eruptions, earthquakes, floods, and tsunamis in the archipelago. Moreover, as impacts of climate change deepen, solutions must also build climate change resilience.

Map 2 shows the 10 provinces in Sumatera covered by the growth corridors, including their capitals. Six provincial capitals are incorporated in one growth corridor line: Banda Aceh, Medan, Riau, Jambi, Palembang, and Bandar Lampung. Meanwhile, four other provincial capitals are covered by branch lines: Padang, Tanjungpinang (and Batam), Bengkulu, and Pangkalpinang. This configuration connects all provincial capitals in Sumatera to each other. Table 2 shows the growth areas.

Map 2: Growth Corridor and Equalization Corridor in Sumatera

Source: Asian Development Bank based on the National Medium-Term Development Plan (RPJMN) 2020–2024.

In addition to the provincial capitals, growth corridors also highlight the importance of growth areas, including SEZs, industrial zones, and national strategic tourism zones. Several other growth areas are being developed and will be developed in the next 5 years (Table 2).

Table 2: Growth Areas in Sumatera Region Development Plan

Special Economic Zone	National Strategic Activity Center	Industrial Zone	National Strategic Tourism Zone	Free Trade Zone and Free Port	Metropolitan Region	Integrated Marine and Fishery Center
Arun Lhokseumawe (Aceh)	Sabang (Aceh)	Kuala Tanjung (Batubara, North Sumatera)	Lake Toba (North Sumatera)	Sabang (Aceh)	Palembang	Sabang (Aceh)
Sei Mangkei (Simalungun, North Sumatera)	Ranai (Natuna, Riau Islands)	Bintan Aerospace (Riau Islands)	Padang-Bukittinggi (West Sumatera)	Batam–Bintan–Karimun (Riau Islands)	Medan	Mentawai (West Sumatera)
Galang Batang (Riau Islands)	Bengkalis (Riau)	Tanjung Enim (Muara Enim, South Sumatera)	Batam-Bintan (Riau Islands)			
Tanjung Api-Api (Banyuasin, South Sumatera)		Kemingking (Muaro Jambi, Jambi)	Bangka Belitung (Bangka Belitung Islands)			
Tanjung Kelayang (Belitung, Bangka Belitung Islands)		Sadai (Bangka Belitung Islands)				
		Tenayan (Riau)				
		Tanggamus (Lampung)				
		Pesawaran (Lampung)				
		Way Pisang (Lampung)				
		Katibung (Lampung)				
		Tanjung Buton (Riau)				
		Ladong (Aceh)				

Source: Based on the National Medium-Term Development Plan (RPJMN) 2020–2024.

RPJMN 2020–2024 focuses on Sumatera's development to downstream processing activities in agriculture, fisheries, and mining-based industries to create added value by processing raw materials into semi-finished and finished products. These will complement the benefits of infrastructure investments in the Trans-Sumatera Toll Road, airports, and ports. The development of economic zones along Sumatera's east coast corridor will also focus on downstream activities in leading commodities such as cacao, coconut, palm oil, rubber, coffee, pepper, nutmeg, sugarcane, gold, tin, petroleum, natural gas, coal, capture fisheries, and aquaculture. These will be processed in export-oriented growth centers supported by the development of Kuala Tanjung as an international hub and trade center in Western Indonesia (Map 3).

Map 3: Indicative Plan for Sumatera

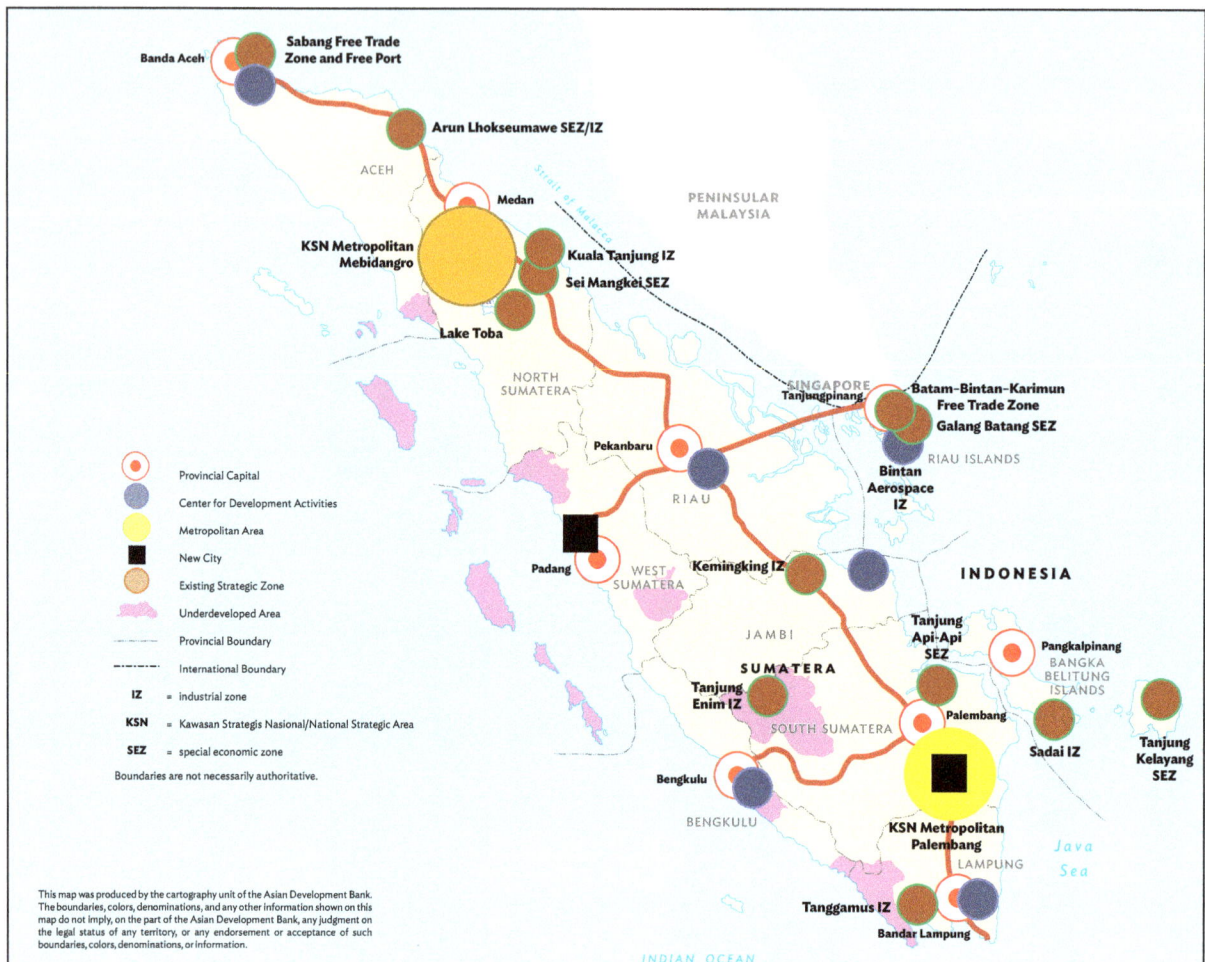

Source: Asian Development Bank based on the National Medium-Term Development Plan (RPJMN) 2020–2024.

To realize Sumatera's regional development plan, RPJMN 2020-2024 emphasized the role of international cooperation initiatives such as the IMT-GT, the Belt and Road Initiative, and the ASEAN Economic Community as a means to expand trade and investment and promote regional and global market diversification. Sumatera would therefore play the role of a primary gateway in international trade (RPJMN 2020–2024, III.39).

The IMT-GT has played an essential role in developing economic corridors in Sumatera, which were identified in the first Road Map for Development 2007–2011 as its flagship programs. These five corridors are

(i)   Extended Songkhla–Penang–Medan Economic Corridor (Nakhon Si Thammarat–Phatthalung–Songkhla–Yala–Pattani–Penang–Medan) (EC1);

(ii)   Strait of Malacca Economic Corridor (covering the western coastal belt from Trang in Southern Thailand to Melaka in Peninsular Malaysia) (EC2);

(iii)   Banda Aceh–Medan–Pekanbaru–Palembang Economic Corridor (a road corridor running from north to south of Sumatera) (EC3);

(iv)   Dumai–Melaka Economic Corridor (a maritime corridor linking Sumatera and Peninsular Malaysia) (EC4); and

(v)   Ranong–Phuket–Aceh Economic Corridor (EC5).[10]

Four of the five economic corridors include provinces in Sumatera. EC1 includes Medan. All provinces in EC3, being a national corridor, are in Sumatera—Banda Aceh, Medan, Pekanbaru, and Palembang. EC4 includes Dumai across Melaka State in Malaysia. EC5 includes Aceh. At the 24th IMT-GT Ministerial Meeting in October 2018, Thailand proposed a sixth economic corridor (EC6) linking Pattani, Yala, and Narathiwat in Thailand, with Perak and Kelantan in Malaysia, and the southern Sumatera provinces in Indonesia.

The member countries requested the Asian Development Bank (ADB) to conduct the review and assessment of IMT-GT economic corridors. The study took stock of the progress made in the five existing economic corridors and assessed the possibility of the proposed EC6. The study consisted of three country reports that present the national perspectives and an integrative report that presents the regional perspective. The Indonesia Country Report covered only the economic corridors which included Sumatera provinces: EC1, EC3, EC4, EC5, and the proposed EC6.

---

[10]   IMT-GT. *Implementation Blueprint 2012–2016*. Accessed from https://www.adb.org/sites/default/files/page/34235/imt-gt-implementation-blueprint-2012-2016-july-2012.pdf.

CHAPTER

3

REVIEW OF THE ECONOMIC CORRIDORS IN INDONESIA

Economic Corridor 1. The Extended Songkhla–Penang–Medan Economic Corridor

Overview

The Extended Songkhla–Penang–Medan Economic Corridor (EC1) consists of three main sections: two overland routes and a maritime route (Map 4). The two overland routes connect (i) the Southern Thailand provinces of Nakhon Si Thammarat, Phatthalung, and Pattani with the international gateway ports in Songkhla, Yala, and Narathiwat; and (ii) Songkhla with Penang (Malaysia) through Perlis and Kedah. The maritime route links Penang with North Sumatera (Map 5).

EC1 is important to Indonesia because it enhances maritime connectivity of Malaysia and Thailand with the western part of Indonesia. North Sumatera province, which is part of EC1, has two important nodes—Medan City and Belawan Port. Medan is the capital city and the main commercial center with a population of 2.26 million (2018). It is the center for the surrounding areas, especially Binjai City and Deli Serdang Regency, which brings the population of the extended area to 4.2 million. In 2018, North Sumatera province contributed 4.9% to the national GDP and had a population of 14.4 million people (Table 3).

Belawan Port is currently the leading international feeder port in EC1. It is located along the Deli River, approximately 12 kilometers (km) from the center of Medan. Belawan Port is Indonesia's busiest port outside of Java, where Tanjung Priok and Tanjung Perak ports—Indonesia's two largest ports—are located. However, there is no direct maritime connection between Penang (Malaysia) and Belawan (Medan, North Sumatera). The Belawan–Penang ferry route had previously existed, but it was terminated in 2010 due to low occupancy rates. To enhance connectivity with neighboring countries, the Government of Indonesia is developing Kuala Tanjung Port as a new international hub port in North Sumatera to support Belawan Port in the shipment of bulk commodities. The Government of Indonesia has also established the Sei Mangkei SEZ in North Sumatera to stimulate economic activities in the corridor.

Status of Physical Connectivity

Land connectivity. Belawan Port is connected with Medan City via the 2x2-lane of the Belawan–Medan–Tanjung Morowa toll road with a length of 12 km (out of 34 km for total toll road length), which has been operating since 1986. From Medan, Belawan Port connects to the eastern Trans-Sumatera National Highway (Jalan Lintas Timur Sumatera) and Trans-Sumatera Toll Road, which is currently being developed.

Maritime connectivity. Belawan Port is located on the Deli River, approximately 12 km from the center of Medan. It is Indonesia's busiest port outside of Java Island. It is able to serve all container types, roll on, roll off (Ro-Ro); bulk; and break-bulk cargo. For container cargo, it serves as an international feeder port to Singapore and Malaysia's bigger ports.

**Map 4: Extended Songkhla–Penang–Medan Economic Corridor
(Economic Corridor 1)**

Source: Asian Development Bank.

Map 5: Extended Songkhla–Penang–Medan Economic Corridor
(Economic Corridor 1) - Indonesia

Source: Asian Development Bank.

Table 3: Economic Corridor 1: Socioeconomic Profile of North Sumatera

Land Area	72,981 km²	**Population**	14.4 million (2018)
GRDP (constant prices in 2010)		Of which, in Medan	2.23 million (16.7%)
2014	33,728	Rank in Sumatera	First
2018	35,409	Share to Sumatera population (%)	24.96
Share to Sumatera (%)	23.0	Share to Indonesia population (%)	5.44
Share to Indonesia (%)	4.9	Population growth rate (2010-2018)	1.27
Growth rate 2014–2018 (%)	1.22	Population density	
Rank in Sumatera	First	1990	139
Rank in Indonesia	Fifth	2000	158
GRDP per capita (constant prices in 2010)		2018	198
2014	2,450	**Share of sectoral employment 2018** (%)	
2018	2,456	Agriculture, veterinary, forestry and fishery	89.61
Growth rate 2014–2018 (%)	0.07	Services	5.01
Rank in Sumatera	Sixth	Trading, hotel, and restaurant	3.95
Rank in Indonesia	14th	Processing industry	1.43

GRDP = gross regional domestic product, km² = square kilometer.
Source: Compiled by the author from various publications of BPS-Statistics Indonesia and Indonesia Industrial Estates Directory (European Union–Indonesia Business Networks. *North Sumatera*. Accessed on 18 October 2021 https://industrialestateindonesia.com/data-province).

Belawan Port is the main sea transportation trade gateway for various industrial products in Sumatera and can support all container types, Ro-Ro, bulk, and break-bulk cargo. Most exports from North Sumatera, Aceh, and West Sumatera are shipped through this port. Belawan Port has four general berths consisting of many smaller berths or jetties used for specific activities (general cargo, bulk cargo, crude palm oil, containers, and passengers). Belawan Port also has a specific berth equipped with modern facilities and equipment for domestic and international container movements. It has 25 warehouses with a total area of 61,474.04 square meters (m²), 23 yards with a total area of 64,386.96 m², and seven container yards with a total area of 262,490 m².

PELINDO I[11] provides Belawan International Container Terminal (BICT) and the Belawan Domestic Container Terminal with container loading and unloading services, temporary stacking services of container loads in open spaces or closed rooms, unloading services, and other container services that include handling, fumigation, labeling, relocation of the container stacking location from the original terminal to the temporary storage place, transfer of ships, and management of document cancellation. At present, due to inadequate depth and lack of vessel channels, BICT functions only as a feeder port to Singapore and Malaysia (Port Klang and Tanjung Pelepas).

The government is currently developing Kuala Tanjung Port as a hub port to handle liquid bulk (e.g., crude palm oil or CPO), dry bulk, and general and container cargo for North Sumatera Province and Aceh Province. It is also designed as an outlet and/or inlet for the Sei Mangkei SEZ. The hinterland of Kuala Tanjung Port is dominated by oil palm plantations in Asahan, Simalungun, Labuhan Batu, and the surrounding areas. Once completed, the port can accommodate 600,000 20-foot equivalent units (TEUs) per year. Kuala Tanjung Port is located in Batubara Regency, about 114 km from Medan.

---

[11]   PELINDO is the acronym for PT Pelabuhan Indonesia or Indonesia Port Corporation, the state-owned enterprise that provides port and harbor services in ten Indonesian provinces. PELINDO I covers the Belawan International Container Terminal.

In addition to Belawan and Kuala Tanjung Ports, the two smaller ports of Tanjung Balai Asahan and Sibolga serve international trade. Tanjung Balai Asahan Port can serve only vessels under 150 gross ton (GT). It is the only port in North Sumatera and Aceh Provinces that serve international ferry routes to Malaysia.[12] Meanwhile, Sibolga Port, located on the west coast of North Sumatera, can accommodate four large ships with a maximum size of 6,000 GT. It is currently serving containers and passengers and will eventually serve liquid bulk cargo in the future.[13] Map 5 shows the extended Songkhla–Penang–Medan Economic Corridor and Table 4 lists the maritime connectivity in Indonesia.

Table 4: Economic Corridor 1: Maritime Connectivity in Indonesia

Port	Link to Ports in Malaysia	Type of Maritime Activity	Remarks
Belawan	Port Klang	Container cargo	Belawan port serves container cargo as well as bulk cargo, especially crude palm oil. Its current status as an international feeder port will end in 2027 when it becomes only an interisland domestic port. Kuala Tanjung Port will replace it as an international hub port in 2027.
	Tanjung Pelepas (Johor)	Container cargo	
Kuala Tanjung	Port Klang (transshipment for Sumatera imports) (Selangor)	Container cargo	Kuala Tanjung has been designated as an international hub port by Presidential Regulation Number 3 of 2016 and Presidential Regulation Number 56 of 2018. Kuala Tanjung has direct calls for container cargo to the Port of Shanghai and liquid bulk for CPO to India.
Tanjung Balai Asahan	Port Klang (Selangor)	Passenger ferry	Six times a week
	Hutan Melintang Port (Perak)	Passenger ferry	Once a week

CPO = crude palm oil.
Source: Compiled by the author from various resources.

Air connectivity. North Sumatera has eight airports, two of which serve international routes (Table 5). These are Kualanamu International Airport (37.7 km from Medan), which has direct flights to Malaysia and Thailand, and Sisingamangaraja XII International Airport (previously known as Silangit International Airport) near Lake Toba as the prominent tourism center in North Sumatera. This airport has direct flight routes to Kuala Lumpur operated by AirAsia.

---

[12] Sri Mas Sari. 2019. Ini Profil Pelabuhan Penumpang & Kargo Tanjung Balai Asahan. *EKONOMI*. 20 February. https://ekonomi.bisnis.com/read/20190220/98/891335/ini-profil-pelabuhan-penumpang-kargo-tanjung-balai-asahan.

[13] Rosiana Haryanti. 2019. Ini Tampilan Pelabuhan Sibolga yang Diklaim Terbaik se-Asia Pasifik. *Kompas.com*. 18 March. https://properti.kompas.com/read/2019/03/18/130000421/ini-tampilan-pelabuhan-sibolga-yang-diklaim-terbaik-se-asia-pasifik-.

Table 5: Economic Corridor 1: Flight Routes in Kualanamu International Airport, North Sumatera

Airlines	Destinations
AirAsia	Kuala Lumpur, Penang
Batik Air	Chennai, Jakarta–Halim Perdanakusuma, Jakarta–Soekarno Hatta, Kuala Lumpur, Madinah
Cathay Dragon	Hong Kong, China
Citilink	Banda Aceh, Bandar Lampung, Batam, Gunung Sitoli, Jakarta–Halim Perdanakusuma, Jakarta–Soekarno Hatta, Kuala Lumpur, Subang, Lhokseumawe, Madinah, Padang Sidempuan, Pekanbaru, Penang, Sibolga, Yogyakarta
Flynas	Charter: Jeddah
Garuda Indonesia	Banda Aceh, Bandar Lampung, Gunung Sitoli, Palembang, Jakarta–Soekarno Hatta, Amsterdam–London
Indonesia AirAsia	Bangkok—Don Mueang, Kuala Lumpur, Penang, Yogyakarta
Jetstar Asia Airways	Singapore
KLM	Amsterdam
Lion Air	Banda Aceh, Bandar Lampung, Batam, Jakarta–Soekarno Hatta, Bandung–Kertajati, Padang, Palembang, Pekanbaru, Penang, Phuket, Yogyakarta
Malaysia Airlines	Kuala Lumpur
Saudia	Jeddah, Madinah
SilkAir	Singapore
SriLankan Airlines	Colombo
Sriwijaya Air	Batam, Jakarta—Soekarno—Hatta, Padang, Penang, Phuket, Surabaya
Susi Air (domestic)	Blangkejeren, Blangpidie, Silangit, Tapaktuan
Thai AirAsia	Phuket
Wings Air	Bengkulu, Dumai, Gunung Sitoli, Jambi, Lhokseumawe, Meulaboh, Padang Sidempuan, Sibolga, Silangit, Simeulue, Takengon

Source: Compiled by the author from https://kualanamu-airport.co.id/.

The connectivity gaps for EC1 in Indonesia are:

(i)   **Maritime**. Since 2018, there has been no existing maritime connectivity between Belawan Port and Penang Port as envisaged in EC1, but Belawan Port has strong maritime links with Port Klang (Selangor), and Tanjung Pelepas (Johor).

(ii)   **Air**. There are direct flights from North Sumatera to Kuala Lumpur, Penang, and Bangkok, but there is no direct flight to the southern part of Thailand (Nakhon Si Thammarat and Songkhla).

Trade

North Sumatera's foreign trade. North Sumatera Province contributed 12% of Sumatera's total foreign trade volume in 2018 and is ranked fifth after Riau, Riau Islands, South Sumatera, and Lampung in terms of GDP contribution. North Sumatera contributed about 20% and ranked third after Riau Islands and Riau Province in terms of trade value. North Sumatera's foreign trade volume and value have grown significantly from the time the economic corridor program was established in 2007 up to the 2014–2018 period (Table 6).

Table 6: Economic Corridor 1: North Sumatera's Foreign Trade Volume
(million tons)

Item	2007	2014	2015	2016	2017	2018	Average 2014–2018	Compound Average Growth Rate 2014–2018 (%)
Total Sumatera	**82.6**	**116. 7**	**119.1**	**108.2**	**125.7**	**140.5**	**122.0**	**4.7**
Exports	69.0	94.5	97.4	87.7	101.6	113.8	99.0	4.8
Imports	13.6	22.2	21.8	20.5	24.1	26.7	23.1	4.7
North Sumatera	**12.6**	**16.5**	**15.9**	**15.2**	**16.0**	**16.9**	**16.1**	**0.6**
Exports	7.8	9.1	9.0	8.4	9.0	9.6	9.0	1.5
Imports	4.8	7.4	6.8	6.9	7.0	7.2	7.0	(0.6)
Share of North Sumatera (%)	**15.2**	**14.1**	**13.3**	**14.1**	**12.7**	**12.0**	**13.2**	–
Exports	114.4	9.6	9.3	9.6	8.8	8.5	9.1	–
Imports	34.9	33.3	31.5	33.2	29.2	27.1	30.6	–

( ) = negative, – = not applicable.
Note: Totals may not sum precisely because of rounding.
Source: Compiled by the author from various publications of BPS-Statistics Indonesia.

Table 7: Economic Corridor 1: North Sumatera's Foreign Trade Value
($ million)

Item	2007	2014	2015	2016	2017	2018	Average 2014–2018	Compound Average Growth Rate 2014–2018 (%)
Total Sumatera	**42,552**	**83,304**	**63,223**	**58,806**	**66,050**	**73,229**	**68,922**	**(3.20)**
Exports	35,150	60,129	44,652	41,833	50,057	50,067	49,347	(4.50)
Imports	7,402	23,175	18,571	16,973	15,993	23,163	19,575	(0.01)
North Sumatera	**9,201**	**14,408**	**11,741**	**11,685**	**13,861**	**14,440**	**13,227**	**0.06**
Exports	7,083	9,361	7,753	7,771	9,225	8,787	8,579	(1.60)
Imports	2,118	5,047	3,988	3,914	4,636	5,652	4,648	2.90
Share of North Sumatera (%)	**21.6**	**17.3**	**18.6**	**19.9**	**21.0**	**20.0**	**19.2**	–
Exports	20.2	15.6	17.4	18.6	18.4	17.5	17.4	–
Imports	28.6	21.8	21.5	23.1	29.0	24.4	23.7	–

( ) = negative, – = not applicable.
Note: Totals may not sum precisely because of rounding.
Source: Compiled by the author from various publications of BPS-Statistics Indonesia.

Most of North Sumatera's traded goods are shipped through Belawan Port. In 2018, 84% of exports and 93% of imports of the province were shipped through Belawan Port. It is also the main gateway for exports of commodities from Aceh (44.6% of total exports in 2018) and West Sumatera. Belawan is Indonesia's third-biggest port for export (2014–2018) after Tanjung Priok in Jakarta and Tanjung Perak in Surabaya (the two latter ports are both in Java Island). As for other trade gateways, Kuala Tanjung Port accounted for 16% of export shipments, while Kualanamu International Airport accounted for less than 1% of North Sumatera's export.

During 2014–2018, container loading (export) and unloading (import) services in Belawan have increased slightly by an average of 1.78% due to an expansion in export activities by 3.4%. Meanwhile, export activities in Kuala Tanjung Port decreased by 3.61% during the same period. Import activities were relatively insignificant, contributing less than 1% of North Sumatera's total import. The export decline in Kuala Tanjung Port indicates that industries around the area, especially in the Sei Mangkei SEZ, still need to be developed and expanded (Table 8).

Table 8: Economic Corridor 1: Foreign Trade Volume Handled by International Gateways in North Sumatera, 2014–2018
(million tons)

Year	2014	2015	2016	2017	2018	Average 2014-2018	Compound Average Growth Rate 2014-2018 (%)	Share of Ports 2018 (%)
North Sumatera	**16.5**	**15.9**	**15.2**	**16.0**	**16.9**	**16.1**	**0.57**	
Exports	9.1	9.0	8.4	9.0	9.6	9.0	1.50	
Imports	7.4	6.9	6.8	7.0	7.2	7.1	(0.60)	
Belawan	**13.8**	**13.5**	**13.0**	**14.1**	**14.8**	**13.8**	**1.78**	**87.60**
Export	7.1	7.2	6.8	7.5	8.1	7.3	3.40	83.60
Import	6.7	6.3	6.2	6.6	6.7	6.5	(0.01)	92.90
Kuala Tanjung	**1.8**	**1.7**	**1.5**	**1.5**	**1.6**	**1.6**	**(3.61)**	**9.20**
Export	1.8	1.7	1.5	1.4	1.6	1.6	(3.61)	16.20
Import	0.0	0.0	0.0	0.0	0.0	0.0	(7.21)	0.01
Kualanamu Airport	**0.0**	**0.1**	**0.1**	**0.0**	**0.0**	**0.0**	**598.19**	**0.04**
Export	0.0	0.1	0.1	0.0	0.0	0.0	(40.07)	0.07
Import	0.0	0.0	0.0	0.0	0.0	0.0	(18.25)	0.00
Others	**0.3**	**0.0**	**0.0**	**0.0**	**0.0**	**0.1**	**(35.89)**	**0.26**
Export	0.2	0.0	0.0	0.0	0.0	0.1	(47.57)	0.18
Import	0.0	0.0	0.0	0.0	0.0	0.0	(2.31)	0.36

( ) = negative.
Note: Totals may not sum precisely because of rounding.
Source: Compiled by the author from various publications of BPS-Statistics Indonesia.

Exports from Sumatera are primarily destined for the Far East and North America. Sumatera's exports consist mainly of mineral fuels, oil products, chemicals, and fertilizers. The top three exports shipped through Belawan Port are palm oil, rubber, and chemicals, while the top three imports shipped through Belawan Port are fertilizers, chemicals, and iron. Since Belawan is only an international feeder port, Singapore and Kuala Tanjung Ports serve as transshipment platforms for goods originating from and destined for Sumatera. Sumatera's exports to Malaysia, and especially Thailand, is minimal compared to its total export volume (Table 9).

Table 9: Economic Corridor 1: Top Three Commodities Traded through Belawan Port, 2018
(tons)

Rank	Export Commodity	Volume (tons)	Share (%)	Import Commodity	Volume (tons)	Share (%)
1	Palm Oil	800,448	9.9	Iron	760,983	11.4
2	Chemicals	760,983	9.4	Fertilizer	494,132	7.4
3	Rubber	576,815	7.2	Chemicals	294,509	4.4

Source: Pelindo 1 Belawan, 2019.

Trade with Malaysia. Malaysia is an important trading partner of North Sumatera. It ranks sixth among North Sumatera's export destinations and third among its sources of imports based on trade value. North Sumatera's top three export partners are the People's Republic of China (PRC), the United States (US) and India; while its top sources of imports are the PRC and Singapore.

North Sumatera's trade volume with Malaysia has been declining. During the period covered by the IMT-GT Road Map 2007–2011, trade volume declined from 1.4 million tons to 1.3 million tons. This trend continued during 2014–2018, during which the average decline in the volume of trade was 9.5%. Although North Sumatera is geographically close to Malaysia, the share of its exports to Malaysia was small—only 4.0%—relative to total export volume in 2014 and this share further declined to 2.3% in 2018. North Sumatera's imports from Malaysia followed the declining trend in exports, although the share of imports from Malaysia was larger in relation to total imports. In 2014, the share of imports from Malaysia was 10.3%, decreasing to 7.4% in 2018. North Sumatera's major exports to Malaysia are seafood, agricultural products, and timber, while major imports from Malaysia are general goods, agricultural products, and used (apparel) goods. North Sumatera has had a negative trade balance with Malaysia since 2007 (Table 10).

Table 10: Economic Corridor 1: North Sumatera's Trade Volume with Malaysia
(million tons)

Item	2007	2011	2014	2015	2016	2017	2018	Average 2014–2018	Compound Average Growth Rate 2014–2018 (%)
North Sumatera	**12.6**	**14.9**	**16.5**	**15.9**	**15.2**	**16.0**	**16.9**	**16.1**	**0.6**
Exports	7.8	8.2	9.1	9.0	8.4	9.0	9.6	9.0	1.5
Imports	4.8	6.7	7.4	6.9	6.8	7.0	7.2	7.1	(0.6)
Trade with Malaysia	**1.4**	**1.3**	**1.1**	**0.8**	**0.8**	**0.7**	**0.8**	**0.8**	**(9.5)**
Exports	0.4	0.6	0.4	0.2	0.2	0.2	0.2	0.2	(11.6)
Imports	1.0	0.7	0.8	0.6	0.5	0.6	0.5	0.6	(8.5)
Share of Trade with Malaysia (%)	**10.9**	**8.9**	**6.8**	**5.3**	**5.0**	**4.5**	**4.5**	**5.2**	**–**
Exports (%)	4.7	7.1	4.0	2.5	2.8	1.8	2.3	2.7	–
Imports (%)	21.3	11.1	10.3	9.0	7.8	7.9	7.4	8.5	–

( ) = negative, – = not applicable.
Source: Compiled by the author based on from various publications of BPS-Statistics Indonesia.

Trade with Thailand. North Sumatera's trade volume with Thailand increased significantly by 153.7% from 2007 to 2011 but fluctuated heavily from 2014 to 2018. During this period, exports from North Sumatera to Thailand were relatively small, contributing less than 1% to the province's total exports; the import share was slightly higher at 3.2%. Export volume to Thailand was 113,920 tons in 2018 with fruits and nuts (37%); alcohols, phenols, phenol-alcohols (22%); and soap (11%) as the top three export commodities (Table 11). This small volume represents an opportunity to boost the trade as North Sumatera and Southern Thailand share similar characteristics as a dominated Muslim community that needs halal products.

Table 11: Economic Corridor 1: North Sumatera's Trade Volume with Thailand
(million tons)

Item	2007	2011	2014	2015	2016	2017	2018	Average 2014–2018	Compound Average Growth Rate 2014–2018 (%)
North Sumatera	**12.6**	**14.9**	**16.5**	**15.9**	**15.2**	**16.0**	**16.9**	**16.1**	**0.6**
Exports	7.8	8.2	9.1	9.0	8.4	9.0	9.6	9.0	1.5
Imports	4.8	6.7	7.4	6.9	6.8	7.0	7.2	7.1	(0.6)
Trade with Thailand	**0.2**	**0.4**	**0.4**	**0.3**	**0.3**	**0.2**	**0.4**	**0.3**	**1.0**
Exports	0.0	0.1	0.1	0.1	0.1	0.0	0.1	0.1	19.7
Imports	0.2	0.3	0.3	0.2	0.2	0.2	0.3	0.2	(3.7)
Share of Trade with Thailand (%)	**1.2**	**2.7**	**2.2**	**1.9**	**1.8**	**1.0**	**2.3**	**1.8**	–
Exports (%)	nil	0.6	0.6	0.8	1.0	nil	1.2	0.7	–
Imports (%)	3.3	5.1	4.2	3.2	2.7	2.2	3.7	3.2	–

( ) = negative, – = not applicable.
Source: Compiled by the author from various publications of BPS-Statistics Indonesia.

Tourism

The development of EC1 does not only promote trade, but also facilitates people mobility. The Belawan–Penang ferry route had previously existed, serviced by KM Langkawi, KM Ekspress Bahagia I, and KM Ekspress Bahagia II, but in 2010 these ferry services were terminated due to low occupancy rates. The only existing international ferry route in North Sumatera is from Tanjung Balai Asahan (approximately 190 km southeast of Medan), which connects Port Klang (Selangor) and Perak in Malaysia.

In recent years, people's mobility has been increasingly facilitated by air travel. The Medan–Penang route is served by AirAsia, Lion Air, and Sriwijaya; while the Medan–Kuala Lumpur route is served by AirAsia, Malaysian Airlines, and Batik Air. There is no direct connectivity from Medan to Southern Thailand. Discussions to open the Medan (Kualanamu Airport)–Hat Yai flight route is ongoing but not yet concluded. For now, North Sumatera connects with Thailand via the Medan–Bangkok route operated by AirAsia.

From 2007 to 2011, the total number of visitor arrivals from Malaysia and Thailand to North Sumatera increased by 66.4%, from 82,335 to 134,217 visitors. Nevertheless, it then declined by 2.3% during 2014–2018. Malaysian visitors dominated foreign visitor arrivals, with a share of about 50% and 60% in 2017 and 2018, respectively. Ninety-seven percent of foreign visitors came through Kualanamu International Airport as the main entry point to North Sumatera. The number of tourists from Thailand is only 1.5% in 2018, although it is ranked third among ASEAN countries with the biggest number of visitors to North Sumatera (Table 12).

Table 12: Economic Corridor 1: Foreign Visitor Arrivals in North Sumatera

Item	2007	2011	2014	2015	2016	2017	2018	Average 2014–2018	Compound Average Growth Rate 2014–2018 (%)
North Sumatera	134,128	223,126	270,837	229,288	233,643	270,792	236,431	248,198	(3.3)
Visitors from Intra-IMT-GT	82,335	134,217	157,233	132,290	118,034	132,449	143,483	136,698	(2.3)
Malaysia	81,347	132,037	152,389	129,203	115,007	128,761	139,878	133,048	(2.1)
Thailand	988	2,180	4,844	3,087	3,027	3,688	3,605	3,650	(7.1)
Share of Visitors from Intra-IMT-GT (%)	61.4	60.2	58.0	57.7	50.5	49.0	60.7	55.1	–
Malaysia	60.7	59.2	56.3	56.4	49.2	47.6	59.2	53.6	–
Thailand	0.7	1.0	1.8	1.4	1.3	1.4	1.5	1.5	–

( ) = negative, – = not applicable, IMT-GT = Indonesia–Malaysia–Thailand Growth Triangle.
Source: Compiled by the author from various publications of BPS-Statistics Indonesia.

Industrial Activities

Medan is a home base for several rubber downstream companies given the vast spread of rubber plantations in North Sumatera. These downstream rubber companies include (i) *Perseroan Terbatas (PT)* Asahan Crumb Rubber, which produces Standard Indonesian Rubber (SIR) 20 natural rubber blocks; (ii) PT Asia Karet, which produces canvas shoes and toys: and (iii) PT Karet Deli, which produces tires. Medan is also known as "Sumatera's coffee axis" (*Poros Kopi Sumatera*), in which coffee beans from Tapanuli, Mandailing, and Simalungun regencies in North Sumatera as well as in the Gayo regency in Aceh are processed into a ready-to-drink product, marketed both domestically and internationally.

Medan also hosts the Sei Mangkei SEZ located in Bosar Maligas subdistrict, Simalungun Regency, North Sumatera, approximately 132 km from Medan, 40 km from Kuala Tanjung Port, and 148 km from Belawan Port. Sei Mangkei SEZ, with a total area of 2,002.77 hectares (ha), consists of three zones—an industrial zone, a logistics zone, and an export processing zone. The SEZ was officially launched on 27 January 2015.

The main products in the zone are palm oil and rubber. Ancillary industries include logistics, energy, electronics, and tourism. The main products manufactured in the zone are fatty acids, fatty alcohol, surfactant, biodiesel, and biogas. Major investors include PT Unilever Oleochemical Indonesia; PT Industri Nabati Lestari; PT Perkebunan Negara III; PT Perusahaan Listrik Negara, PT Pertamina; PT Perkebunan Negara III and Posco Energy; and PT Pertagas and Alternatif Protein. In addition, there are also industrial parks in North Sumatera: Kawasan Industri Medan, Medan Star Industrial Estate, and Pulahan Seruai Industrial Estate.

Overall Assessment

EC1 is a strategic corridor for Indonesia because it serves as a gateway that connects Western Indonesia with the world through ports along the Strait of Malacca. Medan City and Belawan Port are the two major nodes in the existing corridor and serve as the anchor of economic activities for EC1 in Indonesia. Belawan Port has had a significant influence on the development of Medan as a commercial center as well as the hinterlands in North Sumatera and the neighboring provinces of Riau and Aceh, where essential commodities such as rubber, CPO, cocoa, coffee, and other forest products are produced, processed, and shipped for exports. Through the years, improved hinterland connections have emerged with the opening of rail-centered inland container depots that function as dry ports and serve as the catalyst for the further growth of the seaborne transport sector.[14]

Land connectivity between Medan and Belawan Port via toll road is in good condition. Medan, because of its proximity to Belawan Port, is a strategic commercial node in EC1. It is also a part of EC3, which makes it a node intersecting the two corridors. Medan is part of both the Eastern Sumatera National Highway and Trans-Sumatera Toll Road, which connects to all other provinces in Sumatera.

Air connectivity from North Sumatera to Malaysia is adequate, as reflected by the vast number of Malaysian visitors. There are several flights from Kualanamu International Airport in Medan to Kuala Lumpur and Penang. Air connectivity to Thailand is limited as the direct flights are only to Bangkok and there is no regular direct flight from Medan to any city or town in Southern Thailand.

There is no maritime connectivity for container trade between the ports of Belawan and Penang (Malaysia) since 2018, which was originally envisaged in the design of EC1. Until 2010, ferry services were plying the route between the ports of Belawan and Penang (Malaysia), but this was discontinued because of low utilization rates. Therefore, the Extended Songkhla–Penang–Medan economic corridor has not functioned to serve connectivity between North Sumatera (Medan) to Penang and farther to Songkhla.

Belawan Port, however, remains an international trade gateway of Sumatera even though its status is only a feeder port to Singapore Port, Port Klang (Selangor), and Tanjung Pelepas Port (Johor). Most exports from North Sumatera, Aceh, and West Sumatera are shipped through this port. Given the Government of Indonesia's plans to develop Kuala Tanjung Port as the main international hub, Belawan Port will eventually become a domestic (interisland) port.

Belawan Port has been playing an important role in the palm oil and rubber supply chains in the northern Sumatera region. The products transported through Belawan Port are mainly upstream products such as CPO and CPKO (crude palm kernel oil) and downstream products such as cooking oil, margarine and shortening, and oleochemicals (fatty acid, fatty alcohol, and glycerol). CPO-based exports through Belawan Port average about 3.5 million tons per year, the second-highest volume in Sumatera after Dumai Port. As for rubber, the products being shipped through Belawan Port are in the form of crumb rubber, gloves, inner tubes, and outer tires, among others. Most of these products come from several downstream rubber companies located in Medan. Belawan Port is also a gateway for the cement industry from West Sumatera and the fertilizer industry from South Sumatera.

---

14   For instance, the Kereta Api Logistik (logistics railway), a state-owned enterprise company, has established a route from and to Belawan to Sei Mangkei SEZ. It operates every other day with a capacity of 30 TEUs. N. Many. 2018 Developing the port of Belawan as a Modern and International Port. 2018. *IOP Conference Series Earth and Environmental Science* 126(1). 012182. March. https://iopscience.iop.org/article/10.1088/1755-1315/126/1/012182.

Although North Sumatera's major products are mineral fuel (coal), oil products (palm oil), chemicals, fertilizers, and rubber, the main commodities traded with Malaysia are agriculture and seafood products. It is understandable since Malaysia and North Sumatera have similar export commodities, i.e., palm oil and rubber.

Apart from Belawan, there are two smaller ports in North Sumatera that serve international trade, Tanjung Balai Asahan and Sibolga/Gunung Sitoli. Tanjung Balai Asahan Port serves only vessels under 150 GT. It also operates as an international passenger terminal—the only one that serves international ferry routes to Malaysia (footnote 12)—following the closure of Belawan's seaport international passenger terminal. Meanwhile, Sibolga Port, located on the west coast of North Sumatera, can accommodate four large ships with a maximum size of 6,000 GT. It is currently serving containers and passengers and will eventually serve liquid bulk cargo in the future (footnote 13).

Reconfiguration of EC1

In addition to Medan and Belawan, key economic nodes are emerging in the current development of North Sumatera that will play essential roles in EC1 (Table 13). These are (i) Kuala Tanjung Port, (ii) Sibolga, and (iii) Lake Toba.

Kuala Tanjung Port. Kuala Tanjung Port, which is being developed as an alternative international hub port to Belawan Port[15] would eventually become a regional hub port. The main features of the port are

(i)   capacity to accommodate the shipment of palm oil and rubber derivatives estimated to be up to 65% of total goods production in North Sumatera, both containerized and liquid bulk;[16] the port can accommodate 600,000 TEUs per year once completed;

(ii)   vast hinterland dominated by palm oil plantations in Asahan, Simalungun, Labuhan Batu, and the surrounding areas;

(iii)   integrates a harbor with an industrial area of 3,000 ha that include the Sei Mangkei SEZ; its distance from the SEZ is only 40 km, compared to 148 km from Belawan; and

(iv)   accessibility by road through the Trans-Sumatera Toll Road under the segment of Kuala Tanjung–Tebingtinggi–Parapat along 143 km.

At present, trade handled in Kuala Tanjung Port is still small relative to Belawan (10.9% of North Sumatera's total export value). Its role in the supply chain for palm oil and rubber is still limited because the port's development is still in progress. The midterm development of Kuala Tanjung Port is targeted for completion in 2026. It will connect to Tanjung Pelepas, Port Klang, and Penang, which are the other main competitor ports in Malaysia.

Sibolga. The inclusion of Sibolga in EC1 will establish the link between the east and west coasts of North Sumatera. Sibolga City, located on the west coast of North Sumatera facing the Indian Ocean, is part of the Government of Indonesia's plan to develop the Sibolga–Padang–Bengkulu Strategic Development Area (SDA). This SDA will become a center for fishery and tourism that will connect to other development areas of

---

[15]   This policy is stated in Presidential Regulation No. 26/2012 about the Blueprint of National Logistic System Development, and later mentioned in RPJMN 2020-2024 (Annex I, p. III.39).

[16]   A. Kurniawan, W. P. Humang, and R. Sinaga. 2018. Potential Cargo Demand of Kuala Tanjung Port as International Hub Port in Western Indonesia. *MATEC Web of Conferences* 181, 09001. https://doi.org/10.1051/matecconf/201818109001 ISTSDC 2017.

Sibolga–Tebingtinggi (on the east coast near Kuala Tanjung Port), Padang–Pekanbaru, and Bengkulu–Palembang. Sibolga–Padang–Bengkulu will connect to growth or commercial areas on the east coast of Sumatera where Medan, Belawan Port, and the Kuala Tanjung Port are located, thus providing access to the international gateway ports along the Strait of Malacca.

The 2010 census records Sibolga City's population at 84,727 people or 0.65% of the total population of North Sumatera. Fishing is the main economic activity. Fishers who catch fish in various areas such as the waters of the Tapian Nauli Bay, Central Tapanuli, South Tapanuli, Nias, South Aceh, even up to the waters of West Sumatera and Bengkulu bring their catch to the fish reserves in Sibolga City. A well-known product is the Sibolga anchovy, which is exported to Hong Kong, China through Medan and Jakarta.

Sibolga Port is one of the unloading ports for North Sumatera's imports. In 2017, it was the third-biggest unloading port in North Sumatera after Belawan and Kuala Tanjung. A redeveloped and expanded Sibolga Port was launched on 17 March 2019 that featured improvements in the capacity of the container yard (20,000 TEUs per year), fix cranes (40 tons), and passenger terminals (up to 500 people). A liquid bulk berth was also added to accommodate the distribution of CPO. Sibolga is well-connected with the rest of Sumatera through the Trans-Sumatera Toll Road development. It is part of the Prapat–Taruntung–Sibolga segment with a length of about 101 km. The route connects Sibolga with Medan and Kuala Tanjung through Tebingtinggi.

Lake Toba. The tourism potential of Lake Toba is one of the most comprehensive in Indonesia. Its natural environment is pristine and has a distinctive and unique culture, making it one of the main tourist attractions in Indonesia. Located in North Sumatera, about 176 km from Medan City, Lake Toba has contributed around 65% of the total tourist visitors to the province. The Government of Indonesia has designated Lake Toba as one of the 10 "New Bali" sites in the country and will develop it as the National Strategic Tourism Zone under the RPJMN 2020–2024.

Lake Toba has an area of about 1,145 km^2 and a depth of 450 meters. It has been named the largest lake in Southeast Asia. Samosir Island, which is located in the middle of a lake, is as big as Singapore Island and is the center of attraction. Lake Toba offers two categories of tourism activities: nature-oriented activities such as kayaking and camping; and cultural activities such as visiting ethnic villages and watching the iconic Tor-Tor Dance. Various accommodation facilities have been built to cater to different types of tourists.

People can reach Lake Toba by direct flights from Medan and Kuala Lumpur to Sisingamangaraja XII International Airport in North Tapanuli. People can also use land routes via the Medan–Parapat and Medan–Berastagi bus route. Tourists visiting Samosir Island can use the ferry, which runs every hour and a half.

The new configuration for EC1 in North Sumatera will thus comprise five nodes—Medan and Belawan, which are existing nodes, and Kuala Tanjung, Sibolga, and Lake Toba as additional nodes.

Medan will intersect EC1 and EC3 as it is a crucial node in both corridors. In the next development plan, RPJMN 2020–2024, Medan will be developed as Metropolitan Medan, together with Palembang, for the entire Sumatera Island.

Table 13: Economic Corridor 1: Existing and Additional Provinces and Nodes, by Type

Province/State	Node	CAP	COM	BCP	MGP	TOUR
INDONESIA						
North Sumatera	Belawan Port				✓	
	Medan	✓				
	Kuala Tanjung Port*		✓		✓	
	Sibolga*		✓		✓	
	Lake Toba*					✓
MALAYSIA						
Penang	Penang Port • Butterworth • George Town		✓		✓	✓
Kedah	Bukit Kayu Hitam		✓	✓		✓
	Durian Burung		✓	✓		
	Alor Setar	✓				
Perlis	Padang Besar		✓	✓		✓
	Kangar*	✓				
THAILAND						
Songkhla	Songkhla	✓				
	Songkhla Port*				✓	
	Hat Yai		✓			
	Sadao			✓		
	Padang Besa			✓		
	Ban Prakop			✓		
Nakhon Si Thammarat	Nakhon Si Thammarat	✓				
Chumphon*	Chumphon*	✓				
Surat Thani*	Surat Thani*	✓	✓			
	Ko Samui*					✓
Phatthalung*	Phatthalung City*	✓				
Pattani**	Pattani City	✓				
Yala**	Yala City	✓				
Narathiwat**	Narathiwat City	✓	✓			

BCP = border crossing point, CAP = capital, COM = commercial, EC = economic corridor, MGP = maritime gateway port, TOUR = tourism.
Notes: * denotes additional provinces and nodes.
** Pattani, Yala, and Narathiwat were part of the extended EC1 but these provinces have been integrated with the proposed route for EC6 to link with the eastern part of Malaysia.
Source: Study team.

As EC1 also covers Malaysia and Thailand, both countries have their own strategies to develop this corridor. Malaysia's strategy is centered on the development of the Port of Penang, which is expected to become a prominent maritime gateway for North Sumatera and Southern Thailand products to be exported to international markets. In addition, Malaysia is also developing its border area with Thailand in Bukit Kayu Hitam, Durian Burung, and Padang Besar, which is expected to have a major impact on increasing cross-border economic activity in EC1. This Malaysian Border Area is located in the states of Kedah and Perlis. This strategy aligns with Malaysia's Northern Corridor Economic Region Blueprint 2.0 (2016–2025) (footnote 1).

Map 6: Southern Thailand–Northern Malaysia–North Sumatera Economic Corridor (Reconfigured Economic Corridor 1) - Indonesia

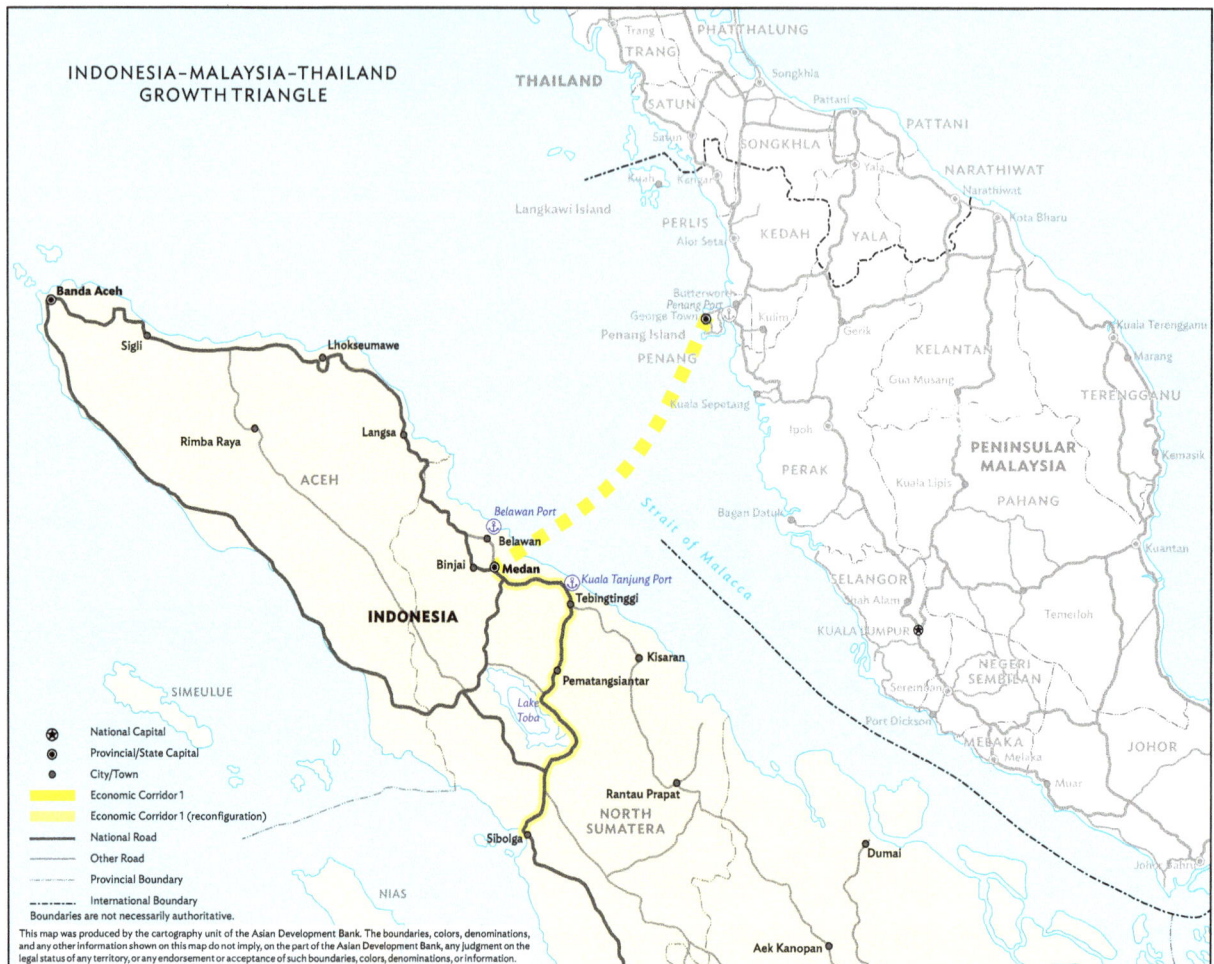

Source: Asian Development Bank.

The reconfigured **EC1 has been renamed Southern Thailand–Northern Malaysia–North Sumatera Economic Corridor** (Map 6).

Meanwhile, Thailand's plan for EC1 development in the region is based on the Southern Economic Corridor (SEC) development strategy. The SEC seeks to integrate production networks for rubber and rubber products with supply chains along with EC1 and the proposed EC6. For this purpose, Thailand plans to develop multimodal connectivity and industrial clusters, both in the form of industrial parks and SEZs. Thailand also plans to establish a tourism network between nodes on EC1 along the Gulf of Thailand and nodes on EC5 adjacent to the Andaman Sea. EC1 can also be linked to EC2 (Krabi, Trang, and Satun), and the proposed EC6 (footnote 1) (Map 7).

Map 7: Southern Thailand–Northern Malaysia–North Sumatera Economic Corridor (Reconfigured Economic Corridor 1)

Source: Asian Development Bank.

Economic Corridor 3. The Banda Aceh–Medan–Pekanbaru–Palembang Economic Corridor

Overview

The Banda Aceh–Medan–Pekanbaru–Palembang Economic Corridor (EC3) is a national corridor passing through four provinces in Sumatera: Aceh, North Sumatera, Riau, and South Sumatera (Map 8). It starts from Banda Aceh and traverses Medan, Pekanbaru, and Palembang via Asian Highway 25. This corridor is part of the ongoing development of the Trans-Sumatera Toll Road covering 2,974 km from Aceh Province in the north to Lampung Province in the south of Sumatera. EC3 covers the eastern coast of Sumatera Island, which has more economic and commercial centers than the western coast. The economic centers include provincial capitals and SEZs, as well as sea and airports (Table 14).

Table 14: Economic Corridor 3: Basic Information on Existing Corridor Nodes

| Province | Nodes | | | Transport Links |
	Commercial	Gateway	Tourism	
Aceh	Banda Aceh SEZ Arun Lhokseumawe	Malahayati Port Sultan Iskandar Muda Int'l Airport	Banda Aceh, Sabang, Singkil Island, Lhokseumawe, Simeulue Island, Meulaboh	Trans-Sumatera Highway Rail links
North Sumatera	Medan SEZ Sei Mangkei	Belawan Port, Kuala Tanjung Port, Kualanamu Int'l Airport	Medan, Lake Toba, Nias Island	Air connectivity from Medan and Banda Aceh to Malaysia and Thailand
Riau	Pekanbaru	Dumai Port Sultan Syarif Kasim II International Airport	Pekanbaru, Bengkalis, Kampar	Ferry service from Dumai (Riau)to Melaka
South Sumatera	Palembang SEZ Tanjung Api-Api	Sultan Mahmud Badaruddin II Int'l Airport	Palembang, Lahat, Pagar Alam, Muara Enim	

SEZ = special economic zone.
Source: Author.

Socioeconomic profile. The four EC3 provinces have a combined population of 34.8 million—about 60% of Sumatera's total population of 57.8 million (Table 15). The respective shares of each province are 25% for North Sumatera, 14.5% for South Sumatera, 11.8% for Riau, and 9% for Aceh. Riau has the highest population growth rate of 2.54%. The massive population of the four provinces reflects a significant market and source of labor that could spur economic growth.

The combined GRDP of the four EC3 provinces was $98.0 billion in 2018 (constant prices) or 63.7% of the Sumatera's GRDP. North Sumatera's share was the highest among the four provinces at 23%, followed by Riau (21.6%), South Sumatera (13.4%), and Aceh (5.7%). Riau had the highest GRDP per capita at $4,885, while Aceh had the lowest number at $1,658 (Table 16).

Map 8: Banda Aceh–Medan–Pekanbaru–Palembang Economic Corridor
(Economic Corridor 3)

Source: Asian Development Bank.

Table 15: Economic Corridor 3: Population and Population Density in Aceh, North Sumatera, Riau, and South Sumatera

	Total area (km²)	1990	2000	2010	2015	2018	Annual Growth Rate 2010–2018 (%)	Share to Sumatera's Population 2018 (%)	Share to Indonesia's Population 2018 (%)
Aceh*	**57,956.0**								
Population (thousand people)		3,416	3,929	4,494.4	5,002.0	5,281.3	2.0	9.1	2.0
Density (people/km²)		66	76	78	86	91			
North Sumatera*	**72,981.2**								
Population (thousand people)		10,252	11,642	12,982	13,938	14,415	1.3	25.0	5.0
Density (people/km²)		139	158	179	191	198			
Riau*	**87,023.7**								
Population (thousand people)		3,279	4,948	5,538.4	6,344.4	6,815	2.5	11.8	2.6
Density (people/km²)		35	52	64	73	78			
South Sumatera*	**91,592.4**								
Population (thousand people)		5,492	6,899	7,450.4	8,052.3	8,370	1.4	14.5	3.2
Density (people/km²)		68	74	82	88	91			
Total Sumatera	**480,793.3**								
Population (thousand people)		36,472	43,269	50,631	53,300	57,765	1.8	100.0	21.8
Density (people/km²)		76	90	105	111	120			

km² = square kilometer.
Note: * indicates the province in the existing corridor.
Source: Compiled by the author from various publications of BPS-Statistics Indonesia.

**Table 16: Economic Corridor 3: GRDP and GRDP per Capita of Aceh,
North Sumatera, Riau, and South Sumatera**
(Constant Prices)

	2007	2014	2015	2016	2017	2018	Growth Rate 2014–2018 (%)	Share to Sumatera (2018) (%)	Share to Indonesia (2018) (%)
Aceh*									
GRDP ($ million)	3,820.3	9,123.0	8,167.2	8,661.4	8,949.0	8,758.0	(1.0)	5.7	1.2
GRDP per capita ($)	905	1,859	1,633	1,700	1,724	1,658	(2.8)	62.2	61.0
North Sumatera*									
GRDP ($ million)	10,594.8	33,727.7	31,964.9	34,517.3	35,985.5	35,409.6	1.2	23.0	4.9
GRDP per capita ($)	842	2,450	2,293	2,448	2,523	2,456	0.1	92.2	90.4
Riau*									
GRDP ($ million)	9,153.1	36,011.8	32,547.4	34,144.8	34,771.3	33,291.0	(1.9)	21.6	4.6
GRDP per capita ($)	1,829	5,819	5,130	5,252	5,223	4,885	(4.3)	183.3	180.0
South Sumatera*									
GRDP ($ million)	5,867.1	19,557.7	18,415.7	19,861.3	20,783.2	20,618.0	1.3	13.4	2.9
GRDP per capita ($)	830	2,463	2,287	2,434	2,514	2,463	0.01	92.4	90.7
Total Sumatera									
GRDP ($ million)	43,353.9	152,264.5	142,161.1	152,201.8	157,422.1	153,962.0	0.3	100.0	21.4
GRDP per capita ($)	903	2,798	2,572	2,712	2,764	2,665	(1.2)	100.0	98.1

( ) = negative, GRDP = gross regional domestic product.
Note: * indicates the province in the existing corridor.
Source: Compiled by the author from various publications of BPS-Statistics Indonesia.

Overall, the growth of the labor force in the four provinces is increasing. The unemployment rate ranged from a high of 6.36% (Aceh) to a low of 4.23% (South Sumatera) in 2018. The school enrollment rate in the four provinces is relatively high for the elementary and junior high school levels (ranging from 94% to 98%), but lower for senior high school (ranging from 70% to 83%). School enrollment in higher education is low, although it is gradually increasing. In 2018, the higher education enrollment in Aceh was 37.6%; Riau, 31.7%; North Sumatera, 30%; and South Sumatera,19%. Education levels in Sumatera would need to be improved significantly for the province to benefit from plans to attract investments and make industries more competitive.

Internet connectivity in Sumatera is low. North Sumatera had the most internet users at 6.3% of the provincial population. Internet users in other Sumatera provinces are much lower: Lampung, 3%; West Sumatera, 2.6%; Riau Islands, 2%; Aceh, 1.5%; Riau, 1.3%; Bangka Belitung and South Sumatera, 0.9%; and Bengkulu and Jambi, 0.6%.[17]

Status of Physical Connectivity

Road connectivity. EC3 is supported by the Eastern Sumatera National Highway (*Jalur Lintas Timur Sumatera*) (Map 9 and Table 17). Most roads in this corridor have two lanes, except the Banda Aceh–Medan section, which has two to four lanes. The Banda Aceh–Medan section is a developed national highway route. This section passes through major towns and cities in Aceh and North Sumatera. The average traveling speed is 40–60 km/hour due to road congestion and road conditions, as well as regular maintenance issues. Roads in all sections in this corridor are classified as Class II. The surface is smooth most of the way but has occasional potholes.

Table 17: Economic Corridor 3: Status of Land Connectivity

Start Point	End Point	Route	Distance (km)	Traffic Lanes	Road classification
Banda Aceh	Medan	AH 25	605	2–4	Class II
Medan	Pekanbaru	AH 25	655	2	Class II
Pekanbaru	Palembang	AH 25	715	2	Class II

AH = Asian Highway, km = kilometer.
Source: Compiled by the author from the Ministry of Transportation's publication and Google Maps.

In addition to the national highway, the government has been developing the Trans-Sumatera Toll Road that will connect all provinces in Sumatera Island, from Aceh to Lampung. The toll road will improve connectivity, reduce logistic costs, and stimulate industrial growth in Sumatera. The development of the toll road has two phases. Phase I consists of eight sections, which are further divided into four initial sections: (i) Medan–Binjai, (ii) Palembang–Indralaya, (iii) Pekanbaru–Dumai, (iv) Bakauheni–Terbanggi Besar; and four additional sections: (v) Terbanggi Besar–Pematang Panggang, (vi) Pematang Panggang–Kayu Agung, (vii) Palembang–Tanjung Api-Api, and (viii) Kisaran–Tebingtinggi. The segments that have been completed and are functional are: (i) Medan–Binjai (17 km) and (ii) Medan-Kualanamu-Tebingtinggi (62 km), both in North Sumatera; (iii) Bakauheni–Terbanggi Besar (140 km) in Lampung; and (iv) Terbanggi Besar–Pematang Panggang–Kayu Agung (185 km) that connects Lampung to Palembang.

There are cargo terminals established in Banda Aceh, Meulaboh, and Langsa. Cargo terminals were built as transit points for trucks from Medan and other locations. The goods were then transferred into smaller trucks before entering the cities. The purpose of cargo terminals is to prevent damage to roads and congestion in cities. The transport department operates all cargo terminals at the respective locations.

---

[17] Based on a survey published by the Indonesian Internet Service Providers Association (*Asosiasi Penyelenggara Jasa Internet Indonesia - APJII*), 16 May 2019.

Map 9: Trans-Sumatera Toll Road

1	Medan–Binjai	17 km	9	Dumai–Simpang Sigambal–Rantau Prapat	175 km
2	Palembang–Indralaya	22 km	10	Rantau Prapat–Kisaran	100 km
3	Bakauheni–Terbanggi Besar	140 km	11	Bukittinggi–Padang	55 km
4	Pekanbaru–Dumai	131 km	12	Batu Ampar–Bandara Hang Nadim	25 km
5	Palembang–Tanjung Api-Api	90 km	13	Jambi–Rengat	190 km
6	Kisaran–Tebingtinggi	60 km	14	Rengat–Pekanbaru	175 km
7	Terbanggu Besar–Pematang Panggang	100 km	15	Betung (Simpang Sekayu)–Tempino–Jambi	191 km
8	Pematang Panggang–Kayuagung	85 km	16	Pekanbaru–Bukittinggi	185 km

17	Indralaya–Muara Enim	88 km
18	Tebingtinggi–Sibolga	200 km
19	Sigli–Banda Aceh	75 km
20	Lubuk Linggau–Curup–Bengkulu	95 km
21	Muara Enim–Lahat–Lubuk Linggau	125 km
22	Binjai–Langsa	110 km
23	Langsa–Lhokseumawe	135 km
24	Lhokseumawe–Sigli	135 km

Source: Asian Development Bank based on the Trans-Sumatera Toll Road Map by Hutama Karya.

Rail connectivity. To connect Aceh and North Sumatera, the Government of Indonesia planned in 2016 to reactivate the 80-km railway from Aceh to North Sumatera along the Besitang to Binjai route, as well as build a new 428-km railway that will pass through Malahayati, Lhokseumawe, and Kuala Langsa, which are major ports in Aceh Province. As of end-2019, the Besitang (Langkat)–Langsa segment of about 35 km has been completed, while the other segments are still being developed. There is also a 28-km railway line from Medan to Kualanamu International Airport. The Government of Indonesia is also developing a 21.5-km railway from Tebingtinggi to Kuala Tanjung to support the Sei Mangkei SEZ. PT Kereta Api Indonesia, a state-owned company operating in Java and Sumatera island, manages railway transport in Aceh and North Sumatera provinces.

To support the railway connection between North Sumatera and Riau, the government is developing the Rantau Prapat–Duri–Pekanbaru railway as one of the national strategic projects starting from 2017. It will connect Rantau Prapat and Kota Pinang in North Sumatera, as well as Dumai and Pekanbaru in Riau. As of end-2019, only the Rantau Prapat–Kota Pinang route in North Sumatera has been developed.

In South Sumatera, the Government of Indonesia has developed the Prabumulih–Kertapati railway for about 80 km since 2015. There is also the 23.4-km light railway transit (LRT) in Palembang, the capital city, which stretches from Sultan Mahmud Badarudin II Airport to Jakabaring Sport Center area, Ogan Permata Indah area and passes over the Musi River. It was launched in 2018 to serve the Asian Games event.

Maritime connectivity. Each of the four provinces in EC3 has its own port (Table 18).

(i)   Aceh-Meulaboh Port on the western coast is the main export gateway, while Kreung Geukeh Port in Lhokseumawe is the main gateway for imports.

(ii)   North Sumatera-Belawan Port (part of EC1) serves as the leading maritime gateway in Sumatera Island. This port is able to support Ro-Ro, container cargo, general cargo, and bulk cargo (especially for CPO). Its current status as an international feeder port would be terminated by 2027 and will only convert into an interisland domestic port. Kuala Tanjung, which is being developed will serve as the international hub port. Kuala Tanjung Port will have the capacity to handle liquid bulk cargo (CPO), dry bulk, container, and general cargo for North Sumatera and Aceh. It will also serve the Sei Mangkei industrial area. The hinterland of Kuala Tanjung Port is dominated by palm oil plantations making it an important gateway for CPO and CPKO exports.

(iii)   Riau Province–Dumai Port is the leading maritime gateway for the province. It is located 177 km from Pekanbaru by the national highway or 131.5 km by the toll road. In 2018, over three-fourths of Riau's exports were shipped from Dumai Port, and one-third of imports were unloaded at the port.

(iv)   South Sumatera-There are three rivers and sea ports for trade activities: Boom Baru in Musi River, Palembang–Kertapati, and Palembang–Plaju. Boom Baru accounted for 83% of South Sumatera's export volume in 2018, followed by Palembang–Kertapati at 13%. Palembang–Kertapati Port is used mainly to export coal from PT Bukit Asam, while Palembang–Plaju is used to export fuel oil from PT Pertamina. Almost all import commodities of the province are unloaded in Boom Baru.

Table 18: Economic Corridor 3: Maritime Links of Ports in Aceh, North Sumatera, Riau, and South Sumatera

Province	Port	Link to Other Ports	Type of Maritime Activity	Remarks
Aceh	Meulaboh	Ports in India, the PRC, and Thailand	Dry bulk	Coal exports
	Kreung Geukeh (Lhokseumawe)	Port Klang (Selangor, Malaysia)	General cargo	Imports
		Port in India	Liquid bulk	Crude palm oil (CPO) exports
North Sumatera	Belawan	Port Klang (Selangor, Malaysia)	Container cargo	Currently an international feeder port for ships bound for Singapore and Malaysia
		Tanjung Pelepas (Johor, Malaysia)	Container cargo	
	Kuala Tanjung	Port Klang (transshipment for import to Sumatera)	Container cargo	Being developed as an international hub port to replace Belawan; Currently, has direct calls for container cargo to Shanghai Port and liquid bulk for CPO to India
	Tanjung Balai Asahan	Port Klang (Selangor, Malaysia)	Passenger ferry	Six times a week
		Hutan Melintang Port (Perak, Malaysia)	Passenger ferry	Once a week
Riau	Dumai	Melaka International Ferry Terminal (Melaka, Malaysia)	Passenger ferry	Ro-Ro service from Sri Junjungan Port (Dumai) to Tanjung Bruas Port (Melaka) being finalized
		Muar Port (Johor, Malaysia)	Passenger ferry	
		Port Klang (Selangor, Malaysia)	Passenger ferry	
			Liquid bulk	
		Port of Port Dickson (Negeri Sembilan)	Passenger ferry	
South Sumatera	Boom Baru	Port Klang (Selangor, Malaysia)	Container cargo General cargo	Container cargo for exporting rubber; general cargo for importing various products

Ro-Ro = roll on, roll off.
Source: Compiled by the author from various sources.

Air connectivity. The four EC3 provinces have their own international airports.

(i) Aceh - Sultan Iskandar Muda International Airport is located 13.5 km southeast of Banda Aceh. This airport is listed as the 23rd busiest airport in Indonesia.

(ii) North Sumatera - Kualanamu International Airport is located in Deli Serdang, 39 km from Medan and 46 km southeast of Belawan Port. It is Indonesia's second-largest airport after Soekarno Hatta International Airport in Jakarta.

(iii) Riau - Sultan Syarif Kasim II International Airport in Pekanbaru serves domestic and international flights. The airport area and the runway are shared with Roesmin Nurjadin Air Force Base.

(iv)   South Sumatera - The only public airport in Palembang is Sultan Mahmud Badaruddin II International Airport. This airport provides domestic routes that connect Palembang with many cities in Indonesia, especially Jakarta, and other towns in South Sumatera, such as Lubuklinggau and Pagaralam.

Several domestic flights are served by these airports within Sumatera and other parts of Indonesia (Table 19). All four airports have flights to Malaysia (mostly Kuala Lumpur, Penang, and Melaka). Only Kualanamu Airport in North Sumatera has flights to Thailand (Bangkok and Phuket).

Table 19: Economic Corridor 3: Flight Routes Served by Airports in Aceh, North Sumatera, Riau, and South Sumatera

Airlines	Destinations
Aceh: Sultan Iskandar Muda International Airport	
AirAsia	Kuala Lumpur–International
Batik Air	Jakarta–Halim Perdanakusuma, Jakarta–Soekarno Hatta
Citilink	Medan
Firefly	Penang
Garuda Indonesia	Jakarta–Soekarno–Hatta
Indonesia AirAsia	Kuala Lumpur–International
Lion Air	Medan
Susi Air	Blangkejeren, Blangpidie, Kutacane, Meulaboh
Malindo Air	Penang
North Sumatera: Kualanamu International Airport	
AirAsia	Kuala Lumpur, Penang
Batik Air	Chennai, Jakarta–Halim Perdanakusuma, Jakarta–Soekarno Hatta, Kuala Lumpur, Madinah
Cathay Dragon	Hong Kong, China
Citilink	Banda Aceh, Bandar Lampung, Batam, Gunung Sitoli, Jakarta–Halim Perdanakusuma, Jakarta–Soekarno Hatta, Kuala Lumpur, Subang, Lhokseumawe, Madinah, Padang Sidempuan, Pekanbaru, Penang, Sibolga, Yogyakarta
Flynas	Charter: Jeddah
Garuda Indonesia	Banda Aceh, Bandar Lampung, Gunung Sitoli, Palembang, Jakarta–Soekarno Hatta, Amsterdam–London
Indonesia AirAsia	Bangkok-Don Mueang, Kuala Lumpur, Penang, Yogyakarta
Jetstar Asia Airways	Singapore
KLM	Amsterdam
Lion Air	Banda Aceh, Bandar Lampung, Batam, Jakarta–Soekarno Hatta, Bandung–Kertajati, Padang, Palembang, Pekanbaru, Penang, Phuket, Yogyakarta
Malaysia Airlines	Kuala Lumpur
Saudia	Jeddah, Madinah
SilkAir	Singapore
SriLankan Airlines	Colombo
Sriwijaya Air	Batam, Jakarta–Soekarno Hatta, Padang, Penang, Phuket, Surabaya
Susi Air (domestic)	Blangkejeren, Blangpidie, Silangit, Tapaktuan
Thai AirAsia	Phuket
Wings Air	Bengkulu, Dumai, Gunung Sitoli, Jambi, Lhokseumawe, Meulaboh, Padang Sidempuan, Sibolga, Silangit, Simeulue, Takengon

continued on next page

Table 19 continued

Riau: Sultan Syarif Kasim II International Airport	
AirAsia	Kuala Lumpur–International
Batik Air	Jakarta–Halim Perdanakusuma, Jakarta–Soekarno Hatta
Citilink	Batam, Jakarta–Halim Perdanakusuma, Jakarta–Soekarno–Hatta, Kuala Lumpur–International, Medan, Palembang, Yogyakarta–Adisutjipto
EastIndo	Charter: Dumai, Jakarta—Pondok Cabe, Pangkalan Kerinci, Singapore
Garuda Indonesia	Batam, Jakarta–Soekarno Hatta
Indonesia AirAsia	Kertajati
Lion Air	Batam, Jakarta–Soekarno Hatta, Kertajati, Medan, Surabaya, Yogyakarta–Adisutjipto, Yogyakarta–International
Malaysia Airlines	Kuala Lumpur–International
Malindo Air	Kuala Lumpur–Subang, Melaka
Scoot	Singapore
Sriwijaya Air	Colombo
Susi Air	Dabo, Pasaman Barat, Tanjung Balai Karimun, Tembilahan
South Sumatera: Sultan Mahmud Badaruddin II International Airport	
AirAsia	Kuala Lumpur–International
Batik Air	Bandung, Jakarta–Halim Perdanakusuma, Jakarta–Soekarno Hatta
Citilink	Bandung, Batam, Jakarta–Halim Perdanakusuma, Jakarta–Soekarno Hatta, Semarang, Surabaya
Garuda Indonesia	Jakarta–Soekarno Hatta, Bandar Lampung, Batam, Bengkulu, Denpasar, Jambi, Medan, Padang, Pangkalpinang, Pekanbaru
Jetstar Asia Airways	Singapore
Lion Air	Batam, Jakarta–Soekarno Hatta, Medan, Padang, Pangkalpinang, Semarang, Surabaya, Yogyakarta
Nam Air	Jakarta–Soekarno Hatta, Pangkalpinang, Yogyakarta
Scoot	Singapore
Sriwijaya Air	Jakarta–Soekarno Hatta
Wings Air	Bandar Lampung, Bengkulu, Jambi, Lubuklinggau, Muara Bungo, Padang, Pagar Alam, Pangkalpinang, Pekanbaru
XpressAir	Bandung, Yogyakarta

Source: Compiled by the author from https://sultaniskandarmuda-airport.co.id/, https://kualanamu-airport.co.id/, https://sultansyarifkasim2-airport.co.id/, and https://smbadaruddin2-airport.co.id/.

Overall status and missing link. In general, the physical connectivity among the four provinces in EC3 is adequate for roads, ports, and airports. The Trans-Sumatera Toll Road is well in-progress to make road transport throughout the island more efficient. Rail connectivity, however, is lagging due to the slow implementation of railway projects. There is still a missing rail link from Pekanbaru to Jambi (402 km), and Jambi to Palembang (233 km). These railway projects are listed as national strategic projects and should have started in 2018. Since 2016, the projects' status has remained in the design preparation stage and environmental impact assessment.

Trade

Foreign trade. EC3 covers 4 of 10 provinces in Sumatera. These four provinces combined contributed 55% of Sumatera's foreign trade volume in 2018. Table 20 shows the ranking of the four provinces and their respective shares to Sumatera's foreign trade in terms of trade volume in 2018.

**Table 20: Economic Corridor 3: Foreign Trade Volume of Aceh,
North Sumatera, Riau, and South Sumatera, 2018**

Rank	Province	Exports (million tons)	Imports (million tons)	Share to Sumatera's Export (%)	Share to Sumatera's Import (%)	Share to Sumatera's Total Trade (%)
	Total Sumatera	**113.8**	**27.7**	**100.0**	**100.0**	**100.0**
1	Riau*	28.3	4.2	24.8	15.7	23.1
2	Riau Islands	23.1	7.1	20.3	26.8	21.6
3	South Sumatera*	21.3	1.1	18.73	4.0	15.9
4	Lampung	13.1	5.3	11.5	19.9	13.1
5	North Sumatera*	9.6	7.2	8.5	27.1	12.0
6	West Sumatera	4.4	1.1	3.9	4.3	4.0
7	Aceh*	5.1	1.0	4.5	0.4	3.7
8	Jambi	5.0	0.2	4.4	0.7	3.7
9	Bengkulu	3.1	0.07	2.7	0.3	2.2
10	Bangka Belitung Islands	0.8	0.2	0.7	0.9	0.8

Notes: * indicates the province is in the existing corridor. Totals may not sum precisely because of rounding.
Source: Compiled by the author from various publications of BPS-Statistics Indonesia.

In terms of both trade volume and value, North Sumatera, Riau, and South Sumatera have stronger trade relations with Malaysia, while Aceh has stronger trade relations with Thailand (Table 21). Aceh, Riau, and South Sumatera enjoyed average trade surpluses with Malaysia and Thailand, while North Sumatera suffered a trade deficit. Major exports from these provinces to Malaysia were pulp and paper, crumb rubber, seafood, and anhydrous ammonia, while exports to Thailand were dominated by coal, vegetable, and fruit.

Table 21: Economic Corridor 3: Foreign Trade Volume and Value of Economic Corridor 3 Provinces with Malaysia and Thailand, 2018

Province	Trade Volume (million tons)					Trade Value ($ million)				
	Total	With Malaysia	Share (%)	With Thailand	Share (%)	Total	With Malaysia	Share (%)	With Thailand	Share (%)
Aceh	**5.2**	**0.0**	**0.4**	**0.7**	**14.2**	**168.3**	**7.5**	**4.5**	**27.4**	**16.3**
Export	5.1	0.0	0.3	0.6	13.1	138.6	4.4	3.2	18.3	13.2
Import	0.1	0.0	7.0	0.1	73.8	29.7	3.1	10.6	9.1	30.7
North Sumatera	**16.8**	**0.7**	**4.5**	**0.4**	**2.2**	**14,439.5**	**746.4**	**5.2**	**390.4**	**2.7**
Export	9.6	0.2	2.3	0.1	1.2	8,787.2	270.2	3.1	173.7	1.9
Import	7.2	0.5	7.4	0.3	3.7	5,652.3	476.2	8.4	216.7	3.8
Riau	**32.5**	**3.1**	**9.5**	**0.2**	**0.8**	**17,499.1**	**1,341.9**	**7.7**	**84.3**	**0.5**
Export	28.3	1.7	6.0	0.1	0.4	15,931.3	1,063.2	6.7	11.6	0.1
Import	4.2	1.4	32.9	0.1	3.4	1,567.8	278.7	17.8	72.7	4.6
South Sumatera	**22.4**	**3.1**	**13.8**	**1.6**	**7.2**	**4,479.2**	**611.3**	**13.6**	**132.6**	**2.9**
Export	21.3	2.9	13.4	1.6	7.6	3,734.5	551.7	14.8	122.7	3.3
Import	1.1	0.2	22.9	0.0	0.0	744.7	59.6	8.0	9.9	1.3
Total EC3	**76.9**	**6.9**	**8.9**	**2.9**	**3.8**	**36,586.1**	**2,707.1**	**7.4**	**634.7**	**1.7**

EC = economic corridor.
Source: Compiled by the author from various publications of BPS-Statistics Indonesia.

Domestic trade. EC3 provinces have supported Sumatera's foreign trade with Malaysia and Thailand and boosted economic activities between commercial nodes within the corridor (Table 22). North Sumatera is the major selling destination for Aceh (99.7%), Riau (48.7%), and South Sumatera (24.1%) because of the presence of Belawan Port, which is an international feeder port to Malaysia and Thailand. The four EC3 provinces contributed 58% of Sumatera's domestic trade value in 2018. North Sumatera, Riau, and South Sumatera were the first, second, and third largest contributors, respectively, in Sumatera's domestic trade.

Table 22: Economic Corridor 3: Domestic Trade of Provinces in Sumatera, 2018
(Rp million)

Province	Purchase	Sale	Total Trade	Share (%)
Aceh*	6,178,667	9,685,601	15,864,268	4.1
North Sumatera*	29,456,930	63,309,856	92,766,786	23.7
West Sumatera	19,051,041	24,181,084	43,232,125	11.1
Riau*	60,520,066	3,519,118	64,039,184	16.4
Jambi	9,469,562	12,632,034	22,101,596	5.7
South Sumatera*	33,027,778	21,614,744	54,642,522	14.0
Bengkulu	3,373,160	6,323,050	9,696,210	2.5
Lampung	19,583,609	24,565,483	44,149,092	11.3
Bangka Belitung Islands	9,890,664	6,820,256	16,710,920	4.3
Riau Islands	18,504,895	9,523,254	28,028,149	7.2
Total Sumatera	**209,056,372**	**182,174,480**	**391,230,852**	

Note: * indicates the province in the existing corridor.
Source: Compiled by the author from various publications of BPS-Statistics Indonesia.

Domestic trade relations among the four EC3 provinces in 2018 indicate the following:

(i)   North Sumatera was the largest domestic trade partner for Aceh, both for purchases (67.74%) and sales (99.97%). The Banda Aceh–Medan road segment plays a major role in the trade between the two provinces.

(ii)   For North Sumatera, Riau was the main trade partner in EC3, contributing 43.5% of its total domestic sale in 2018. Aceh is also an important source of domestic purchases, especially of CPO, which is processed in the downstream and upstream industries in North Sumatera.

(iii)   For Riau, North Sumatera was the main domestic trade partner, both as a selling destination (55.4%) and a purchase source (23.5%). CPO is the main commodity for Riau's domestic trade as Dumai is one of the centers for the palm oil industry. Moreover, the land route of the eastern Trans-Sumatera Highway (AH 25), with more than 600 km, is crucial for transporting palm oil between Riau and North Sumatera.

(iv)   For South Sumatera, the main trading partners—Jambi and Lampung—are not within EC3.

The four EC3 provinces also have strong trade relations with some provinces in Java Island: Jakarta, East Java, and West Java. EC3 has established links between Sumatera Island with Java Island, which is the center of Indonesia's economy (Table 23).

Table 23: Economic Corridor 3: Domestic Trade among Economic Corridor 3 Provinces in Sumatera and with Java, 2018

Province	Purchases			Sales		
	Main Origin	Share (%)	Main Commodities	Main Destination	Share (%)	Main Commodities
Aceh	North Sumatera	67.7	Cars, motorcycles, and LNG	North Sumatera	99.9	CPO, mining products, and CPKO
	Jakarta	29.2		Gorontalo	0.03	
	East Java	2.7		Central Kalimantan	0.00	
North Sumatera	Jakarta	42.5	Cars, CPO, and corn	Riau	43.5	Poultry food, paper, and PVC pipe
	Aceh	20.5		Jakarta	16.9	
	East Java	12.7		West Sumatera	9.6	
Riau	Jakarta	52.3	CPO, cars, and PKO	North Sumatera	55.4	CPO, packed coconut milk, and car and truck tires
	North Sumatera	23.5		Jakarta	28.5	
	Jambi	9.4		Jambi	4.4	
South Sumatera	Jakarta	39.8	Rubber-based products, cars, and processed rubber	Jakarta	30.4	Coal, urea fertilizer, and CPO
	Jambi	37.1		Lampung	28.0	
	West Java	8.3		Jambi	9.23	

CPO = crude palm oil, CPKO = crude palm kernel oil, LNG = liquefied natural gas, PKO = palm kernel oil, PVC = polyvinyl chloride.
Source: BPS-Statistics Indonesia, 2019.

Land transportation is used mostly for trade activities in EC3, especially in Aceh, where 99% of sales are with North Sumatera with which it shares land borders. The Trans-Sumatera Highway that connects Aceh and North Sumatera has shorter mileage with relatively lower costs. Riau also uses 95% of land transportation to send goods to North Sumatera and West Sumatera. The Trans-Sumatera Highway has greatly assisted the development of trade among commercial nodes in the EC3 provinces. The rate of utilization of land transportation in all commercial nodes is higher than water and air transportation. South Sumatera uses about 14% of its water transportation for domestic sales (Table 24).

Table 24: Economic Corridor 3: Transportation Usage for Domestic Trade Activities, 2018
(% share)

Transportation	Purchase Activities			Sale Activities		
	Road	Water	Air	Road	Water	Air
Aceh	99.5	0.0	0.5	100.0	0.0	0.0
North Sumatera	81.9	10.6	7.5	84.5	11.7	3.8
Riau	96.9	0.5	2.6	95.0	5.0	0.0
South Sumatera	98.8	0.9	0.3	86.1	13.9	0.02

Note: Totals may not sum precisely because of rounding.
Source: BPS-Statistics Indonesia, 2019.

Supply chains. Domestic and foreign trade activities have contributed to the development of supply chains in EC3. Banda Aceh is the home base for several tuna processing companies. Yellowfin tuna coming from Meulaboh, Pulau Aceh, Laweng, and Ulee Lheue are processed into frozen tuna and tuna loin, then sold domestically and exported to Japan, the Republic of Korea, and Thailand. Value-added for tuna exports could still be enhanced, since 90% of captured tuna are sent to Medan still unprocessed. Banda Aceh is also a home base for the coffee bean processing industry. Specialty products such as robusta coffee from Ulee Kareng (in Banda Aceh itself) and Arabica coffee from Gayo Highland (Aceh Tengah and Bener Meriah Regencies) are marketed to other Sumatera provinces and Kalimantan. Aceh also sells *pinang* (betel nut), CPO, and Arabica coffee to North Sumatera. In terms of foreign trade, Banda Aceh's main export is tuna, including to Thailand. In Aceh Province, coal is the main commodity exported to Thailand and other countries such as India.

In North Sumatera, Medan is the home base for several downstream rubber companies. These include PT Asahan Crumb Rubber producing SIR 20 natural rubber block, PT Asia Karet producing canvas shoes and toys, and PT Karet Deli producing tires. Medan is also known as "Sumatera's coffee axis" (*Poros Kopi Sumatera*) where the coffee from Tapanuli, Mandailing, and Simalungun regencies in North Sumatera, as well as Gayo in Aceh, are processed for the domestic and export markets.

In South Sumatera, Palembang is the center for the rubber processing industry, with raw materials coming from Muara Enim, Ogan Ilir, and other surrounding regencies. South Sumatera has the widest rubber plantation in Indonesia—837,000 ha or 23.6% of the total national area planted, producing 991,000 tons of dried natural rubber (28% of total national production) in 2018. The industry, however, focused mainly on upstream and midstream activities such as the production of crumb rubber or SIR 20. Rubber-based products are then exported through four loading ports all located in Palembang: Boom Baru, Palembang-Kertapati, Palembang-Plaju, and Sultan Mahmud Badaruddin II (airport). These ports ship the goods to the PRC, Malaysia, and the US. In addition to rubber, South Sumatera also has large CPO plantations covering 1.19 million ha CPO is sold to North Sumatera to be reprocessed in downstream industries. South Sumatera's major export commodities are mineral fuels (coal), pulp, and rubber and its derivative products. For domestic trade, CPO, urea fertilizer, and coal are being transported to other provinces such as North Sumatera, Lampung, and Bengkulu.

Tourism

Tourism is an essential sector in EC3. In 2018, North Sumatera had the highest foreign visitor arrivals among the four EC3 provinces; South Sumatera had the lowest (Table 25). Malaysians dominate the foreign visitor composition in all four provinces, mainly because of several flights between major cities in EC3 and Penang and Kuala Lumpur, as well as Melaka (from Riau). In 2018, foreign tourist arrivals at Kualanamu International Airport in Medan reached 236,431, increasing by 6.9% from the previous year. Almost 60% of the tourists came from Malaysia. Tourists from Thailand to North Sumatera were only 3,605 people (less than 2%), although Thailand ranked third among ASEAN countries in terms of the number of visitors to the province. Visitors from Thailand are low in the absence of direct flights from Southern Thailand to the EC3 provinces in Sumatera. Only Kualanamu Airport in Medan has a direct flight to Bangkok via Lion Air. For Riau Province, there are international ferry services from Malaysia (Melaka International Ferry Terminal, Port of Port Dickson, Muar Port, and Port Klang) to Dumai Port. About 13,000 Malaysians (8.8% of total visitor arrivals) visited Riau in 2018.

Table 25: Economic Corridor 3: Foreign Visitor Arrivals in Aceh, North Sumatera, Riau, and South Sumatera, 2018

Province	Total	From Malaysia	Share (%)	From Thailand	Share (%)
Aceh[a]	29,213	24,210	83.0	268	0.9
North Sumatera	236,431	139,878	59.2	3,605	1.5
Riau[b]	146,935	31,915	21.7	286	0.2
South Sumatera[c]	13,862	7,817	56.4	195	1.4

[a]   Only through Sultan Iskandar Muda International Airport.
[b]   Only through Sultan Syarif Kasim II International Airport (19,006) + through Dumai Port (12,909).
[c]   Only through Sultan M. Badaruddin II International Airport.

Source: BPS-Statistics Indonesia, 2019; Ministry of Tourism and Creative Economy, 2019 (Ministry of Tourism and Creative Economy. *Data Kunjungan Wisatawan Mancanegara Bulan Desember Tahun 2018*. http://www.kemenpar.go.id/asset_admin/assets/uploads/media/pdf/media_1564113468_Laporan_Wisman_Bulan_Desember_2018_V_2_-_Klasik_12.pdf.

Industrial Activities and Special Economic Zones

Three major SEZs are being developed by the Government of Indonesia along EC3 in Sumatera: (i) Arun Lhokseumawe (Aceh), (ii) Sei Mangkei (North Sumatera), and (iii) Tanjung Api-Api (South Sumatera). The SEZs aim to encourage investments by dynamic firms in industries where the participating provinces can provide proximity of access to raw materials and help lower trade costs to convenient access gateway ports so that they can be competitive in global value chains (Table 26).

Arun Lhokseumawe SEZ is strategically located along the trading routes to ASEAN and South Asia and is expected to benefit from the revitalization of the maritime economy with the development of the Maritime Silk Road. The Arun Lhokseumawe SEZ is projected to reach an investment value of $3.8 billion and employ 40,000 workers by 2021.

The Sei Mangkei SEZ is currently hosting several companies with strategic interests in palm oil derivatives. PT Unilever Oleochemical Indonesia exports its products to 42 countries, while PT Industri Nabati Lestari exports olein, refined bleached palm oil, stearin, and fatty acid to Argentina, Bangladesh, India, Papua New Guinea, the PRC, Senegal, and the US. In 2019, the total export value from Sei Mangkei reached Rp3.2 trillion ($228.6 million).

Tanjung Api-Api SEZ is expected to serve as a gateway port for South Sumatera's foreign trade since the existing ports such as Boom Baru Port located in the Musi River face the challenges of silting. Downstream industry products in the zone will address the lack of rubber processing industry in South Sumatera to boost the province's export performance.

In addition to the major SEZs, there are also some industrial parks around EC3, especially in North Sumatera and Riau. The Medan Industrial Estate and Pulahan Seruai Industrial Estate are located in North Sumatera, while Dumai and Tanjung Buton Industrial Zones are located in Riau.

For future development, it is noted that those SEZs still dominantly depend on fossil fuel-based energy such as LNG and coal. However, an eco-friendly initiative has also been made, such as the establishment of PLTG with environmentally friendly power plant or clean energy in Sei Mangkei. The stakeholders need to encourage similar initiatives in other SEZs. Therefore, the development of the SEZ in EC3 will be in line with Indonesia's commitment to reduce carbon emissions at the global level.

Table 26: Economic Corridor 3: Special Economic Zones

Physical Features	Industry Focus and Potentials	Other Features
Arun Lhokseumawe SEZ[a] (Aceh)		
Location: • North Aceh District and Lhokseumawe City, Aceh Province • Approximately 264 kilometers (km) from Aceh and 340 km from Medan • Crossed by the Sea Lanes of Communication and the Strait of Malacca Area: 2,622.48 hectares (ha) Management: • a consortium composed of PT Pertamina (oil and gas), PT Pupuk Iskandar Muda (petrochemicals), PT Pelindo 1 (logistics), Regional Development Company of Aceh (agro-industry), covering three areas: the Arun refinery complex, Dewantara subdistrict, and Desa Jamuan	Main industries: energy, petrochemical, agro-industry-supporting food security, logistics, and kraft paper-producing industries The energy sector (oil and gas): liquefied natural gas (LNG) regasification, LNG hub and/or trading, LPG hub and/or trading, mini LNG plant, PLTG with environmentally friendly power plant or clean energy solutions Agro-industries: processing of palm oil, coffee, cocoa, rubber, coconut, other essential oils Potential industries: aquatic ecosystems and capture fisheries	Logistics infrastructure is being developed to support the oil and gas, petrochemical, and agro-industries by enhancing international port and dock infrastructure.
Sei Mangkei SEZ (North Sumatera)		
Location: • Bosar Maligas district, Simalungun Regency • 119.77 km from Medan • Built along with Port of Kuala Tanjung as part of the strategy to turn North Sumatera into an international hub Area: 2,002.77 ha Zones: • industrial zone • logistics zone • export processing zone	Main industries: palm oil and rubber Ancillary industries: logistics, energy, electronics, and tourism Main manufactured products: fatty acid, fatty alcohol, surfactant, biodiesel and biogas	
Tanjung Api-Api SEZ (South Sumatera)		
Location: • Banyuasin, Rimau Sungsang, Palembang • 67.9 km from Palembang City • near the Indonesian archipelago lanes and the Strait of Malacca • has a good potential of water supply from the nearby Banyuasin and Telang River Area: 2,030 ha Main investors: • PT Indo-Rama Synthetics • PT Palembang GMA Refinery Consortium	Main industries: downstream industrial center of resource-based sectors such as seed rubber, palm oil, and coal	Supply chain. The special economic zone is expected to play a significant role in processing rubber, palm oil, and coal to boost the province's exports.

PLTG = Pembangkit Listrik Tenaga Gas (gas power plant).
[a] Arun Lhokseumawe SEZ was established by Government Regulation No. 5 of 2017.
Source: Compiled by the author from Indonesia's National Council for Special Economic Zones, 2020.

Overall Assessment

The four EC3 provinces are well-connected by roads, ports, and airports. Land transportation is the main transport route to support trade activities between commercial nodes. The road condition in the corridor is relatively good; roads in all sections are classified as Class II and have smooth surfaces most of the way, although there are occasional potholes. The transport backbone of the corridor is part of the Trans-Sumatera Toll Road. Some segments have been completed connecting Bakauheni Port in Lampung near Java Island to Palembang in South Sumatera. It suggests the possible inclusion of South Sumatera and Lampung in EC3. Meanwhile, despite a comprehensive plan to develop a Trans-Sumatera Railway, the development of rail links has lagged behind the construction of the Trans-Sumatera Toll Road, leaving some vital rail links that still need to be completed.

The four provinces contributed 55% of Sumatera's foreign trade and 58% of Sumatera's domestic trade in 2018, signifying relatively vibrant commercial activities in EC3. The ongoing development of the Trans-Sumatera Toll Road should be accelerated since road transport is used more than 90% in domestic trade, supporting supply chains in essential commodities. The development of Kuala Tanjung Port as an international hub is expected to boost foreign trade to harness the full trade potential of Sumatera, especially for palm oil and rubber-based products, through a potential increase in downstream processors located in the SEZs.

Basic supply chain linkages have developed among the four provinces, with Medan, Dumai, and Palembang as important nodes. Coffees from Gayo Highland regencies in Aceh and Tapanuli, Mandailing, Simalungun regencies in North Sumatera are processed in Medan—Sumatera's Coffee Axis—and marketed in both domestic and export markets. Medan is a home base for several rubber downstream companies sourcing their raw materials from several plantations in North Sumatera. Dumai in Riau Province is a center for CPO-based industries, both upstream and downstream. Palembang in South Sumatera is a center for the rubber processing industry with raw materials coming from Muara Enim, Ogan Ilir, and other surrounding regencies. The rubber processing industry in South Sumatera focuses mainly on upstream products (e.g., crumb rubber or SIR 20) exported through loading ports in Palembang. South Sumatera also has large CPO plantations where raw materials are sold to North Sumatera to be reprocessed in downstream industries.

Firms located in the SEZs in the EC3 provinces play an essential role in linking the local supply chains to global value chains, especially for CPO-based and rubber products. Availability of raw materials from plantations that are processed into upstream products by local enterprises and the presence of international ports in each province have provided SEZ firms with a cost advantage to become competitive in the international market. At present, Belawan remains the main gateway port not only for North Sumatera, but also for other provinces. For example, around 45% of Aceh's export value is shipped mainly through Belawan Port in North Sumatera.

Well-developed air connectivity between the EC3 provinces and Malaysia has brought an enormous number of Malaysian visitors. It has also enabled people from the provinces to go to Malaysia for leisure, medical treatment, and education. Air connectivity with Thailand is limited with few direct flights, and only to Bangkok and Phuket.

Reconfiguration of EC3

The Sumatera region has 10 provinces—8 provinces in mainland Sumatera, and 2 archipelagic provinces outside the mainland. The four provinces currently included in EC3 are located along mainland Sumatera's eastern coast, which are relatively more economically developed than provinces along the western coast.

The reconfiguration of EC3 aligns with the government's development plan for Sumatera based on RPJMN 2020–2024 (Map 10). The Government of Indonesia will develop a growth corridor in Sumatera covering all 10 provinces based on the plan. Six provinces will be connected through a growth corridor along the east coast region: Aceh, North Sumatera, Riau, Jambi, South Sumatera, and Lampung. Four provinces will be covered through a branch line of growth connecting to West Sumatera and Bengkulu in the west coast region, as well as Riau Islands and Bangka Belitung Islands, which are archipelagic provinces outside Sumatera Island.

The reconfiguration brings together all eight provinces in Sumatera Island into EC3. It will include the four existing provinces and four additional provinces: Jambi, Lampung, West Sumatera, and Bengkulu. Jambi and Lampung are two provinces belonging to the eastern coast growth corridor, while West Sumatera and Bengkulu belong to the branch line of growth along the western coast. The two archipelagic provinces—Riau Islands and Bangka Belitung Islands—have been proposed for inclusion under EC6.

The eight provinces, through their respective capitals, will all be connected by the Trans-Sumatera Toll Road. There are also various types of growth areas along the corridor—5 SEZs, 12 industrial zones, and 2 free trade zones and free ports. Based on its expanded scope, **EC3 has been renamed as Trans-Sumatera Economic Corridor**. Table 27 shows the existing and proposed additional nodes in EC3, given its expanded coverage.

Table 27: Economic Corridor 3: Existing and Additional Provinces and Nodes, by Type

Province	Node	Type				
		CAP	COM	INT	MGP	TOUR
INDONESIA						
Aceh	Banda Aceh	✓	✓	✓		✓
	Arun Lhokseumawe SEZ*		✓		✓	
North Sumatera	Medan	✓	✓	✓		✓
	Belawan Port				✓	
	Sei Mangkei SEZ		✓			
	Kuala Tanjung Port*		✓		✓	
Riau	Pekanbaru	✓	✓	✓		
	Dumai				✓	
	Tanjung Buton Port*		✓		✓	
West Sumatera*	Padang*	✓	✓			✓
	Bukittinggi*		✓			✓
Jambi*	Jambi*	✓	✓			
South Sumatera	Palembang	✓	✓			✓
	Tanjung Api-Api Port		✓		✓	✓
Bengkulu*	Bengkulu*	✓	✓			
Lampung*	Bandar Lampung*	✓	✓			
	Bakauheni Port*				✓	

CAP = capita, COM = commercial, INT = inter-change, MGP = maritime gateway port, SEZ = special economic zone, TOUR = tourism.
Note: * denotes additional provinces and nodes.
Source: Author.

Map 10: Trans-Sumatera Economic Corridor
(Reconfigured Economic Corridor 3)

Source: Asian Development Bank.

Additional nodes in existing provinces. These are Kuala Tanjung Port in North Sumatera and Tanjung Buton in Riau.

(i)   **Kuala Tanjung Port** is being developed to become an international port hub that will eventually replace Belawan Port—currently the main sea trade gateway of import and export of various industrial products in Sumatera Island. Once developed, Kuala Tanjung Port will be able to boost exports of CPO and CPKO, as well as other palm oil-based products through its expanded capacity to handle liquid bulk and dry bulk cargo and larger container cargo volumes.

(ii)   **Tanjung Buton**[18] is a designated 5,000-hectare industrial zone and port facility in Siak Regency, Riau Province. It is expected to promote industries in Riau such as CPO, forest products, pulp and derivatives, petrochemicals, coconut-based products, rubber products, fisheries, oil and gas, as well as small and medium industries. It will serve as a gateway for charcoal, a prominent industry in Siak Regency, especially for the domestic market. Trade activities in the port is estimated to have a capacity of 5.9 million tons per year.[19] Tanjung Buton currently serves ferry routes to Selat Panjang and other destinations within Riau Province, Batam, and Karimun in Riau Islands Province, as well as Belitung in Bangka Belitung Islands Province.[20]

Additional provinces and nodes. The four additional provinces and their respective nodes in the reconfigured EC3 are described below:

West Sumatera

West Sumatera Province is along Sumatera's western coastline, facing the Indian Ocean**.** It has a land area of 42,013 km and a population of 5.4 million (2018) or (9.32% of Sumatera's total population). GRDP stood at $11,325 million in 2018, or 7.36% to Sumatera's GRDP. GRDP per capita of $2,104 is the fourth lowest in Sumatera. The proposed nodes in West Sumatera are Padang City and Bukittinggi.

Padang, the provincial capital hosts about one-fifth of West Sumatera's total population. It is traversed by the western Trans-Sumatera Highway (*Jalan Lintas Barat Sumatera*), which connects Padang with the nearby cities of Bengkulu and Banda Lampung as well as with all other provinces in Sumatera. Teluk Bayur Port in Padang is the main maritime gateway port of the city. Exports are dominated by palm oil (40.8%), cement (around 40%), and crumb rubber (3.14%), which are shipped to major destinations like India and the US. Trade with Malaysia shipped through the port comprises only 4.3% of the province's total trade, while trade with Thailand even recorded a smaller share at less than 1%. Linking West Sumatera with provinces along the eastern coast can significantly increase trade with Malaysia and Thailand through ports along the Strait of Malacca. Under RPJMN 2020–2024, the Padang–Pekanbaru section (254.8 km) and the Padang–Sicincin section (36 km) are scheduled to be contracted.

Bukittinggi is the city with the second-largest GRDP in West Sumatera, after Padang and has a population of around 128,000 (2018). Bukittinggi can be reached from Padang by road along 85 km (2–3 hours drive) or from Pekanbaru along 220 km. The city is also connected to the city of Sibolga via the western Sumatera highway. It will be traversed by the Trans-Sumatera Toll Road. The Minangkabau International Airport serves

---

18   Tanjung Buton is one of the designated industrial zones that will be developed for the next 5 years under RPJMN 2020–2024.

19   Dinas Penanaman Modal dan Pelayanan Terpadu Satu Pintu Kabupaten Siak. *Kawasan Industri Tanjung Buton*. Accessed on 3 July 2020 from https://web.siakkab.go.id/peluang-investasi/.

20   Government of Siak Regency, Riau. *Pelabuhan Tg. Buton-Siak*. Accessed in 3 July 2020 from https://web.siakkab.go.id/pelabuhan-tg-buton-siak/.

domestic routes to Sumatera's main cities such as Batam, Medan, Pekanbaru, Jambi, Palembang, and Bengkulu, as well as international routes to Kuala Lumpur and Singapore. Bukittinggi is one of the largest wholesale centers on Sumatera Island. Trading activities are concentrated in Ateh Market, Bawah Market, and Aur Kuning Market.

Bukittinggi is a well-known tourist destination in the Sumatera region. Under the RPJMN 2020–2024, the city has been designated as part of the National Strategic Tourism Zone. West of Padang is the Mentawai Island, which has been chosen as an Integrated Marine and Fishery Center in Sumatera, together with Sabang in Aceh. Some famous tourist attractions include the Sianok Canyon and the clock tower The city is also famous as a center for ethnic Minangkabau souvenirs. The city is most famous for is its authentic culinary delights, such as "Nasi Kapau," which is hard to find in other areas.

Jambi

Jambi Province is located on the east coast of central Sumatera and spans to the Barisan Mountains in the west. The province has a land area of 50,160.05 km^2 and a sea area of 3,274.95 km^2. The estimated population in mid-2019 is 3.6 million, the fifth-biggest after North Sumatera, Lampung, South Sumatera, and Riau. Jambi Province contributed 6.4% to Sumatera's GDP. GDP per capita is $2,766, the third-highest in Sumatera after Riau Islands and Riau.

Jambi City, the capital and largest city, has a population of 598,103 (2018), or 16.7% of Jambi's total population. Based on RPJMN 2020–2024, Jambi City is part of the growth corridor of Sumatera. It is located in the main eastern Trans-Sumatera National Highway, connecting Pekanbaru and Palembang. The Trans-Sumatera Toll Road will connect Jambi to Palembang under section 15 and to Pekanbaru under sections 13 and 14. Water transport is used via the river-based ports in Muara Sabak and Kuala Tungkal. The Sultan Thaha Airport serves domestic flights to Medan, Batam, Padang, Pekanbaru, Palembang, Bandar Lampung, and Jakarta. There is no international flight route to Malaysia, Singapore, and Thailand.

Jambi City is the center for the rubber processing industry given that Jambi Province has the third largest rubber plantation area in Indonesia. Major rubber processing companies include PT Remco and PT Angkasa that exports SIR 20 to Japan, India, the PRC, Canada, Germany, Poland, and the US through the Saicom Rubber company based in Singapore. The development of Kemingking Industrial Zone for about 2,000 ha, 20 km from Jambi City, is also being developed for agro-processing industries.

Jambi province's share to Sumatera's total trade in 2018 was 3.67%, with exports volume dominating imports by 26 times. Exports to Malaysia contributed 5.93% of Jambi's total exports, while the exports share to Thailand is 5.39%. Vegetable oil, mineral fuels, and coal are the main exports to Malaysia, while betel nut (*pinang*), mineral fuels, and coal are the main exports for Thailand. Malaysia is the third-biggest import partner (with a 15.2% share) after Canada and the PRC while Thailand's share of imports is insignificant. Major import commodities from Malaysia are parts of machinery plant, soya beans, and ethylene polymers aseptic bag.

Jambi Province uses Belakang Padang Port located in Riau Islands as its main export gateway. It also ships commodities through Belawan Port and Kualanamu Airport in North Sumatera; Teluk Bayur Port in West Sumatera; the Musi River and Plaju Ports in South Sumatera, and Panjang Port in Lampung. Smaller trading ports located in the Jambi Province are Muara Sabak and Talang Duku.

Bengkulu

Bengkulu Province is located on the southwest coast of Sumatera, facing the Indian Ocean. In 2020, Bengkulu's population was estimated at 1.9 million persons from 1.7 million persons in 2010, growing at an average annual rate of 2.51%. It is divided into nine regencies spread over 19,813 km^2 of land area. The province contributed 1.98 % of Sumatera's GRDP in 2018. The per capita income of the province was $1,554 in 2018, the lowest in Sumatera.

Bengkulu City, the capital, had a population of 376,000 in 2018, or about 20% of the province's population. Under RPJMN 2020–2024, Bengkulu will be connected with Palembang through the Trans-Sumatera Toll Road as part of the Lubuk Lingau–Curup–Bengkulu section for 95.8 km. This toll section is expected to be operational by 2022.

Bengkulu is a rich source of captured fish from the Indian Ocean, rubber, wood, and palm oil. Grouper and tuna are exported to Malaysia, while palm oil shells are exported to Thailand and the PRC. Pulau Baai Port, 16 km from Bengkulu city, is the main gateway for Bengkulu's exports (49.3%), followed by Teluk Bayur Port in West Sumatera (24%). Bengkulu's contribution to the Sumatera's foreign trade was 2.2% in 2018 in terms of trade volume. Exports to Malaysia and Thailand contributed 16.7% and 7.3%. For domestic trade, CPO, kernel, and coffee are the main commodities sold to other provinces in Indonesia.

Lampung

Lampung Province is located on the southern tip of Sumatera, having a short border with Bengkulu to the northwest, and a long border with South Sumatera to the north. The province covers a land area of 35,376 km^2 and has an estimated population of about 8.5 million as of mid-2019. Lampung is the second-most populous province in Sumatera after North Sumatera. Its per capita income is $1,915.75 in 2018, the third-lowest among Sumatera's 10 provinces, only better than Bengkulu and Aceh.

Lampung is connected to Java Island through the Bakauheni Port—a port located in Cilegon, Banten, on the northwestern tip of Java—that serves Ro-Ro ferry routes to Merak Port. Lampung is also connected to other provinces in Sumatera via the Trans-Sumatera Highway and the Trans-Sumatera Toll Road. The existing sections for this toll road are Bakauheni–Terbanggi Besar (140 km) and Terbanggi Besar–Pematang Panggang–Kayu Agung (185 km). Lampung Province has a railway line between Bandar Lampung–Palembang, which is part of a railway network in South Sumatera operated by Kereta Api Indonesia. The Raden Inten II Airport services flights to Bengkulu, Palembang, Jambi, and Batam in Sumatera, as well as Jakarta, Bandung, and Yogyakarta in Java. There are also flight routes to Kuala Lumpur by Citilink Airways. Under RPJMN 2020–2024, Lampung will be developed as part of the growth corridor of Sumatera. Four industrial zones in Lampung will be developed for the next 5 years: Tanggamus, Pesawaran, Way Pisang, and Katibung.

Lampung is famous as the base of the sugar industry in Indonesia. It contributes around 38% of national sugar production (750,000–800,000 tons per year). Established sugarcane plantations are spread in Lampung Tengah, Tulang Bawang, and Lampung Utara regencies, while young plantations are in Mesuji and Lampung Timur regencies. Lampung sugar is marketed domestically throughout Sumatera and other regions in Indonesia.

Lampung was the fourth biggest contributor to Sumatera's foreign trade in 2018, with a share of 8.6%. Trade with Thailand contributed 7.2% of the volume of Lampung's foreign trade; the share of Malaysia is lower at 3.1%. Lampung's major exports are pepper and coffee, forest products, and sugar and confectionery. Lampung's contribution to domestic trade was 11.3% of Sumatera's total domestic trade in 2018. Lampung's major domestic trading partners were DKI Jakarta and South Sumatera. Tapioca flour, instant coffee, and rubber latex are the main commodities sold from Lampung.

Bandar Lampung and Bakauheni Ports are the two important nodes in Lampung. **Bandar Lampung**, the capital, is located near Sunda Strait which is a strategic waterway for Indonesian Sea Lanes of Communication 1. The city's population in 2018 was estimated at 1.03 million people, or 12.4% of Lampung's total population. Two main gateway ports—Panjang Port and Tarahan Coal Port (for coal exports from PT Bukit Asam)—are located in the city.

(i)   **Panjang Port** is located at the international trade lane together with the Strait of Malacca. Its deeper channel and basin enables it to be developed as a deep seaport without the need for dredging. It has dedicated terminals for container, dry bulk, Ro-Ro, and multipurpose terminals. As the trade gateway within the province, it is being developed to serve as a hub port equipped with modern digital facilities and well-connected to various modes of transport. Mother vessels of some of the world's leading shipping companies have opened direct service to this port. Logistics business players are eyeing Lampung Province to be the center of logistics activities in southern Sumatera.

(ii)   **Tarahan Coal Port** is a coal terminal. In 2015, the Tarahan coal terminal expanded the port's facilities to accommodate ships at a maximum capacity of 210,000 dead weight ton (DWT) from the previous 80,000 DWT. The maximum capacity of the terminal will be further enlarged to 240,000 DWT.

Bakauheni Port is located in South Lampung Regency, covering around 75 ha. Located at the southern end of the Trans-Sumatera Toll Road, Bakauheni Port connects to the Port of Merak on the western tip of Java, which is separated by the Sunda Straits for about 14.7 miles. The ferry service that links the ports of Merak and Bakauheni through a distance of about 28 km is an essential interisland route connecting Java—where Jakarta, the national capital, is located—and Sumatera with its abundant natural resources. The ferry service plays a key role in the movement of passengers and freight between the two islands. In 2016, 30 ferries were serving the Bakauheni–Merak route, which can take 112 trips per day, loading 17,544 of four-wheel vehicles per day in peak season.[21] In 2019, the Bakauheni–Merak line carried the second-highest number of passengers and the highest freight volume in Indonesia, after the Ketapang–Gilimanuk line connecting Java and Bali Islands.[22] The role of Bakauheni Port has become more important because of the cancellation of the Sunda Straits bridge development plan.

---

[21]   T. K. Utami. 2020. Kajian Evaluasi Lintas Penyeberangan Merak –Bakauheni. *Warta Penelitian Perhubungan*. 32 (1). pp. 43–52. http://dx.doi.org/10.25104/warlit.v32i1.1543.

[22]   R. Tri. 2019. *Libur Natal dan Tahun Baru, 2 Lintas Penyeberangan Paling Padat*. 1 December. https://bisnis.tempo.co/read/1278757/libur-natal-dan-tahun-baru-2-lintas-penyeberangan-paling-padat.

Economic Corridor 4. The Melaka–Dumai Economic Corridor

Overview

The Melaka–Dumai Economic Corridor (EC4) is primarily a maritime corridor that connects Sumatera Island and the Malay Peninsula through the two strategic ports of Dumai and Melaka located opposite each other, adjacent in one of the narrowest stretches of the Strait of Malacca (Map 11). This maritime corridor has a long tradition of freight and passenger traffic between Sumatera and Malaysia.

EC4 involves Riau Province on the Indonesian side of the corridor, one of the richest provinces of Indonesia, with abundant palm oil plantations and on–shore oil and gas resources (Table 28).

Table 28: Economic Corridor 4: Socioeconomic Profile of Riau Province

Land Area	87,024 km²	**Population***	6.8 million (2018)
GRDP (constant prices)		Of which, Pekanbaru	1.1 million (16.4%)
2014	Rp447.99 trillion ($36.0 billion)	Rank in Sumatera	Fourth highest
2018	Rp482.09 trillion ($33.3 billion)	Share to Sumatera population (%)	11.8
Share to Sumatera (%)	21.6	Share to Indonesia population (%)	2.57
Share to Indonesia (%)	4.6	Population growth rate (2010–2018)	2.54
Growth rate 2014–2018 (%)	1.85	Population density	
Rank in Sumatera	Second	1990	35
Rank in Indonesia	Sixth	2000	52
GRDP per capita ($ in constant prices)		2018	78
2014	Rp72.39 million ($5,819)	**Share of sectoral employment 2018** (%)	
2018	Rp70.74 million ($4,885)	Agriculture, veterinary services, forestry and fishery	89.82
Growth rate (%)	–0.58	Trading, hotel and restaurants	4.33
Rank in Sumatera	Second	Services	3.47
Rank in Indonesia	Fifth	Manufacturing industry	1.34
		Mining	1.04

* = based on population projection, GRDP = gross regional domestic product, km² = square kilometer.
Source: Compiled by the author from various publications of BPS-Statistics Indonesia and Indonesia Industrial Estates Directory. https://industrialestateindonesia.com/.

Map 11: Melaka–Dumai Economic Corridor
(Economic Corridor 4)

Source: Asian Development Bank.

The two existing nodes in Riau Province are (i) Dumai, which is a commercial and gateway node; and (ii) Pekanbaru, which is the capital of the province. The 10 other areas are classified as regencies.[23] Although Dumai comprises only less than 2% of the province's land area, it contributed close to 6% of the province's revenue in 2017.[24] Dumai is principally a trading port for exports of palm oil-related products and imports of general cargo, fertilizer, cement, and rice.[25] Dumai and Riau have the highest GDP per capita in Sumatera, reaching $4,861 in 2018. Dumai is also called *kota minyak* (oil city) due to the presence of large fossil fuel companies such as Chevron and Pertamina, as well as palm oil industries such as PT Bukit Kapur Reksa. Dumai has a developed oil refinery and palm oil processing industries promoted in five industrial estates: Pelintung, Lubuk Gaung, Dock Yard, Bukit Kapur, and Bukit Timah. There are big palm oil processing factories in these estates, among them Asian Agri, Sinarmas, and Energi Unggul Persada.

**Map 12: Melaka–Dumai Economic Corridor
(Economic Corridor 4) - Indonesia**

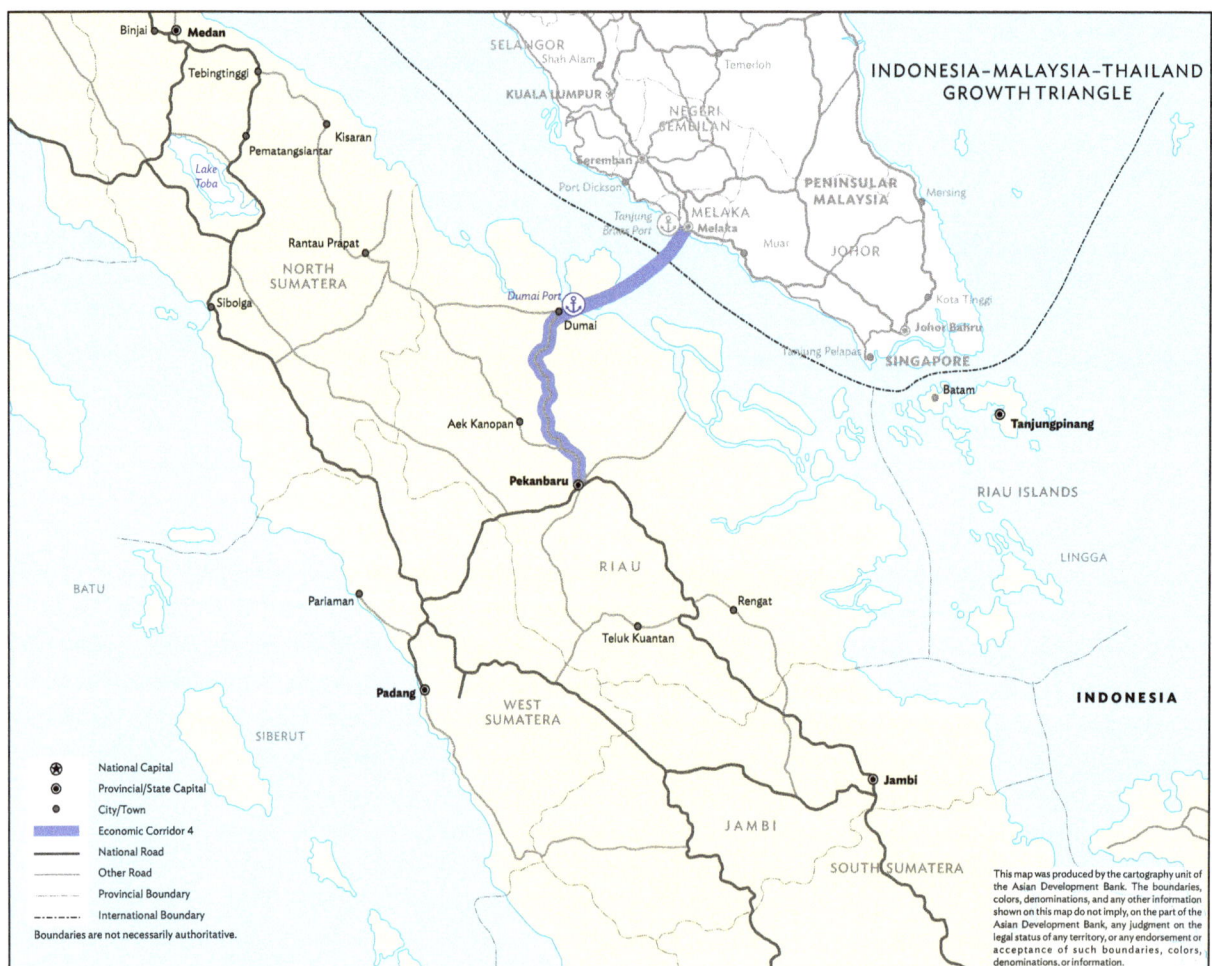

Source: Asian Development Bank.

---

[23]   BPS-Statistics Indonesia. 2019. *Provinsi Riau dalam Angka 2019*. Pekanbaru: BPS Provinsi Riau. p. 25.

[24]   BPS-Statistics Indonesia. 2019. Provinsi *Riau dalam Angka 2019*. Pekanbaru: BPS Provinsi Riau. pp. 10 and 55.

[25]   IMT-GT. 2017. *IMT-GT Vision 2036*. Putra Jaya: CIMT. p. 61.

Dumai Port is located in Dumai City, next to the Strait of Malacca. It has terminals for liquid bulk, dry bulk, container, and passengers. It also has a shorter distance (approximately 67 miles) to the Malaysian Peninsula, compared to other major ports in mainland Sumatera. The port is protected from huge sea waves by Rupat Island, making it an ideal international port.

Dumai Port is the main international trade gateway of Riau Province, serving as a transit point for goods and passengers from different areas in Riau, which are transported by road to the ports for shipment to overseas destinations. Dumai Port is the biggest gateway for CPO exports in Sumatera with an average shipment of 6 million tons per year, compared to Belawan Port's volume of only export 3.5 million tons per year.[26] For imports, general cargo, fertilizer, cement, and rice are the main commodities coming through Dumai Port.[27] Dumai Port also serves daily ferry trips to the International Ferry Terminal and port of Port Dickson.[28] The Pinang Kampai Airport serves commercial flights from Dumai to Batam and Medan (by Wings Air) as well as to Jakarta–Halim Perdanakusuma (by TransNusa Air Service).

Pekanbaru is the capital city and commercial center of Riau Province with a population of 1.1 million or 16.4% of total population in Riau Province (2018).[29] Pekanbaru is strategically located in the middle of Sumatera Island, connecting the northern region (Aceh and North Sumatera) with the southern region (South Sumatera, Jambi, Lampung), as well as connecting the western region (West Sumatera) and the eastern region (Riau Islands). The distance between Dumai and Pekanbaru is 129 km. There are two alternative routes between the two cities. One is the 177-km section of the eastern Trans-Sumatera Highway. The other is the 131.5-km toll road, which became operational in 2020. The Pekanbaru–Dumai toll road is one of the 15 segments of Trans-Sumatera Toll Road that will eventually connect Aceh at the northernmost part to Lampung at the southernmost part of Sumatera Island.[30] This segment is divided into six sections: Pekanbaru–Minas (9.5 km), Minas–Kandis Selatan (24.1 km), Kandis Selatan–Kandis Utara (16.9 km), Kandis Utara–Duri Selatan (26.5 km), Duri Selatan–Duri Utara (29.54 km), and Duri Utara–Dumai (25.05 km).[31] Pekanbaru is also a node in EC3.

There are three trading ports in Pekanbaru—Perawang, Pekanbaru, and Rumbai—out of a total of 17 trading ports in Riau Province. Vegetable (palm oil) and wood are dominant products being exported through Pekanbaru. Thailand is Pekanbaru's top export destination in 2018, contributing 90.71% of total export volume, followed by Malaysia. Vegetable products, animal and/or vegetable fats and oils, as well as wood and articles of wood are the main export commodities. Malaysia is the top source of imports (65.6%), with Thailand trailing behind with only 2.2%. Wood and articles of wood, iron and steel, and machinery and mechanical appliances are the main import commodities for Pekanbaru.

---

[26] *Wartaekonomi*. 2017. 2018, Pelindo I Akan Tingkatkan Kapasitas Pelabuhan Dumai. 22 October. https://www.wartaekonomi.co.id/read158458/2018-pelindo-i-akan-tingkatkan-kapasitas-pelabuhan-dumai.

[27] IMT-GT. 2012. *IMT-GT Implementation Blueprint 2012–2016*. Putra Jaya: CIMT. p. 16.

[28] These services are facilitated by three docks: Dock A (350 meters) for general cargo and passengers, Dock B (500 meters) for loading liquid bulk and transporting CPO, and Dock C (500 meters) for container ships also for dry bulk.

[29] BPS-Statistics Indonesia. 2019. *Provinsi Riau dalam Angka 2019*. Pekanbaru: BPS Provinsi Riau. p. 67.

[30] Komite Percepatan Penyediaan Infrastruktur Prioritas. 2019. *Laporan KPPIP Semester I 2019*. Jakarta: KPPIP. p. 80.

[31] Murti Ali Lingga. 2019. *Hutama Karya Targetkan Tol Pekanbaru-Dumai Beroperasi Awal 2020*. Kompas.com. 5 September. https://money.kompas.com/read/2019/09/05/142900426/hutama-karya-targetkan-tol-pekanbaru-dumai-beroperasi-awal-2020.

Status of Physical Connectivity

Land route. Currently, the main access from Dumai to Pekanbaru is via the Trans-Sumatera Highway along AH 25. It has two lanes which are fully asphalted. The Government of Indonesia has also invested Rp16.21 trillion ($1.16 billion) to build the 131.5 km, four-lane Pekanbaru–Dumai toll road, which has been operational since 25 September 2020. This section of the toll road is part of both EC4 and EC1.

Maritime links. Dumai Port is the biggest gateway for CPO export in Sumatera handling 6 million tons per year, compared to Belawan Port in Medan that can only handle 3.5 million tons per year (footnote 26). General cargo, fertilizer, cement, and rice are the main import commodities handled in Dumai Port.[32]

Dumai Port has maritime links with a number of ports in Malaysia. It exports stearin[33] to Port Klang (Selangor) and routinely serves three shipments per month to that port. There are also ferry services from Dumai Port to the Melaka International Ferry Terminal, port of Port Dickson (Negeri Sembilan), Muar Port (Johor), and Port Klang (Table 29). The ferry services facilitate people mobility to support tourism.

Table 29: Economic Corridor 4: Maritime Connectivity of Dumai Port

Link from Dumai Port to Ports in Malaysia	Type of Maritime Activity	Remarks
Melaka International Ferry Terminal (Melaka)	Passenger ferry	Ro-Ro ferry service between Sri Junjungan Port in Dumai to Tanjung Bruas Port in Melaka has started for goods with limited capacity
Muar Port (Johor)	Passenger ferry	
Port Klang (Selangor)	Passenger ferry Liquid bulk	Exports of stearin
Port of Port Dickson (Negeri Sembilan)	Passenger ferry	

Ro-Ro = roll on, roll off.
Source: Study team.

The governments of Indonesia and Malaysia have planned the Dumai–Melaka Ro-Ro ferry service to promote a more efficient maritime transport link. Sri Junjungan Port is the designated port in Indonesia, while Tanjung Bruas Port is the designated port in Malaysia. The two countries are in the process of finalizing harmonized regulations on cross-border vehicles. Under existing arrangements, vehicles from Dumai loaded into the Ro-Ro until the designated port is not permitted to go beyond Tanjung Bruas Port, and vice versa. This requires the commodities to be transferred to another vehicle licensed or registered in the receiving country, which would significantly increase the cost and time to trade. Pending the resolution of this issue, the Ro-Ro service has been limited only to goods (up to 1,000 GT) and not passengers during the initial phase.

Dumai Port is the center for at least five feeder ports: Bagansiapiapi, Tanjung Lumba-Lumba, Tanjung Medang, Sinaboi, and Panipahan.[34] It has three docks: Dock A (350 meters) for general cargo and passengers, Dock B (500 meters) for loading liquid bulk and transporting CPO, and Dock C (500 meters) for container ships also

---

[32] IMT-GT. 2012. *IMT-GT Implementation Blueprint 2012–2016*. Putra Jaya: CIMT. p. 16.

[33] Stearin is the solid fraction of palm oil that is produced by partial crystallization at controlled temperature.

[34] Pelindo 1 Cabang Dumai. *Pelabuhan Pusat dan Pelabuhan Feedernya di Riau*. Accessed on 5 October 2019. http://dumai.pelindo1.co.id/pelindodumai/hal-feeder-port.html.

for dry bulk commodities (footnote 26). These three docks are facilitating key marine and logistics services as shown in Table 30.

Table 30: Economic Corridor 4: Main Services in Dumai Port

Marine Service	Port/Terminal Operator
• Scouting	• Terminal for liquid bulk
• Delaying	• Terminal for dry bulk
• Anchoring	• Terminal for container
• Mooring	• Terminal for passenger
	• Land, building, water, and electricity
Logistic Service	**Other Services**
• Container depots	• Hospital
• Shipyards	• Health clinic

Source: Pelindo I Cabang Dumai, 2019 (Pelindo 1 Cabang Dumai. *Segmen Usaha / Jasa PT Pelabuhan Indonesia I (Persero) Cabang Dumai.* http://dumai.pelindo1.co.id/pelindodumai/hal-port-service.html.

Air connectivity. Sultan Syarif Kasim II International Airport in Pekanbaru connects Riau with Melaka by Malindo Air (Table 31). The airport also serves international routes to other destinations in Malaysia: Kuala Lumpur and Selangor. The Pinang Kampai Airport in Dumai serves only domestic flights from Dumai to Pekanbaru, Batam, and Medan, as well as to Jakarta.

Table 31: Economic Corridor 4: Flight Routes Served by Airports in Riau Province

Airlines	Destinations
Sultan Syarif Kasim II International Airport	
AirAsia	Kuala Lumpur International Airport
Batik Air	Jakarta–Halim Perdanakusuma, Jakarta–Soekarno Hatta
Citilink	Batam, Jakarta–Halim Perdanakusuma, Jakarta–Soekarno Hatta, Kuala Lumpur-International, Medan, Palembang, Yogyakarta–Adisutjipto
EastIndo	Charter: Dumai, Jakarta–Pondok Cabe, Pangkalan Kerinci, Singapore
Garuda Indonesia	Batam, Jakarta–Soekarno Hatta
Indonesia AirAsia	Kertajati
Lion Air	Batam, Jakarta–Soekarno Hatta, Kertajati, Medan, Surabaya, Yogyakarta–Adisutjipto, Yogyakarta–International
Malaysia Airlines	Kuala Lumpur International Airport
Malindo Air	Kuala Lumpur–Subang, Melaka
Scoot	Singapore
Sriwijaya Air	Colombo
Susi Air	Dabo, Pasaman Barat, Tanjung Balai Karimun, Tembilahan
Pinang Kampai Airport	
Wings Air	Pekanbaru, Batam, Medan
TransNusa Air	Jakarta–Halim Perdanakusuma

Source: Compiled by the author from https://sultansyarifkasim2-airport.co.id/ and http://hubud.dephub.go.id/hubud/website/BandaraListing.php.

Trade

Riau's foreign trade. Riau's foreign trade volume decreased by 1.9% on average during 2014–2018 (Table 32). This notwithstanding, the province was the highest contributor to Sumatera's foreign trade volume (23.1%) and second-highest in terms of value (about 24%) in 2018. Riau has been generating a constant trade surplus since 2007 (the first year of economic corridor implementation) until 2018 (Table 32).

Table 32: Economic Corridor 4: Riau Province's Foreign Trade Volume
(million tons)

	2007	2014	2015	2016	2017	2018	Average 2014–2018	Compound Average Growth Rate 2014–2018 (%)
Total Sumatera	**82.66**	**116.69**	**119.13**	**108.22**	**125.70**	**140.48**	**122.04**	**4.8**
Exports	69.03	94.48	97.36	87.67	101.62	113.82	98.99	4.8
Imports	13.63	22.20	21.77	20.55	24.08	26.67	23.05	4.7
Riau	**23.74**	**35.04**	**30.33**	**30.04**	**32.00**	**32.47**	**31.98**	**(1.9)**
Exports	22.36	32.17	27.62	26.81	28.29	28.27	28.63	(3.2)
Imports	1.38	2.88	2.71	3.23	3.71	4.19	3.34	9.9
Share of Riau (%)	**28.7**	**30.0**	**25.5**	**27.8**	**25.5**	**23.1**	**26.2**	–
Exports	32.3	1.5	3.0	3.1	3.2	3.3	29.0	–
Imports	10.1	13.0	12.5	15.7	15.4	15.7	14.5	–

( ) = negative, – = not applicable.
Note: Totals may not sum precisely because of rounding.
Source: Compiled by the author from various publications of BPS-Statistics Indonesia.

Table 33: Economic Corridor 4: Riau Province's Foreign Trade Value
($ million)

	2007	2014	2015	2016	2017	2018	Average 2014–2018	Compound Average Growth Rate 2014–2018 (%)
Total Sumatera	**42,552.5**	**83,304.3**	**63,222.7**	**58,805.9**	**66,050.98**	**73,229.39**	**68,922.4**	**(3.20)**
Exports	35,150.0	60,129.4	44,651.6	41,832.6	50,056.6	50,066.6	49,347.4	(4.50)
Imports	7,402.4	23,175.0	18,571.1	16,973.3	15,993.4	23,162.7	19,575.1	(0.01)
Riau	**11,970.1**	**23,581.9**	**15,712.7**	**15,008.9**	**17,682.7**	**17,499.1**	**17,897.1**	**(7.20)**
Exports	11,080.5	21,865.2	14,371.7	13,706.2	16,207.3	15,931.3	13,230.1	(7.60)
Imports	8,896.6	1,716.8	1,341.0	1,302.7	1,475.4	1,567.8	1,480.7	(2.20)
Share of Riau (%)	**28.1**	**28.3**	**24.9**	**25.5**	**26.8**	**23.9**	**26.0**	–
Exports (%)	31.5	1.5	49.0	4.1	28.7	2.7	26.8	–
Imports (%)	12.0	7.4	7.2	7.8	9.2	6.8	7.6	–

( ) = negative, – = not applicable.
Note: Totals may not sum precisely because of rounding.
Source: Compiled by the author from various publications of BPS-Statistics Indonesia.

About 80% of exports and 42.11% of Riau's imports, in terms of volume, are shipped through the Dumai Port. The value of exports shipped through Dumai Port reached $12.5 billion in 2018 of which 21% ($2.66 billion) were oil and gas. The top three export destinations are India, the PRC, and the Netherlands. Other goods include animal and/or vegetable fats and oils amounting (63.5%), crude oil (18.5%), and various chemical products (11.7%). Malaysia is the fourth largest export partner in Asia for Dumai city after India, the PRC, and Pakistan. For imports, Malaysia is the largest trading partner and Thailand is on the sixth place.

Table 34: Economic Corridor 4: Main Trading Ports in Riau Province, 2018

Port	Trade Volume (million tons)				Trade Value ($ million)			
	Export	Share (%)	Import	Share (%)	Export	Share (%)	Import	Share (%)
Dumai	22.61	80.0	1,77	42.1	12,497.72	78.5	557.58	35.6
Buatan (Siak)	2.68	9.5	0.79	18.8	1,463.04	9.2	399.46	25.5
Perawang (Siak)	1.52	5.4	1.42	34.0	1,366.08	8.6	436.90	27.9

Source: BPS-Statistics Indonesia, 2018.

Trade with Malaysia. The volume of trade with Malaysia grew by an average of 14.6% during 2014–2018. The volume of exports were consistently higher than imports although Riau's imports grew by 36.0%, compared to exports, which grew at a much slower pace of 5.4% (Table 36). Animal and vegetable fats and oils are the major exports, while general cargo, fertilizer, cement, and rice are the main imports. Malaysia is the fourth largest export destination in Asia after India, the PRC, and Pakistan in 2018. For imports, Malaysia is the largest country of origin, while Thailand ranks a far sixth. Dumai Port also exports CPO's derivative product, stearin, to Port Klang (Selangor), as well as palm kernel expeller and palm kernel shells to Thailand.

Table 35: Economic Corridor 4: Riau's Trade Volume with Malaysia
(million tons)

Item	2007	2014	2015	2016	2017	2018	Average 2014–2018	Compound Average Growth Rate 2014–2018 (%)
Riau	**23.7**	**35.0**	**30.3**	**30.0**	**32.0**	**32.5**	**32.0**	**(1.9)**
Exports	22.4	32.2	27.6	26.8	28.3	28.3	28.6	(3.2)
Imports	14.4	2.9	2.7	3.2	3.7	4.2	3.3	9.9
Trade with Malaysia	**1.8**	**1.8**	**1.7**	**2.8**	**2.8**	**3.1**	**2.5**	**14.6**
Exports	1.6	1.4	1.4	2.4	1.7	1.7	1.7	5.4
Imports	0.2	0.4	0.3	0.5	1.1	1.4	0.8	35.9
Share of Trade with Malaysia (%)	**7.3**	**5.1**	**5.8**	**9.5**	**8.8**	**9.5**	**7.9**	**–**
Exports (%)	7.3	0.7	1.5	5.3	1.1	4.1	6.0	–
Imports (%)	15.4	14.1	11.6	15.3	30.9	32.8	22.4	–

( ) = negative, – = not applicable.
Source: Compiled by the author from various publications of BPS-Statistics Indonesia.

Table 36: Economic Corridor 4: Riau's Trade Value with Malaysia
($ million)

Item	2007	2014	2015	2016	2017	2018	Average 2014–2018	Compound Average Growth Rate 2014–2018 (%)
Riau	11,970.1	23,582.0	15,712.7	15,008.9	17,682.7	17,499.1	17,897.1	(7.2)
Exports	11,080.5	21,865.2	14,371.7	13,706.2	16,207.3	15,931.3	16,416.3	(7.6)
Imports	889.6	1,716.8	1,341.0	1,302.7	1,475.4	1,567.8	1,480.7	(2.2)
Trade with Malaysia	603.6	1,296.8	959.3	1,314.0	1,268.3	1,341.9	1,180.3	(4.8)
Exports	520.5	1,048.2	802.0	1,136.7	1,001.2	1,063.3	797.6	0.4
Imports	83.1	248.6	157.3	177.4	267.0	278.7	225.8	2.9
Share of Trade with Malaysia (%)	5.0	5.5	6.1	8.8	7.2	6.1	6.6	–
Exports (%)	4.7	4.8	5.6	8.3	6.2	6.7	4.9	–
Imports (%)	9.3	14.5	11.7	13.6	18.1	17.8	15.3	–

( ) = negative, – = not applicable.
Source: Compiled by the author from various publications of BPS-Statistics Indonesia.

Tourism

Air and maritime connectivity in EC4 has facilitated the mobility of people. Malaysians comprised about 64% (19,000) of foreign visitor arrivals at Sultan Syarif Kasim II International Airport in Pekanbaru in 2018 (Table 37). Around 13,000 Malaysians also visited Riau by international ferry from the Melaka International Ferry Terminal, Port of Port Dickson, Muar Port, and Port Klang in 2018. Visitors from Thailand contributed less than 2% of foreign visitors coming to Riau due to limited flights.

Table 37: Economic Corridor 4: Foreign Visitor Arrivals in Riau's Sultan Syarif Kasim II International Airport, 2015–2018

Item	2015	2016	2017	2018	Average 2015–2018	Compound Average Growth Rate 2015–2018 (%)
Riau	27,810	32,810	40,105	29,776	26,100	(7.3)
Visitors from Intra-IMT-GT	18,861	18,682	22,631	19,292	15,893	0.8
Malaysia	18,549	18,301	22,125	19,006	15,596	0.8
Thailand	312	381	506	286	297	(2.9)
Share of Visitors from Intra-IMT-GT (%)	67.8	100.7	123.7	87.2	60.9	–
Malaysia	66.7	55.8	55.2	63.8	60.0%	–
Thailand	1.1	2.1	2.8	1.3	1.1	–

( ) = negative, – = not applicable, IMT-GT = Indonesia–Malaysia–Thailand Growth Triangle.
Source: Compiled by the author from various publications of BPS-Statistics Indonesia.

Industrial Activities and Special Economic Zones

Under RPJMN 2020–2024, Dumai City is included in the growth corridor of Sumatera connected with other provincial capitals through the Trans-Sumatera Toll Road. Dumai is one of the 21 industrial and/or special economic zones designated by the national government outside Java Island.

There are three major industrial estates in Dumai's Industrial Growth Center for palm oil industry cluster.

(i) Pelintung Industrial Estate or Dumai Industrial Estate covering 5,084.53 ha. As of 2018, 10 companies were located in the estate, including the biggest nitrogen, phosphorus, and potassium fertilizer company in Southeast Asia.

(ii) Lubuk Gaung Industrial Estate covering 2,158 ha. There were at least 15 companies in the estate in 2018 engaged in CPO refineries, palm kernel oil, biodiesel, and small ports operations.

(iii) Pelindo Port Industrial Estate covering 115 ha with 12 companies as of 2018 engaged in CPO refineries, edible oil, and fatty acids, among others.[35]

In addition, there are also companies outside the industrial estates processing CPO derivative products, some of which are invested by Malaysians. The Riau provincial government is contemplating on the development of an SEZ in North Rupat Island and Pekanbaru City for tourism. The local government also prepares some industrial areas (e.g., Kuala Enok, Tenayan Raya, and Teknopolitan) outside the industrial growth centers for interested investors. The IMT-GT Business Center in Indonesia is based in Pekanbaru, with Riau Province serving as coordinator in promoting trade and commerce among the 10 IMT-GT provinces.

Overall Assessment

The two-lane road connecting Dumai with Pekanbaru along the Trans-Sumatera Highway is adequate and will be further enhanced with the completion of the four-lane Trans-Sumatera Toll Road. When the whole length of the Trans-Sumatera Toll Road is completed, EC4 can interface with EC3 through Penkanbaru, which is a key node in both corridors. Maritime connectivity between Dumai Port and ports in Malaysia (Melaka International Ferry Terminal, port of Port Dickson, Muar Port, and Port Klang) are mostly passenger ferry services, except that stearin (liquid bulk) is also exported to Port Klang. The Ro-Ro ferry service between Sri Junjungan Port and Tanjung Bruas Port is only partially operational for goods, not passengers, pending the finalization of regulations for transit vehicles. The full operationalization of the Ro-Ro ferry service is expected to boost trade between Sumatera and Malaysia due to the reduction in the time and cost to trade, which will benefit especially small and medium-sized enterprises to export their goods in small shipments. Air connectivity is served from Sultan Syarif Kasim II International Airport but flights to Malaysia are limited, with only one airline serving direct flights to Melaka, although there are three airlines with direct flights to Kuala Lumpur.

Dumai City has developed industrial estates to support industry clusters for palm oil with facilities and infrastructure to make them more efficient and competitive in export markets. Palm oil processing industries export their products to worldwide destinations through Dumai Port, which is the largest international gateway for CPO in Indonesia. Under the National Logistics System Blueprint 2012, Dumai will be developed further

---

[35] Regulation of Riau Province No.9/2018 on the Industrial Development Plan of Riau Province 2018–2038. https://ppid.riau.go.id/download/19/1543366590rpip-gabungan-fix.pdf.

to be the main port for CPO-based commodities.[36] Pelindo I has recently announced its plans to turn Dumai Port, as well as Belawan Port in North Sumatera, into CPO export centers as part of the government's plan to further exploit the potentials of the palm oil industry and move up the value chain.[37] Pekanbaru also plays an important role in the export of palm oil, as well as wood, through smaller ports in Perawang, Pekanbaru, and Rumbai.

Dumai Port has contributed significantly to the robust growth in Riau's foreign trade with around 80% of exports, both in terms of volume and value, being shipped through the port. Riau has maintained a constant trade surplus since 2007. Malaysia ranks fourth among Riau's export partners but prospects are promising with trade growing at an average of 14.6% during 2014–2018. Malaysia is also Riau's top source of imports.

Melaka's proximity to Dumai accounts for the large number of Malaysian visitors to the province traveling by ferry and by plane. Most Malaysian visitors to Riau are tourists. At the same time, there are also a good number of people from Riau traveling to Malaysia for leisure, education, or medical treatment. Plans to develop Riau Province's outer islands for tourism is expected to increase Malaysian and other foreign visitors to Riau that can augment the demand for maritime and air transport in the future.

The full implementation of the Melaka–Dumai Ro-Ro project remains to be stalled and this has been a set back in achieving the maritime objective of EC4. The project was initiated in 2008 to increase the volume of trade between Indonesia and Malaysia through the Ro-Ro mode of shipping designed to carry rolling cargoes that do not require quay cranes for loading or off-loading and eliminates cargo handling labor. The project was envisaged to boost the export potentials of small and medium enterprises in Riau who will be spending less for sea transport costs and benefit from faster service. Although the Ro-Ro service has started limited operations last October 2020, albeit restricted to a maximum capacity of 1,000 MT for goods only (not passengers), several issues are still being resolved before the Ro-Ro service can operate fully. Agreement has not been reached between Indonesia and Malaysia regarding the technical specifications of trucks and/or four-wheeled vehicles that can enter and exit ports and cross the border areas of the two countries; safety standards and customs formalities to be applied, among others. Moreover, Tanjung Bruas Port is a cargo port whereas Sri Junjungan Port is a passenger port, thus requiring adjustments in facilities and service capacities in the latter. Sri Junjungan Port is located approximately 6 km from Dumai Port, or 19 km from the entry point of Dumai–Pekanbaru toll road.

The Melaka–Dumai Economic Corridor, which includes only Riau Province, has not been used to full advantage considering the province's enormous economic growth potential. There is scope for including nodes in the surrounding islands of Rupat, Bengkalis, and Rangsang, in line with the government's priority to develop Indonesia's outermost islands to maintain its national interests on defense, prosperity, and the environment.

---

[36]   The Ministry of Transport, Ministry of State-Owned Enterprises, National Development Plan Agency, Ministry of Trade, Ministry of Industry, Ministry of Public Works, and Ministry of Agriculture are responsible for implementing the plan.

[37]   A. Gunawan and M. A. Iswara. 2020. Pelindo to Upgrade Dumai, Belawan Ports to Accommodate Growing CPO Exports *The Jakarta Post*. 7 February. https://www.thejakartapost.com/news/2020/02/06/pelindo-to-upgrade-dumai-belawan-ports-to-accommodate-growing-cpo-exports.html.

Reconfiguration of EC4

The reconfiguration of EC4 in Sumatera includes: (i) the designation of Sri Junjungan Port and Rupat Island as additional nodes in Riau Province, and (ii) the addition of West Sumatera Province with Padang and Bukittinggi as additional nodes. West Sumatera has also been added to the new configuration of EC3, as discussed in the previous section. On the Malaysian side, the reconfiguration of EC4 extended the corridor up to Johor.

The reconfigured **EC4 has been renamed Central Sumatera–Southern Malaysia Economic Corridor** (Maps 13 and 14).

**Map 13: Central Sumatera–Southern Malaysia Economic Corridor
(Reconfigured Economic Corridor 4) - Indonesia**

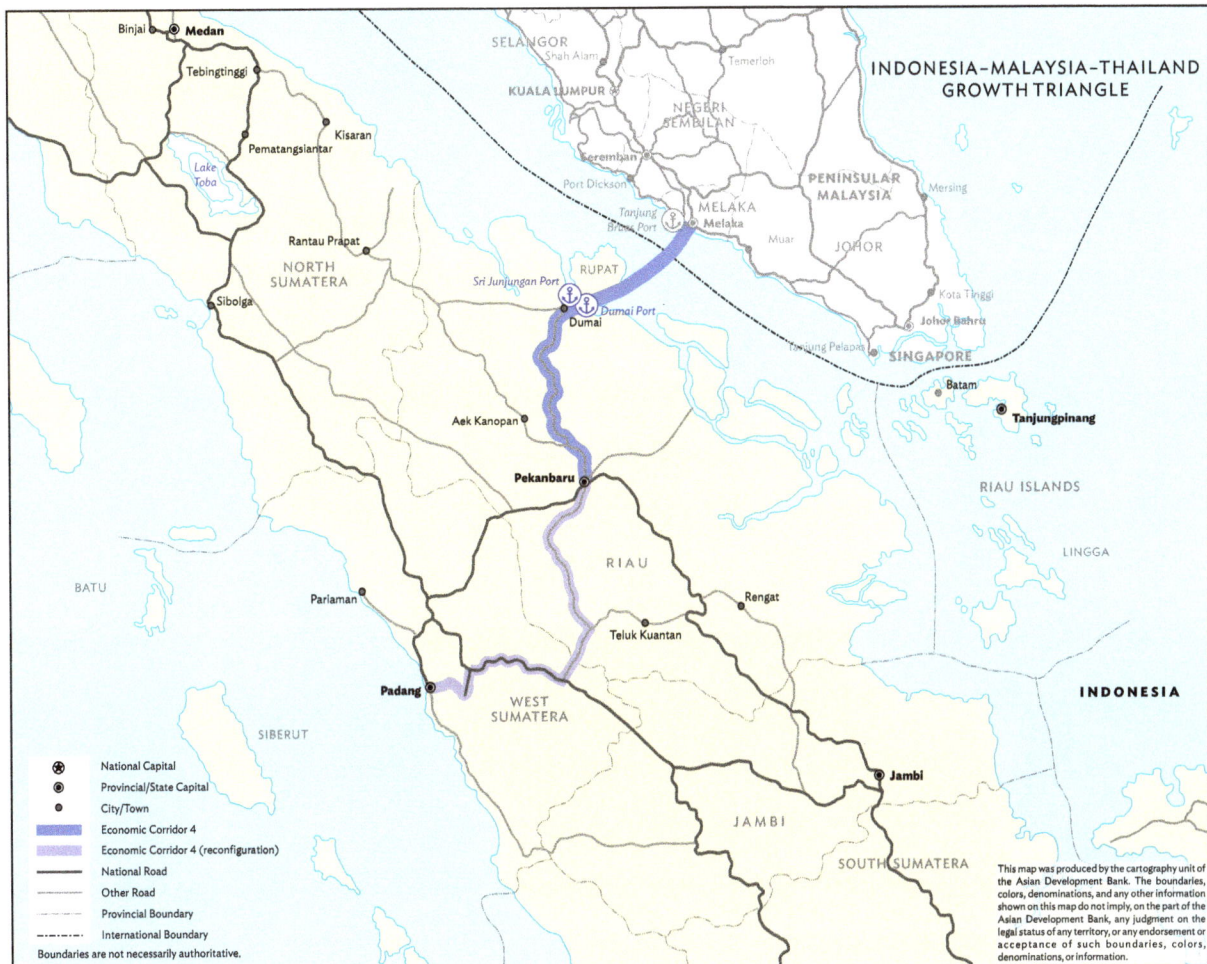

Source: Asian Development Bank

Map 14: Central Sumatera–Southern Malaysia Economic Corridor
(Reconfigured Economic Corridor 4)

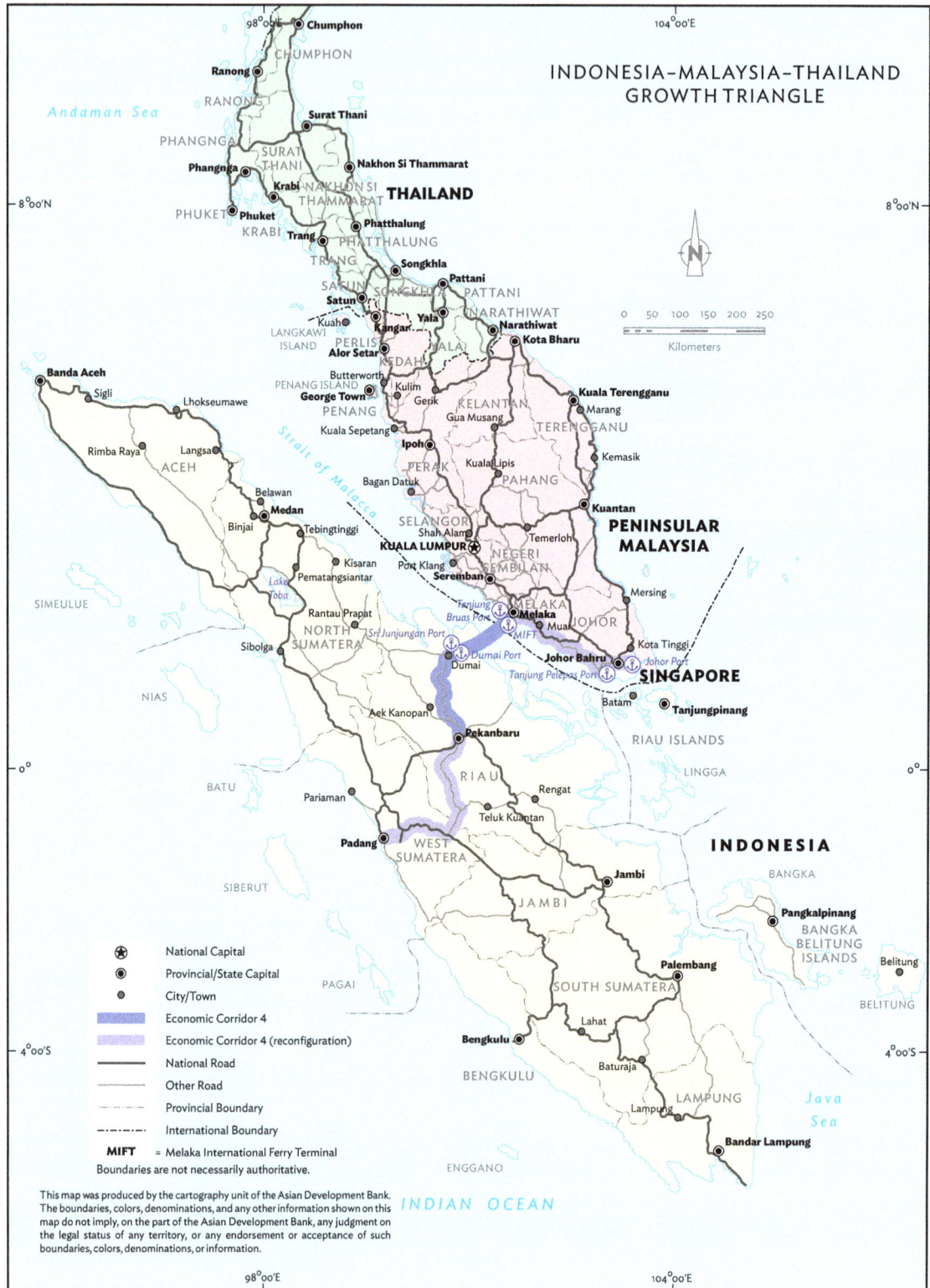

Boundaries are not necessarily authoritative.

This map was produced by the cartography unit of the Asian Development Bank. The boundaries, colors, denominations, and any other information shown on this map do not imply, on the part of the Asian Development Bank, any judgment on the legal status of any territory, or any endorsement or acceptance of such boundaries, colors, denominations, or information.

Source: Asian Development Bank.

Two Additional Nodes in Riau Province

Sri Junjungan Port in Dumai, which is the designated port on the Indonesian side for the Melaka–Dumai Ro-Ro ferry project was included as additional maritime gateway nodes in EC4. Sri Junjungan Port serves the domestic ferry route as well as logistics services for agricultural products, especially rice, from Rupat Island.

Rupat Island, which is in front of Dumai City and part of the Bengkalis Regency, will be a tourism node, as part of the Ministry of Tourism and the local government's plan to develop an SEZ for tourism in North Rupat. The island is already a popular destination for marine tourism. Based on Presidential Decree No. 6/2017, Rupat, Bengkalis, and Rangsang Islands in Riau are regarded as Indonesia's Outermost Islands and as such are given priority location (*lokpri*) status for development. It is also part of the National Strategic Tourism Zone. Local people in these islands are also engaged in cross-border activities with Malaysia considering the short travel time of 30 minutes by boat.[38] There are two Ro-Ro ferries serving the route from Batu Panjang Port in Rupat Island to Sri Junjungan Port in Dumai, as well as a fast ferry from Tanjung Medang in Rupat to Dumai Port. Customs, immigration, quarantine, and security facilities are being developed in these ports to facilitate legal border crossing activities between Indonesia and Malaysia.

Apart from its tourism potential, Rupat Island has a huge economic potential that can benefit from its proximity to Dumai. It plays an important role in the agriculture supply chain for rice, coconut, rubber, palm oil, and betel nut. It is a rich source of sea sand, which has been exploited by PT Logomas. Studies indicate that it also has a potential for silica mining, with 100 km^2 of land having the highest concentrated silica in Indonesia. Bengkalis Regency is a major contributor to Riau's trade, ranking fourth as the province's largest exporter, and fifth largest importer.

Rupat's inclusion as a new node in EC4 is crucial in the context of developing small islands through a more environmentally friendly approach. So far, many residents of Rupat Island and its surroundings (Rangsang and Bengkalis) have depended on their livelihood from cutting down mangrove trees for charcoal production. In fact, mangrove trees are crucial in maintaining the ecosystem of the islands. Due to the massive and uncontrolled felling of mangrove trees, Rupat and two other islands have suffered serious abrasion. The Government of Indonesia through the Coordinating Ministry for Maritime Affairs and Investment needed a budget of around Rs1.4 trillion (around $98 million) to overcome the abrasion since 2019. Rupat's inclusion as an EC4 node can help divert the livelihoods of local residents from making charcoal made from mangroves that could damage the ecosystem and consequently, the tourism industry. The development plan for Rupat Island and its surroundings have recently become more environmentally friendly as stakeholders consider replacing mining with other sectors that are in line with the nature of the island.

Inclusion of West Sumatera

West Sumatera[39] is located west of Riau Province, facing the Indian Ocean, and its inclusion in EC4 can help enhance economic linkages with the growth corridor along the eastern coast of Sumatera. Connectivity with Riau Province will enable West Sumatera to tap into more developed palm oil and rubber supply chains and expand trade with Malaysia through Dumai Port. Padang, the capital, can potentially benefit from the

---

[38]   During the virtual national consultation on 5 June 2020 conducted as part of this study, the local government had proposed the inclusion of West Sumatera Province in EC4.

[39]   West Sumatera is subdivided into 12 regencies and 7 autonomous cities and has a population of about 5 million people (2018). See the detailed information on BPS-Statistics Indonesia. 2019. *Provinsi Sumatera Barat dalam Angka 2019*. Padang: BPS-Statistics Indonesia.

development of the tourism SEZ being planned at Rupat. Both Rupat and Padang are part of the National Strategic Tourism Zone and can collaborate in the packaging, promotion, and marketing of tourism products in their territories as well as in Melaka. West Sumatera belongs to the equalization corridor under the National Indicative Plan for Sumatera. The Trans-Sumatera Highway connects Padang, West Sumatera's capital, with Pekanbaru and Dumai. Once completed, the Padang–Pekanbaru segment of the Trans-Sumatera Toll Road will enable faster and more efficient transport between the two cities. West Sumatera, with its capital Padang, and Bukittingi, has also been included in EC3, as discussed in the preceding section. Table 38 shows the provinces and nodes covered in the new configuration of EC4.

Table 38: Economic Corridor 4: Existing and Additional Provinces and Nodes, by Type

Province/State	Node/Type	Type			
		CAP	COM	MGP	TOUR
INDONESIA					
Riau	Dumai Port			✓	
	Dumai City		✓		
	Sri Junjungan Port*			✓	
	Rupat Island*				✓
	Pekanbaru	✓	✓		
West Sumatera*	Padang*	✓	✓		
MALAYSIA					
Melaka	Tanjung Bruas Port (Port of Melaka)			✓	
	Melaka International Ferry Terminal*			✓	✓
	Melaka City*	✓	✓		✓
Johor*	Johor Bahru*	✓	✓		
	Tanjung Pelepas Port, Gelang Patah*			✓	
	Johor Port, Pasir Gudang*			✓	

CAP = capital, COM = commercial, MGP = maritime gateway port, TOUR = tourism.
Note: * denotes additional provinces and nodes.
Source: Study team.

As Indonesia's partner in EC4, Malaysia has involved the state of Melaka since the beginning of EC4. However, the ongoing development shows great potential for the development of domestic links between Melaka and Johor, which can then amplify Malaysia's economic network with Central Sumatera (Riau and West Sumatera), Southern Sumatera, and Singapore. Therefore, Johor needs to be included in EC4, especially for several strategic nodes such as the city of Johor Bahru, Tanjung Pelepas Port, and Johor Port (footnote 1).

Economic Corridor 5. The Ranong–Phuket–Aceh Economic Corridor

Overview

The Ranong–Phuket–Aceh Economic Corridor (EC5) is envisaged to enhance the connectivity between Sumatera and Southern Thailand primarily through maritime mode (Maps 15 and 16). Connectivity will be established through the development of facilities in key ports in Aceh,[40] Sabang, and Malahayati, to be connected with Phuket Port in Southern Thailand. Despite very limited trade between Southern Thailand and Aceh, tourism possibilities exist and could be developed between Phuket and Sabang, which has a lot of unspoiled places to offer. Ranong Port located at the extremity of the corridor in Southern Thailand at the mouth of Kraburi River in Ranong Province, basically serves as a supply base for oil and gas offshore exploitation.[41]

EC5 involves the Aceh Province in Sumatera, with the following nodes (Table 39):

(i)   Banda Aceh - capital and commercial node

(ii)   Ulee Lheue Port (mainland Aceh) - the main ferry port

(iii)   Malahayati Port (mainland Aceh) - main cargo terminal

(iv)   Sabang (We Island) - tourism node

(v)   Sabang Port (Sabang) container port and free port, port of call for cruise ships

(vi)   Balohan Port (Sabang) - the main ferry port

Table 39: Economic Corridor 5: Existing Nodes in Aceh Province by Type

Province/State	Node	Type			
		CAP	COM	MGP	TOUR
Aceh	Banda Aceh	✓	✓		✓
	Sabang City		✓		✓
	Ulee Lheue Port			✓	
	Malahayati Port			✓	
	Sabang Port		✓	✓	✓
	Balohan Port			✓	

CAP = capital, COM = commercial, MGP = maritime gateway port, TOUR = tourism.
Source: Author.

Aceh is the westernmost province of Indonesia on the northern end of Sumatera. It has a land area of 58,376.81 km^2 and a population of 5.8 million (Table 40). Aceh is surrounded by water on three sides: the Indian Ocean to the west and north, and the Strait of Malacca to the east. The dominant sectors are oil and gas and mining, and agriculture and fisheries. Coal is the main commodity exported to Thailand and other countries such as India (Table 40).

---

[40]   IMT-GT. 2017. *IMT-GT Vision 2036*. Putra Jaya: CIMT. p. 61.

[41]   IMT-GT. 2012. *IMT-GT Implementation Blueprint 2012–2016*. Putra Jaya: CIMT. p. 17.

**Map 15: Ranong–Phuket–Aceh Economic Corridor
(Economic Corridor 5)**

INDONESIA–MALAYSIA–THAILAND
GROWTH TRIANGLE

Chumphon
CHUMPHON
Ranong
Ranong Port
RANONG
Andaman Sea
Surat Thani
PHANGNGA
SURAT THANI
Nakhon Si Thammarat
Phangnga
Phangnga
PHUKET
NAKHON SI THAMMARAT
THAILAND
Krabi
Phuket
Phuket Port
KRABI
Trang
Phatthalung
TRANG
PHATTHALUNG
SATUN
Songkhla
SABANG ISLAND
Sabang Port
Satun
SONGKHLA
Pattani
PATTANI
Yala
NARATHIWAT
Balohan Port
Malahayati Port
LANGKAWI ISLAND
Kangar
YALA
Narathiwat
Banda Aceh
Alor Setar
PERLIS
Kota Bharu
Ulee Lheue Port
Sigli
Lhokseumawe
KEDAH
Butterworth
Kulim
KELANTAN
Kuala Terengganu
Langsa
PENANG ISLAND
George Town
Gerik
Marang
Rimba Raya
ACEH
PENANG
Gua Musang
TERENGGANU
Kuala Sepetang
Belawan
Kuala Lipis
Kemasik
Medan
Ipoh
Binjai
Tebingtinggi
PERAK
PAHANG
Kisaran
Kuala Kubu
Kuantan
Pematangsiantar
Bagan Datuk
Lake Toba
SELANGOR
PENINSULAR
Shah Alam
Temerloh
MALAYSIA
SIMEULUE
KUALA LUMPUR
NEGERI SEMBILAN
Rantau Prapat
Seremban
Mersing
NORTH SUMATERA
Port Dickson
Sibolga
Melaka
MELAKA
NIAS
Muar
JOHOR
Dumai
Kota Tinggi
Johor Bahru
SINGAPORE
Aek Kanopan
Tanjungpinang
Pekanbaru
RIAU ISLANDS
RIAU
LINGGA
BATU
Pariaman
Rengat
Teluk Kuantan
INDONESIA
BANGKA
Padang
WEST SUMATERA
Jambi
Pangkalpinang
SIBERUT
JAMBI
BANGKA BELITUNG ISLANDS
Belitung
PAGAI
BELITUNG
SOUTH SUMATERA
Palembang
Lahat
Bengkulu
BENGKULU
Baturaja
LAMPUNG
Java Sea
Lampung
ENGGANO
Bandar Lampung
INDIAN OCEAN
Strait of Malacca

Andaman Sea

98°00'E   104°00'E

8°00'N   8°00'N

0°   0°

4°00'S   4°00'S

N

0 50 100 150 200 250
Kilometers

98°00'E   104°00'E

⊛ National Capital
◉ Provincial/State Capital
● City/Town
━ Economic Corridor 5
━ National Road
━ Other Road
─·─ Provincial Boundary
─··─ International Boundary
Boundaries are not necessarily authoritative.

This map was produced by the cartography unit of the Asian Development Bank.
The boundaries, colors, denominations, and any other information shown on this
map do not imply, on the part of the Asian Development Bank, any judgment on
the legal status of any territory, or any endorsement or acceptance of such
boundaries, colors, denominations, or information.

Source: Asian Development Bank.

**Map 16: Ranong–Phuket–Aceh Economic Corridor
(Economic Corridor 5) - Indonesia**

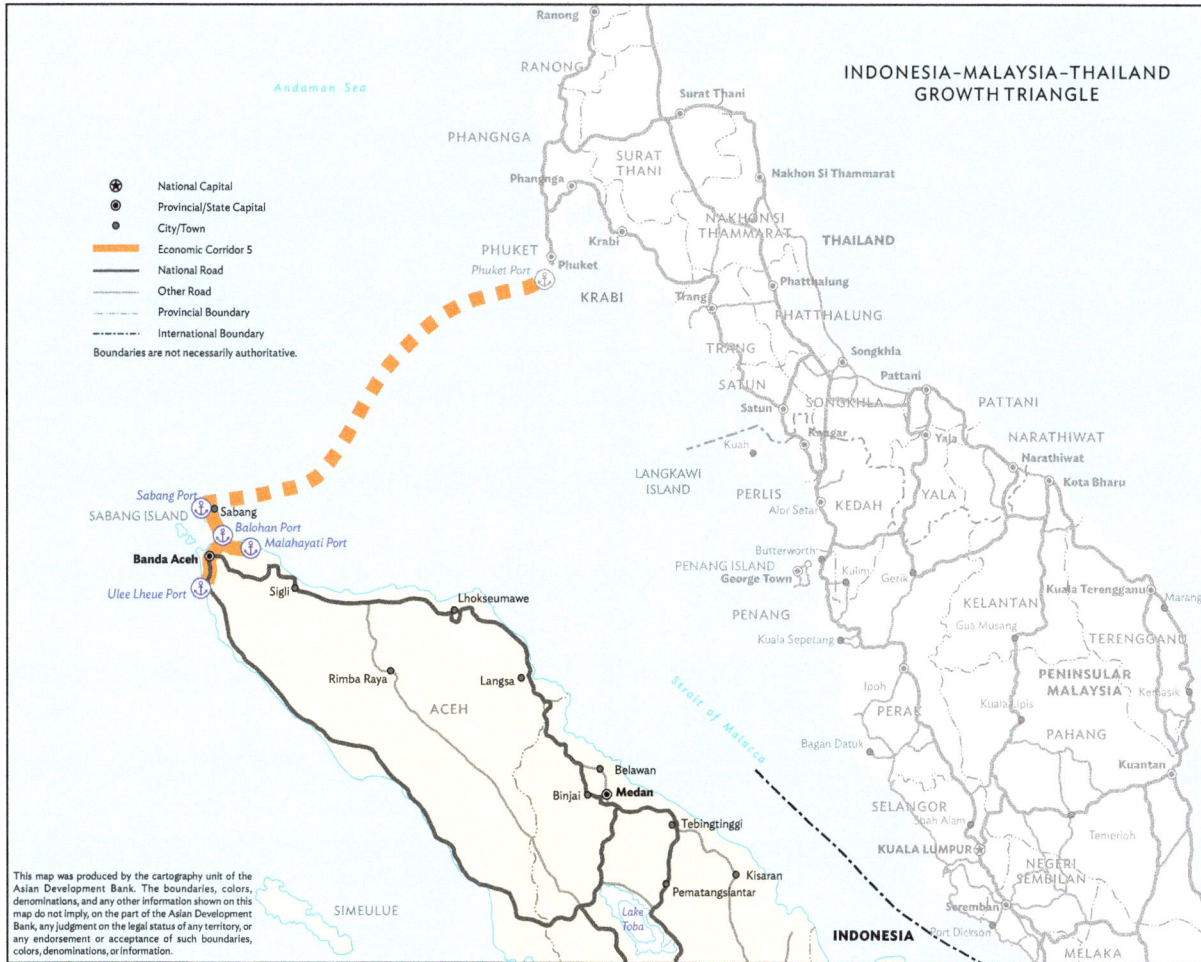

Source: Asian Development Bank.

Table 40: Economic Corridor 5: Socioeconomic Profile of Aceh Province

Land Area	57,956 km²	Population*	5.8 million
GRDP (constant prices)		**Of which, Banda Aceh**	**265,000**
2014	Rp113.49 trillion ($9.1 billion)	Rank in Sumatera	Sixth
2018	Rp126.82 trillion ($8.8 billion)	Share to Sumatera population (%)	9.14
Share to Sumatera (%)	5.69	Share to Indonesia population (%)	1.99
Share to Indonesia (%)	1.22	Population growth rate (2010-2018)	1.96
Growth rate 2014-2018 (%)	2.82	Population density	
Rank in Sumatera	Eighth	1990	76
Rank in Indonesia	19th	2000	90
GRDP per capita		2018	120
2014	Rp23.13 million ($1,859)	**Share of sectoral employment 2018** (%)	
2018	Rp24.01 million ($1,658)	Agriculture, veterinary, forestry, and fishery	40.34
Growth rate (%)	0.94	Trading, hotel, and restaurant	19.42
Rank in Sumatera	Ninth	Processing industry	7.57
Rank in Indonesia	27th	Services	0.86

GRDP = gross regional domestic product, km² = square kilometer, Rp = Indonesian rupiah.
* Population estimate based on the 2010 census.
Source: Compiled by the author from various publications of BPS-Statistics Indonesia and Indonesia Industrial Estates Directory.

Banda Aceh, the capital of Aceh Province has a population of 265,000 in 2018, or 5% of the Aceh Province's total population. In addition to its role as a commercial node, Banda Aceh is also a popular destination for halal tourism, especially among Indonesians and Malaysians. Banda Aceh is at the northernmost tip of the existing Trans-Sumatera Highway and the ongoing Trans-Sumatera Toll Road project. It is close to Malahayati Port in Aceh Besar Regency where domestic logistics distribution and export–import activities take place. Sultan Iskandar Muda International Airport serves domestic flight routes to Medan and Jakarta, as well as international flights to Kuala Lumpur, Penang, Jeddah, and Medina. Banda Aceh is also a node in EC3 (Table 40).

Banda Aceh is a home base for several tuna processing companies. Yellowfin tuna coming from Meulaboh, Pulau Aceh, Laweng, and Ulee Lheue are processed into frozen tuna and tuna loin. These products are marketed domestically and also exported to Japan, the Republic of Korea, and Thailand. There is scope for further value-addition to tuna exports since the bulk of tuna transported to Medan are still unprocessed. Banda Aceh is also a home base for the coffee bean processing industry, especially robusta coffee from Ulee Kareng in Banda Aceh and Arabica coffee from Gayo Highland (Aceh Tengah and Bener Meriah regencies). The products are marketed to other Sumatera provinces and Kalimantan. Aceh also sells betel nut (*pinang*), CPO, and Arabica coffee to North Sumatera.

Ulee Lheue Port is a ferry port located in Banda Aceh. It serves the Ulee Lheue Port–Balohan Port (Sabang) route, mainly for tourists to go to Sabang. There are no commodities trading in this port. It only provides logistics services between Banda Aceh and Sabang. There are no plans to further develop this port in the RPJMN 2020–2024 or in the National Logistics System Blueprint.

Express ferries are operated by private vessels KM Bahari 3, Km Cantika 89, Bahari 89, and Bahari 2F. *Angkutan Su-ngai Danau dan Penyeberangan* (ASDP)—a state-owned enterprise—is operating two Ro-Ro ferries: (i) KMP BRR, 911 GT in capacity, which can load 450 passengers, 25 cars, and 100 motorcycles; and (ii) KMP Tanjung Burang, with a capacity of 507 GT which can load 200 passengers, 15 cars, and 50 motorcycles.

Malahayati Port is the main cargo terminal for Banda Aceh, located about 23 km from the city. It has a depth of 9.5 meters and a dock of 384 meters, which can accommodate three 100-meter ships with a load of 300 TEU containers at a time. It is supported by loading and unloading equipment, three forklift units, and six container transport trucks, and others. Malahayati Port receives consumer goods in containers from ships operated by Tempuran Emas Line (Tanjung Priok–Belawan–Malahayati) once per week and Kanaka Line (Tanjung Priok–Belawan–Lhokseumawe–Malahayati) twice per month. This is part of the effort to make Malahayati Port as a feeder to Belawan Port based on the Indonesian national agenda of sea toll development (*tol laut*).[42] Malahayati port is being used by PT Samana to export pozzolan (a mixture of cement) to India since 2018, and will also export pozzolan to Dubai in 2020. Pozzolan mining is located in Aceh Besar regency, close to Malahayati Port. As regards imports, Malahayati Port is the entry point of liquid asphalt coming from Singapore.

Since 2014, Malahayati Port has played an increasing role in import activities compared to exports. Imports coursed through Malahayati originate from Singapore. There are no further development plans for this port under RPJMN 2020–2024 or in the National Logistics System Blueprint.

Sabang is located in We Island located northwest of Sumatera. We Island is separated from the main Sumatera Island but administratively under Aceh Province. Sabang is 39 km from Banda Aceh, near the Strait of Malacca, and is the westernmost city in Indonesia, bordering Malaysia, Thailand, and India. It has a population of 34,570 or less than 1% of Aceh's population. Its GRDP is also less than 1% of the provincial GRDP. Travel from Sabang City to Banda Aceh takes about 45 minutes by fast regular ship or 2 hours by ferry.

Under RPJMN 2020–2024, Sabang has been identified as a strategic location for several programs. It has been designated as a National Strategic Activity Center (*Pusat Kegiatan Strategis Nasional*) due to its location as the northernmost Indonesian border area. Sabang is a free trade zone and free port for Aceh's imports. It is also a part of the Integrated Marine and Fishery Center in Sumatera, together with Mentawai Islands in West Sumatera. This center will provide Sabang with the infrastructure and support facilities to promote marine tourism in Indonesia.

Because of the small size of the island (120.67 km^2), Sabang has no significant natural resources and no big industries. Agriculture is the main economic activity, with coconuts and cloves as the principal crops. Other regencies and/or cities in Aceh Province do not use Sabang Port for exports. Sabang, however, has a free port, which is the second biggest import gateway for Aceh Province (24.5% of total imports) after Lhokseumawe.

---

[42] Sea toll is a concept to improve connectivity between islands in Indonesia to reduce the basic prices of commodities throughout the archipelago and eliminate the price gap between western part of Indonesia, which is more developed compared to the eastern part. It was launched by President Joko Widodo in 2014.

Sabang Port is managed by *Badan Pengusahaan Kawasan Sabang* (BPKS) and is part of the Sabang free port and free trade zone. The port, which has a depth of 20 meters and a shipping lane length of 1,400 meters, has potential to be a strategic transshipment port. At present, Sabang Port has two container terminals.[43] Container Terminal 1 (CT-1) has the capacity to accommodate up to 30,000 DWT, while Container Terminal 3 (CT-3) can accommodate up to 100,000 DWT. There was no export activity in Sabang Port from 2014–2018 but it is the second biggest port after Lhokseumawe, for handling Aceh's imports from Singapore. With limited trade activity, Sabang Port is currently focusing on developing cruise calls from ships visiting Langkawi (e.g., Marella cruise ship) and Phuket (e.g., Seabourn cruise ship).

Balohan Port is a ferry port located in Sabang, We Island. It provides the main access from Sabang to Banda Aceh, especially for tourists who are traveling to Jakarta, Medan, Kuala Lumpur, and Penang through the Iskandar Muda International Airport. There are no commodities being traded in this port. It only facilitates logistics flow between Banda Aceh and Sabang. The port is being revitalized with a total budget of Rp221 billion. This includes a port area widening from 1 ha to 4.5 ha. It is expected that Balohan will be an international port after the revitalization has been completed, although the international route has yet to be determined.

Status of Physical Connectivity

Land route. The road from Banda Aceh City to Malahayati Port covering 33 km has two asphalt lanes. It is the main transport route for imported goods entering through Malahayati container port to Banda Aceh and its surrounding areas.

Maritime links. There are no commercial ferries or cargo ships from Aceh or Sabang to Ranong or Phuket in Thailand as envisaged in EC5 (Table 41). The IMT-GT Implementation Blueprint 2012–2016 stated that "Ulee Lheue is a newly-reconstructed port … and can accommodate, with some minor adjustments, passenger vessels and Ro-Ro services from the south of Thailand (Phuket)." As of end-November 2019, this plan has not materialized. After the tsunami in 2004, there were Ro-Ro services from Kreunggukuh in Lhokseumawe to Penang, as well as express ferry from Langsa (Aceh) to Penang, but both services have stopped due to low occupancy rates. The operator had hoped to subsidize the operational costs by transporting export–import commodities, but cumbersome requirements for export–import licenses did not make the plan viable.[44]

Among the four ports in Aceh, only Malahayati and Sabang Port operate as an international commercial seaport, although in a limited capacity. Malahayati Port specifically handles exports of pozzolan to India and Dubai, and imports of liquid asphalt from Singapore. Ulee Lheue Port in mainland Aceh, and Balohan Port in Sabang, basically provide ferry services between them. Sabang Port handles only Aceh's imports from Singapore. Given limited trade, the port is currently focusing on developing cruise calls from ships visiting Langkawi and Phuket.

---

[43]   Container Terminal 1 (CT-1) has two docks (170 meter x 41 meter and 32 meter x 9.5 meter), both 15 meters deep and could accommodate an up to 30,000 DWT vessel. CT-1 also has stacking field with an area of 10,850 meters and warehouses with an area of 3,150 meters. Container Terminal 3 (CT-3) has a 423 meter x 70 meter dock, 23 meters deep and could accommodate 100,000 DWT. In addition to container, CT-3 also has been docked by cruise ships and yachts.

[44]   *Bakri*. 2013. Ferry Kembali Layari Langsa–Penang. 19 November. https://aceh.tribunnews.com/2013/11/19/ferry-kembali-layari-langsa-penang.

Table 41: Economic Corridor 5: Status of Maritime Connectivity of Ports in Aceh

Port	Link to Other Ports	Type of Maritime Activity	Remarks
Malahayati	Singapore	Liquid bulk	Import of liquid asphalt
	India	Dry bulk	Export of pozzolan
	Belawan	Container cargo	Domestic shipping route
Ulee Lheue	Balohan	Passenger express and Ro-Ro ferry	Serves domestic route only
Balohan	Ulee Lheue	Passenger express and Ro-Ro ferry	Serving domestic route only
Sabang	Singapore	Container cargo	Import of general goods
		Passenger cruise	
	Laem Chabang, Thailand	Passenger cruise	
	Langkawi, Malaysia	Passenger cruise	

Ro-Ro = roll on, roll off
Source: Compiled by the author from various sources.

Air connectivity. There are two airports in Banda Aceh. Sultan Iskandar Muda International Airport,[45] located 13.5 km southeast of Banda Aceh, serves domestic routes to major cities in Sumatera and Jakarta, as well as international routes from Banda Aceh to Penang and Kuala Lumpur (Table 42). Maimun Saleh Airport in Sabang, We Island is a small airport that belongs to the Indonesian military. Previously, the airport was used to serve domestic flights from Sabang to Medan but this was stopped in November 2018 due to the difficulty of coordinating operating hours for commercial and military activities.

Table 42: Economic Corridor 5: Flight Routes in Sultan Iskandar Muda International Airport, Aceh

Airlines	Destinations
AirAsia	Kuala Lumpur-International
Batik Air	Jakarta–Halim Perdanakusuma, Jakarta–Soekarno–Hatta
Citilink	Medan
Firefly	Penang
Garuda Indonesia	Jakarta–Soekarno–Hatta
Indonesia AirAsia	Kuala Lumpur-International
Lion Air	Medan
Susi Air	Blangkejeren, Blangpidie, Kutacane, Meulaboh
Malindo Air	Penang

Source: https://sultaniskandarmuda-airport.co.id/.

Overall, the status of physical connectivity in EC5 falls short of meeting the objective to establish maritime connectivity between Aceh or Sabang and Ranong or Phuket. There is no direct shipping line for trade between Malahayati Port and Phuket Port; nor a passenger ferry line between Ulee Lheue Port or Sabang Port and Phuket Port or Ranong Port. The ports on the Indonesian side have limited international trading activity due to lack of demand. There are also no plans for further developing the ports in the next 5 years based on government plans. Sabang Port has the potential to become a strategic transshipment port because of its location, but because of limited trade, it is currently focusing on promoting port calls by cruise ships from Singapore as home port. There are direct flights to Kuala Lumpur and Penang but none to Thailand.

---

[45]   Sultan Iskandar Muda International Airport is listed as the 23rd busiest airport in Indonesia and has been awarded the World's Best Airport for Halal Travelers in the World Halal Tourism Awards 2016.

Trade

Foreign trade. From 2014 to 2018, the volume of Aceh's foreign trade fluctuated and showed no clear pattern. From 3.8 million tons in 2007, the first year of the IMT-GT Road Map 2007–2011, Aceh's trade volume dropped to about 418,500 in 2016, but recovered in 2018 to 5 million or 3.6% of Sumatera's total trade. On average, the value of exports exceeded imports during 2014–2018. In 2018, Aceh ranked seventh in terms of contribution to Sumatera's foreign trade volume (3.6%), but recorded the smallest contribution (0.23%) in terms of trade value (Table 43).

Table 43: Economic Corridor 5: Aceh's Foreign Trade Volume, 2007, 2014–2018
(million tons)

Item	2007	2014	2015	2016	2017	2018	Average 2014–2018	Compound Average Growth Rate 2014–2018 (%)
Total Sumatera	**82.7**	**116.7**	**119.1**	**108.2**	**125.70**	**140.5**	**122.0**	**4.8**
Exports	69.0	94.5	97.4	87.7	101.6	113.8	99.0	4.8
Imports	13.6	22.2	21.8	20.6	24.1	26.7	23.1	4.7
Aceh	**3.9**	**0.9**	**1.3**	**0.4**	**2.6**	**5.1**	**2.1**	**54.2**
Exports	3.6	0.72	1.2	0.3	2.5	5.1	0.9	63.3
Imports	0.3	0.2	0.2	0.1	0.1	0.1	0.1	(14.9)
Share of Aceh (%)	**4.7**	**0.8**	**1.1**	**0.5**	**2.1**	**3.6**	**1.7**	–
Exports	5.2	0.8	1.2	0.3	2.5	4.5	1.0	–
Imports	2.3	0.8	0.7	0.6	0.4	0.4	0.6	–

( ) = negative, – = not applicable.
Note: Totals may not sum precisely because of rounding.
Source: Compiled by the author from various publications of BPS-Statistics Indonesia.

Table 44: Economic Corridor 5: Aceh's Foreign Trade Value, 2007, 2018–2018
($ million)

Item	2007	2014	2015	2016	2017	2018	Average 2014–2018	Compound Average Growth Rate 2014–2018 (%)
Total Sumatera	**42,552.4**	**83,304.3**	**63,222.7**	**58,805.9**	**66,050.0**	**73,229.3**	**68,922.4**	**(3.20)**
Exports	35,150.0	60,129.4	44,651.6	41,832.6	50,056.6	50,066.6	49,347.4	(4.50)
Imports	7,402.4	23,175.0	18,571.1	16,973.3	15,993.4	23,162.7	19,575.1	(0.01)
Aceh	**1,884.9**	**547.9**	**210.2**	**51.9**	**117.0**	**168.3**	**219.1**	**(25.50)**
Exports	1,854.2	507.4	93.3	22.9	77.7	138.6	124.7	(27.70)
Imports	30.7	40.5	116.8	29.0	39.3	29.7	51.1	(7.50)
Share of Aceh (%)	**4.4**	**0.7**	**0.3**	**0.09**	**0.2**	**0.2**	**0.3**	–
Exports	5.3	0.9	0.2	0.05	0.2	0.3	0.3	–
Imports	0.4	0.2	0.6	0.2	03	0.1	0.3	–

( ) = negative, – = not applicable.
Note: Totals may not sum precisely because of rounding.
Source: Compiled by the author from various publications of BPS-Statistics Indonesia.

Meulaboh Port was the main gateway for export with a share of 99% in terms of volume or 93.5% in value. Coal was the main commodity exported through Meulaboh. There was no import activity recorded in this port in 2018. Import activities were concentrated in Lok Nga Port (57.74% in volume or 6.11% in value) and Lhokseumawe (22.94% in volume or 36.46% in value). Malahayati Port and Sabang Port were also important import gateways for liquid asphalt and general cargo, both from Singapore. The contribution of both ports were higher in terms of trade value than trade volume (Table 45).

Table 45: Economic Corridor 5: Major Trade Gateways in Aceh, 2018

Ports	Volume (million tons)				Value (million US$)			
	Export	Share (%)	Import	Share (%)	Exports	Share (%)	Imports	Share (%)
Meulaboh	5.0	99.0	0.0	0.0	129.6	93.5	0.0	0.0
Malahayati	0.02	0.4	0.01	13.5	0.2	0.1	537	17.8
Lhokseumawe	0.02	0.5	0.02	22.9	7.6	5.5	10.8	36.5
Blang Lancang (Arun)	0.01	0.11	0.00	0.00	0.8	0.6	0.0	0.0
Kuala Langsa	0.0	0.0	0.0	34.4	0.1	0.1	4.5	15.2
Blang Bintang (U)	0.0	0.0	0.0	0.0	0.3	0.2	0.1	0.17
Lok Nga	0.0	0.0	0.1	57.7	0.0	0.0	1.8	6.1
Sabang	0.0	0.0	0.0	2.4	0.0	0.0	7.2	24.4
Total	**5.1**	**100.0**	**0.1**	**100.0**	**138.6**	**100.0**	**29.7**	**100.0**

Note: Totals may not sum precisely because of rounding.
Source: BPS-Statistics Indonesia. 2019. *Statistik Perdagangan Luar Negeri Aceh 2018 Banda Aceh: 2019*. pp. 28 and 55.

Trade with Thailand. Aceh's trade with Thailand is quite strong. In 2018, Thailand was the third largest export partner for Aceh after India and the PRC. Exports to Thailand accounted for 13%, both in volume and value terms. Exports to Thailand were mainly through Meulaboh Port, which was the main gateway for mineral fuel exports. As for imports, Thailand was the largest country of origin in 2018 by volume (73.8%). Lok Nga Port in Aceh Besar Regency is the main gateway for imports from Thailand. This port is located in the area of PT Lafarge Holcim Indonesia, the biggest cement producer in Aceh. This factory requires large quantities of gypsum, which is imported from Thailand.[46] One of the gypsum suppliers to PT Lafarge Holcim Indonesia was the Southern Group, which has two loading ports: (i) in Tambon Tha Thong, Amphoe Mueang, Surat Thani Province; and (ii) in Nongtalea Sub-District, Muang District, Krabi Province.[47] In terms of trade value, Thailand had the second-largest contribution 30.7%, after Singapore (Tables 46 and 47).

---

[46] PT Semen Andalas Indonesia. 2006. *Summary Environmental Impact Assessment Project Number: 39932-01 Indonesia: Reconstruction of Cement Production Facility in Aceh Project*. December. https://www.adb.org/sites/default/files/project-document/66600/39932-ino-seia.pdf.

[47] Southern Group. *Loading Port*. Accessed from https://www.southerngroup-thai.com/loading-port in 2 July 2020.

Table 46: Economic Corridor 5: Aceh Trade with Thailand

(million tons)

Item	2007	2014	2015	2016	2017	2018	Average 2014–2018	Compound Average Growth Rate 2014–2018 (%)
Aceh	**3.9**	**0.9**	**1.3**	**0.4**	**2.6**	**5.2**	**2.1**	**54.9**
Exports	3.6	0.7	1.2	0.3	2.5	5.1	2.0	63.3
Imports	0.3	0.2	0.2	0.1	0.1	0.1	0.1	(14.9)
Trade with Thailand	**0.02**	**0.1**	**0.1**	**0.1**	**0.14**	**0.7**	**0.2**	**60.8**
Exports	0.01	0.00	0.01	0.00	0.07	0.67	0.15	624.7
Imports	0.01	0.10	0.08	0.09	0.07	0.07	0.08	(7.7)
Share of Trade with Thailand (%)	**0.5**	**11.1**	**6.9**	**21.0**	**5.3**	**14.2**	**11.0**	–
Exports	0.17	0.03	1.01	0.63	2.82	13.07	7.66	–
Imports	4.33	53.48	53.58	70.42	71.54	73.81	62.34	–

( ) = negative, – = not applicable.
Note: Totals may not sum precisely because of rounding.
Sources: BPS-Statistics Indonesia (BPS-Statistics Indonesia. 2019. *Statistik Perdagangan Luar Negeri Aceh 2018*. Banda Aceh; BPS-Statistics Indonesia. 2018. *Statistik Perdagangan Luar Negeri Aceh 2017*. Banda Aceh; BPS-Statistics Indonesia. 2017. *Statistik Perdagangan Luar Negeri Aceh 2016*. Banda Aceh; BPS-Statistics Indonesia. 2016. *Statistik Perdagangan Luar Negeri Aceh 2015* Banda Aceh; BPS-Statistics Indonesia. 2015. *Statistik Perdagangan Luar Negeri Aceh 2014* Banda Aceh).

Table 47: Economic Corridor 5: Aceh Trade with Thailand

($ million)

Item	2007	2014	2015	2016	2017	2018	Average 2014–2018	Compound Average Growth Rate 2014–2018 (%)
Aceh	**1,884.9**	**547.9**	**210.2**	**51.9**	**117.0**	**168.3**	**2,191.0**	**(25.5)**
Exports	1,854.2	507.4	93.3	22.9	77.7	138.6	168.0	(27.7)
Imports	30.6	40.5	116.8	29.0	39.3	29.7	51.1	(7.5)
Trade with Thailand	**5.8**	**7.6**	**10.1**	**2.6**	**6.2**	**27.5**	**10.8**	**(13.5)**
Exports	1.9	0.04	5.8	0.6	44.4	18.3	5.8	377.2
Imports	4.0	7.6	4.3	2.0	1.8	9.1	5.0	4.9
Share of Trade with Thailand (%)	**0.3**	**1.4**	**4.8**	**4.9**	**5.3**	**16.3**	**6.0**	–
Exports	0.10	0.01	6.2	2.5	5.6	13.2	3.5	–
Imports	13.0	18.6	3.6	6.9	4.5	30.7	9.6	–

( ) = negative, – = not applicable.
Note: Totals may not sum precisely because of rounding.
Sources: BPS-Statistics Indonesia (BPS-Statistics Indonesia. 2019. *Statistik Perdagangan Luar Negeri Aceh 2018*. Banda Aceh; BPS-Statistics Indonesia. 2018. *Statistik Perdagangan Luar Negeri Aceh 2017*. Banda Aceh; BPS-Statistics Indonesia. 2017. *Statistik Perdagangan Luar Negeri Aceh 2016*. Banda Aceh; BPS-Statistics Indonesia. 2016. *Statistik Perdagangan Luar Negeri Aceh 2015*. Banda Aceh; BPS-Statistics Indonesia. 2015. *Statistik Perdagangan Luar Negeri Aceh 2014*. Banda Aceh).

In 2018, Aceh's major exports to Thailand were coal, anhydrous ammonia, and vegetable materials used primarily for plaiting. Gypsum (salt, sulfur, lime) and sugar-confectionery were the main import commodities (Table 48).

Table 48: Economic Corridor 5: Top Exports and Imports of Aceh with Thailand, 2018

Rank	Export Commodity	Volume (tons)	Share (%)	Import Commodity	Volume (tons)	Share (%)
1	Coal, whether or not pulverized but not agglomerated, other coal	663,825	99.78	Gypsum (salt, sulfur, lime)	56,100	77.89
2	Anhydrous ammonia	1,367	0.21	Oats	15,000	20.83
3	Other vegetable materials used primarily for plaiting, other than 14011000 - 14012090	126	0.02	Sugar and confectionery	800	1.11

Source: BPS-Statistics Indonesia. 2019. *Statistik Perdagangan Luar Negeri Aceh 2018.* Banda Aceh. pp. 32–33; 62–63.

Tourism

The number of Thai visitors to Aceh was relatively small—less than 1% of total foreign visitors—in 2017 and 2018. The largest number of visitors was from Malaysia, contributing about 75% on average or more than 24,000 people each year in 2017 and 2018. Because of limited data, it was not possible to observe the trend in the number of visitors from the two countries in the last 5 years. Data for 2017 and 2018, however, shows Thailand visitors increasing, while the number of Malaysian visitors coming to Aceh is relatively stable (Table 49).

Table 49: Economic Corridor 5: Foreign Visitor Arrivals in Aceh, 2017–2018

Item	2017	2018	Average 2017–2018	Growth Rate 2017–2018 (%)
Aceh	**33,105**	**33,276**	**33,191**	**0.5**
Visitors from Intra-IMT	25,133	24,509	24,821	(2.5)
Malaysia	24,874	24,213	24,544	(2.7)
Thailand	259	296	278	14.3
Share of Visitors from Intra-IMT (%)	**75.9**	**73.7**	**74.8**	–
Malaysia	75.1	72.8	73.9	–
Thailand	0.8	0.9	0.8	–

( ) = negative, – = not applicable, IMT = Indonesia–Malaysia–Thailand.
Note: Totals may not sum precisely because of rounding.
Sources: BPS-Statistics Indonesia, 2018 and 2019 (BPS-Statistics Indonesia. 2018. *Statistik Kunjungan Wisatawan Mancanegara Provinsi Aceh 2017.* Banda Aceh; BPS-Statistics Indonesia of Aceh Province. 2018. BPS-Statistics Indonesia. 2019. *Statistik Kunjungan Wisatawan Mancanegara Provinsi Aceh 2018.* Banda Aceh: BPS-Statistics Indonesia of Aceh Province).

The number of visitors to Sabang as a transit point for some cruise ship lines has shown no clear trend (Tables 50 and 51). The number of yachts calling on the port showed a steady increase driven mainly by the Sabang–Phuket–Langkawi (SAPULA) route.

Table 50: Economic Corridor 5: Number of Visitor Arrivals to Sabang, 2013–2017

Year	Domestic Visitors	International Visitors
2013	401,224	2,569
2014	512,992	3,564
2015	623,635	5,582
2016	724,923	10,038
2017	736,725	6,032

Source: Sabang Management and Development Agency (BPKS), 2019.

Table 51: Economic Corridor 5: Number of Cruise Ships and Yacht Arrivals to Sabang

Year	Cruise Ships	Yachts
2016	11	63
2017	3	84
2018	7	96

Source: Sabang Management and Development Agency (BPKS), 2019.

Industrial Activities and Special Economic Zones

The nearest SEZ to EC5 is in Arun Lhokseumawe located in Lhokseumawe City, North Aceh District. It was established by Government Regulation No. 5 of 2017. The SEZ's location is crossed by the Sea Lane of Communication and the Strait of Malacca and provides it with a comparative advantage to become part of the global production network.

Arun Lhokseumawe SEZ is a node in EC3 as described in the earlier section (Table 27). The SEZ focuses on several sectors: energy, petrochemical, agro-industry, logistics, and kraft paper industries. The energy sector (oil and gas) will develop LNG regasification, LNG hub and/or trading, LPG hub and/or trading, mini LNG Plant PLTG, together with the development of environmentally friendly power plants or clean energy solutions. Logistics infrastructure through the enhancement of international ports and dock infrastructure will be developed to support these industries.

Arun Lhokseumawe SEZ has the potential to become a rich and productive aquatic ecosystem with the development of the capture fisheries industry. Agro-processing industries located in the zone can also benefit the hinterlands that are planted to high-value commodities such as palm oil, coffee, cocoa, rubber, coconut, essential oil, and others. The revitalization of the marine economy through the Maritime Silk Road will provide Arun Lhokseumawe with access to Southeast Asian and South Asian trading markets in the near future.

The Aceh provincial government has proposed a new SEZ in the west coast—the Basela (*Barat Selatan*), which means "'southwest" Aceh. This SEZ is designed to develop the west coast area facing the Indian Ocean, which is relatively left behind by the more prosperous areas on the east coast.

Overall Assessment

EC5 has fallen short of its objective to establish closer economic relations between Aceh and Southern Thailand. No commercial links have developed between Sultan Iskandar Muda International Airport, Malahayati Port, and Ulee Lheue Port with counterpart facilities in Ranong or Phuket. The only identified maritime connectivity is between Lok Nga Port in Aceh Besar Regency and Nongtalea Port in Krabi Province. However, Krabi is not part of EC5.

Although trade between Aceh and Thailand has been increasing over the past 5 years, exports to Thailand are shipped mainly through Meulaboh Port which is the main gateway for mineral fuel exports, while imports are shipped through Lok Nga Port in Krabi.

Malaysian visitors to Aceh far outnumber Thai visitors because of the availability of direct flights from Aceh to Kuala Lumpur and Penang, whereas there are no direct flights to Ranong and Phuket nor Bangkok. Visitors traveling through marine transport have been increasing with a growing number of yachts coming to Aceh from Phuket and Langkawi. Moreover, cruise ships coming from the homeport in Singapore, Langkawi (Malaysia), and Laem Chabang (Thailand) have been making frequent calls recently in Sabang Port.

To improve the performance of EC5, the following measures may be pursued: The role of Meulaboh Port in the west coast of Aceh, which serves as the main export gateway for coal (93.5%) and other mineral fuels, should be further developed. Malahayati Port and Sabang Port are also important import gateways for liquid asphalt and general cargo, both from Singapore, although these ports do not have links with Phuket or any part of Thailand.

Plans for the Aceh–Phuket Ro-Ro service, which will use the Ulee Lheue Port in Banda Aceh, should be revisited. Plans to open the Ro-Ro service were mentioned in the IMT-GT Blueprint 2012–2016, but this has not materialized as of end-2019. As an alternative, air connectivity between Banda Aceh and Phuket should be explored.

The cruise tourism program that will connect Sabang with Langkawi and Phuket should be promoted through attractive tourism packages. The IMT-GT working group on tourism should involve Sabang in developing these packages together with cruise ship operators. Tour packages could include visits to Banda Aceh featuring its authentic cuisine, cultural heritage, and the tsunami memorial.

Proposed Reconfiguration of EC5

Apart from the measures mentioned above, there is no additional node proposed for EC5 in Sumatera. However, Krabi Province in Thailand has been added as part of the corridor to recognize existing maritime links between Lok Nga Port in Aceh and Nongtalea Port in Krabi. In Malaysia, Langkawi in Kedah State has also been added as part of the corridor for effective coordination of tourism activities under the SAPULA program (Table 52). These proposed additional provinces and nodes are discussed in the Malaysia and Thailand country reports.

Table 52: Economic Corridor 5: Existing and Additional Provinces and Nodes, by Type

Province/State	Node	CAP	COM	MGP	TOUR
INDONESIA					
Aceh	Banda Aceh	✓			
	Sabang City		✓		
	Ulee Lheue Port			✓	
	Malahayati Port			✓	
	Sabang Port		✓	✓	✓
	Balohan Port			✓	
MALAYSIA					
Kedah	Langkawi*				✓
	Teluk Ewa Port*			✓	
THAILAND					
Ranong	Ranong City	✓	✓		✓
	Ranong Port			✓	
Phuket	Phuket City	✓	✓		✓
	Phuket Port			✓	
Krabi*	Krabi City*	✓	✓		✓
Phangnga*	Phangnga City*	✓			

CAP = capital, COM = commercial, MGP = maritime gateway port, TOUR = tourism.
Note: * denotes additional provinces and nodes.
Source: Study team.

For Thailand, the development of EC5 is in line with the SEC strategy to develop tourism in Southern Thailand by connecting areas along the Andaman Sea (EC5) and tourism destinations in the Gulf of Thailand (EC1). For this reason, in addition to the existing nodes in Phuket and Ranong, Thailand also plans to add Krabi and Phangnga as new nodes in EC5. In addition to tourism, Thailand is also trying to develop a production network for rubber latex, rubberwood, and halal food through EC5 connectivity with EC1 and EC6 (footnote 1).

Malaysia previously had no nodes on EC5. However, the rapid development of tourism around the Strait of Malacca and the Andaman Sea, especially cruise ship tourism, has prompted IMT-GT to develop the SAPULA trilateral tourism zone in EC5. The cruise line includes Langkawi in Malaysia as one of the attractive nodes. Therefore, the inclusion of Langkawi in EC5 can help Malaysia seize the opportunity to continue the development of the tourism industry which has been the leading economic sector of the region. In addition, there is Teluk Ewa Port on Langkawi Island, which has links with ports in Palembang, South Sumatera, and ports in Krabi, Thailand. The inclusion of Teluk Ewa Port can help Malaysia develop its trade sector with Indonesia and Thailand in EC5 (footnote 1).

The reconfigured **EC5 has been renamed Southwestern Thailand–Northern Sumatera–Northwestern Malaysia Economic Corridor**.

Map 17: Southwestern Thailand–Northern Sumatera–Northwestern Malaysia Economic Corridor (Reconfigured Economic Corridor 5)

Source: Asian Development Bank.

CHAPTER

4

PROPOSED ROUTE FOR
ECONOMIC CORRIDOR 6

Background

The sixth economic corridor (EC6) was proposed by Thailand in the 24th Ministerial Meeting held in Melaka on 1 October 2018. The ministers directed that a study be conducted to determine the proposed route for this corridor. The proposed route for EC6 is envisaged to link Thailand's southern provinces of Pattani, Yala, and Narathiwat with the east coast of Malaysia through Perak and Kelantan, and with Indonesia in the southern part of Sumatera.[48]

There are two alternatives that could link southern Sumatera with Malaysia and Thailand in EC6:

- Alternative I: Songkhla–Pattani–Yala–Narathiwat→Kelantan–Perak→Strait of Malacca Economic Corridor→Melaka–Dumai Economic Corridor→Riau. Under this alternative, no new province in Sumatera will be included in the proposed EC6. Sumatera will be linked with EC6 through EC4 (Melaka–Dumai Economic Corridor) and EC3 (Banda Aceh–Medan–Pekanbaru–Palembang Economic Corridor).

- Alternative II: Songkhla–Pattani–Yala–Narathiwat→Kelantan–Perak→Strait of Malacca Economic Corridor→Riau Islands→Bangka Belitung→South Sumatera→other southern Sumatera provinces (Bengkulu, Lampung, and Jambi). This alternative would accommodate provinces in the southern Sumatera region that are not currently covered by the existing IMT-GT's economic corridors—both the archipelagic provinces (Riau Islands and Bangka Belitung Islands) as well as mainland provinces (Bengkulu, Lampung, Jambi, and South Sumatera).

Development Strategies

Under the RPJMN 2020–2024, Sumatera Island development will focus on downstream activities in agriculture, fisheries, and mining-based industries to create added value through processing raw materials into semi-finished and finished materials, which could drive export-oriented growth along the eastern coast. This could be achieved by optimizing the benefits of infrastructure such as the Trans-Sumatera Toll Road, airports, and ports. In addition, the development of economic zones along the east coast corridor of Sumatera is expected to generate investments in downstream industries that could enhance export-oriented growth. The leading commodities identified in RPJMN 2020–2024 are cacao, coconut, palm oil, rubber, coffee, pepper, nutmeg, sugarcane, gold, tin, petroleum, natural gas, coal, capture fisheries, and aquaculture. Downstream activities in these commodities will be promoted in SEZs, industrial zones, free trade zones, and free ports.

Regional development in Sumatera is carried out through two main approaches—the growth approach and the equity approach. These two approaches are reflected in the designated growth corridor and the island-based equalization or equal distribution corridor. The growth corridor is oriented toward stimulating national economic growth by accelerating the development of growth areas. The growth areas that have been identified in the plan are designated as national activity centers, regional activity centers, SEZs, industrial zones, national strategic tourism zones, as well as cities and urban agglomeration areas in districts and cities located in the growth corridor. The equal distribution corridor is oriented toward more equitable provision of basic services through the establishment of regional activity centers and local activity centers that can provide a wider reach in areas covered in the corridor.

---

48   Point 3 of the Joint Statement of the 24th Ministerial Meeting of Indonesia–Malaysia–Thailand Growth Triangle (IMT-GT), 1 October 2018, Melaka, Malaysia. https://subregional.ekon.go.id/wp-content/uploads/2018/12/Joint-Statement-24th-IMT-GT-Ministerial-Meeting.pdf.

The growth and equalization corridors in Sumatera have been facilitated by the development of Trans-Sumatera Toll Road. The reconfiguration of EC3 in the previous part of this report has been synchronized with this toll road route in mainland Sumatera Island. Since the toll road will not connect the mainland provinces with archipelagic provinces of Riau Islands and Bangka Belitung Islands, the plan is to include these two provinces in EC6 to open wider economic opportunities for them through connectivity with Malaysia and Thailand.

Riau Islands and Bangka Belitung Islands play strategic roles in Sumatera's development. Batam and Tanjungpinang in Riau Islands are strategic nodes in the growth corridor, while Pangkalpinang, Natuna, and Tanjung Pandan in Bangka Belitung Islands are strategic nodes in the equalization corridor. Batam and Tanjungpinang are connected to Pekanbaru (Riau) via commercial flights, while Pangkalpinang and Tanjung Pandan are connected to Palembang via regular flights and scheduled ferries. SEZs are located in these provinces—the Galang Batang SEZ near Tanjungpinang (Bintan Island) and Tanjung Kelayang SEZ in Belitung Islands. Batam-Bintan and Bangka Belitung also have been designated as National Strategic Tourism Zones in RPJMN 2020–2024. Batam (Riau Islands), Tanjungpinang (Bintan), Pangkalpinang (Bangka), and Tanjung Pandan (Belitung) have core economic activities that could be further developed through linkages with EC6 and EC3 as well as other economic corridors. The EC6 intersects with EC3 in Palembang.

In the context of spatial planning, the term "southern Sumatera" (*Sumatera Bagian Selatan*) refers to the five provinces of South Sumatera, Jambi, Bengkulu, Lampung (located in mainland southern Sumatera island), and Bangka Belitung Islands. Meanwhile, Riau Island is regarded as part of the northern Sumatera.[49] The four provinces in mainland southern Sumatera are proposed to be part of the EC6 route.

The Proposed Route for EC6

In Thailand, EC6 will traverse the three provinces of Pattani, Yala, and Narathiwat. The strategy is to integrate provincial production networks in the three provinces with halal and other food supply chains in Songkhla and nearby areas (EC1). Because of security issues in these provinces that limit outside investments, agricultural produce is transported to nearby factories or exported directly through the Thai–Malaysian borders. Enhancing the domestic value chain will boost the productivity and economic resiliency of provinces in Southern Thailand. The three provinces can also leverage their shared culture and history to expand tourism opportunities.

In Malaysia, the strategy for EC6 is aligned with the government's strategy to develop the East Coast Economic Region in seven priority development areas: (i) tourism; (ii) oil, gas, and petrochemicals; (iii) manufacturing: (iv) agribusiness; (v) human capital development; (vi) logistics; and (vii) services. The development of the eastern region will be boosted with the construction of the East Coast Rail Link (ECRL), which will provide the peninsula's eastern coast with a more efficient means of access to the west coast along the Strait of Malacca. The route in Malaysia will traverse eight states: Kelantan, Terengganu, Pahang, Perak, Selangor, Melaka, Negeri Sembilan, and Johor. There are two alternative routes in Malaysia from Kelantan: one passes through Terengganu, Pahang along the eastern coast, crossing to Selangor (EC2) and Melaka (EC4) and onward to Johor (EC4); the other route links Kota Bharu (the start point of ECRL) and passes through Perak, Selangor (Port Klang, which is the endpoint of ECRL) and up to Melaka and Johor.

---

49   Meanwhile, Riau Island is considered as part of the northern Sumatera. See the details on the Ministry of Agrarian Affairs and Spatial Planning-Republic of Indonesia. 2012. *Empat Kementerian Dorong DPRD Percepat Perda* RTRW. Retrieved 4 December 2020 from https://tataruang.atrbpn.go.id/Berita/Detail/2752.

The proposed configuration of EC6 on the Indonesian side considers Alternative II, which includes the two archipelagic provinces of Riau Islands and Bangka Belitung Islands with links to the four provinces in the southern part of Sumatera: South Sumatera, Jambi, Bengkulu, and Lampung (Map 19).

South Sumatera is part of the existing EC3 and Jambi, Bengkulu, and Lampung have been included in the reconfigured EC3. By designating the strategic links between the two archipelagic islands and southern Sumatera, EC6 can generate greater synergies between the growth corridor and the equalization corridor, consistent with the development strategy for Sumatera.

The nodes in the proposed EC6 will include the following:

(i)   Riau Islands – Batam, Tanjungpinang (Bintan)

(ii)   Bangka Belitung Islands – Pangkalpinang (Bangka), Tanjung Pandan (Belitung)

(iii)   South Sumatera – Palembang

(iv)   Jambi – Jambi City

(v)   Bengkulu – Bengkulu City

(vi)   Lampung – Bandar Lampung

The two archipelagic islands—Riau Islands and Bangka Belitung Islands—will be part of the route for EC6. These two island groups are participating provinces in the IMT-GT but are not part of any corridor. Riau Islands is located in one of the world's busiest shipping lanes along the Strait of Malacca, sharing water borders with neighboring countries—Brunei Darussalam, Malaysia, and Singapore. Several Thai fishing vessels also operate near the Natuna Sea (around 17.4% of foreign vessels).[50] As Riau Islands Province is bordering West Kalimantan Province in Borneo Island, EC6 will potentially establish connectivity with the West Borneo Economic Corridor in Brunei Darussalam–Indonesia–Malaysia–Philippines East ASEAN Growth Area (BIMP-EAGA).

Riau Islands Province has existing maritime links with Malaysia. Because of their location, the ports in Riau Islands and Bangka Belitung are linked primarily to Singapore and Johor. Economic ties between Johor and Batam dates back to the 1980s with the establishment of the Singapore, Johor (in Malaysia), and Riau Islands (SIJORI) Growth Triangle—the first regional cooperation framework in Southeast Asia. Although SIJORI has been inactive for some years, it has brought about significant infrastructure and industrial development in Batam and Tanjungpinang (Bintan) pursuant to Indonesia's objective to make Batam a regional center for industry, logistics, and tourism. Malaysia's proposal to include Johor in EC4 will allow revisiting opportunities for collaboration between Johor and Riau Islands.

The long distance between southern Sumatera and Southern Thailand has made it difficult to establish strong economic ties between the two areas. Riau Islands have no direct maritime and air links with Southern Thailand. Riau Island's trade with Thailand is small—contributing an average of only 1.14% to the province's exports from 2014–2018, and less than 1% for imports.

---

[50]   Based on data from Ministry of Marine and Fishery Affairs 2017, out of 1,605 ex-foreign fishing vessels, 280 (17.4%) are from Thailand. Kementerian Kelautan dan Perikanan Indonesia. 2017. *Laut Masa Depan Bangsa: Kedaulatan, Keberlanjutan, Kesejahteraan.* Jakarta: KKP RI. p. 41.

Nevertheless, Riau Islands could serve as a transit point for foreign trade from southern Sumatera which has a significant share of trade with Thailand, especially Jambi (12.89%), Lampung (4.63%), and Bengkulu (2.98%). For Bengkulu, it will need Palembang (South Sumatera) to transport their commodities by land to seaport in the east coast of Sumatera. Riau Islands also could be a transit point for Bangka Belitung Islands, as its compound average growth rate of trade with Thailand in 2014–2018 was high at 44.06%, making it promising to boost trade performance in the future.

EC6 could play a domestic supply chain, in which upstream and midstream products from southern Sumatera provinces, such as CPO, rubber, white pepper, and raw fishery products, could be processed in industrial parks and special economic zones located in Riau Islands. It will be in line with the Government of Indonesia's plan to make Batam as an international logistic hub for Indonesia.

The inclusion of southern Sumatera provinces (Bangka Belitung Islands, South Sumatera, Jambi, Bengkulu, and Lampung) together with Riau Islands as a transit point and center for industrial zones, has great potential in strengthening economic linkages between Malaysia and Thailand through the network of IMT-GT economic corridors.

EC6 would be called as Southeastern Thailand–Eastern Malaysia–Southern Sumatera Economic Corridor (Maps 18 and 19).

Socioeconomic Profile of Provinces in EC6

Riau Islands Province (*Kepulauan Riau*) comprises 1,796 islands scattered between Sumatera, Malaysian Peninsula, and Borneo. It is situated along the Strait of Malacca where the province shares water borders with neighboring countries such as Malaysia, Singapore, and Viet Nam. The Riau Islands have a relatively large potential for mineral resources, energy, as well as marine resources. Capture fisheries is the dominant industry with 122,433 tons of production in Karimun and Tanjungpinang in 2018. Fish processing factories in Batam, Tanjungpinang, and Natuna produce frozen fish meat, salted fish, as well as fish chips. Other fresh marine products include grouper fish exported to Hong Kong, China and seaweeds exported to the PRC, Viet Nam, and Singapore. Other major products are Chinese cabbage (Batam and Bintan), chili (Batam), rubber (Karimun and Lingga), and coconut (Natuna).

Map 18: Southeasternmost Thailand–Eastern Malaysia–Southern Sumatera Economic Corridor (Proposed Route for Economic Corridor 6)

Source: Asian Development Bank.

Map 19: Southeastern Thailand–Eastern Malaysia–Southern Sumatera Economic Corridor (Proposed Route for Economic Corridor 6) - Indonesia

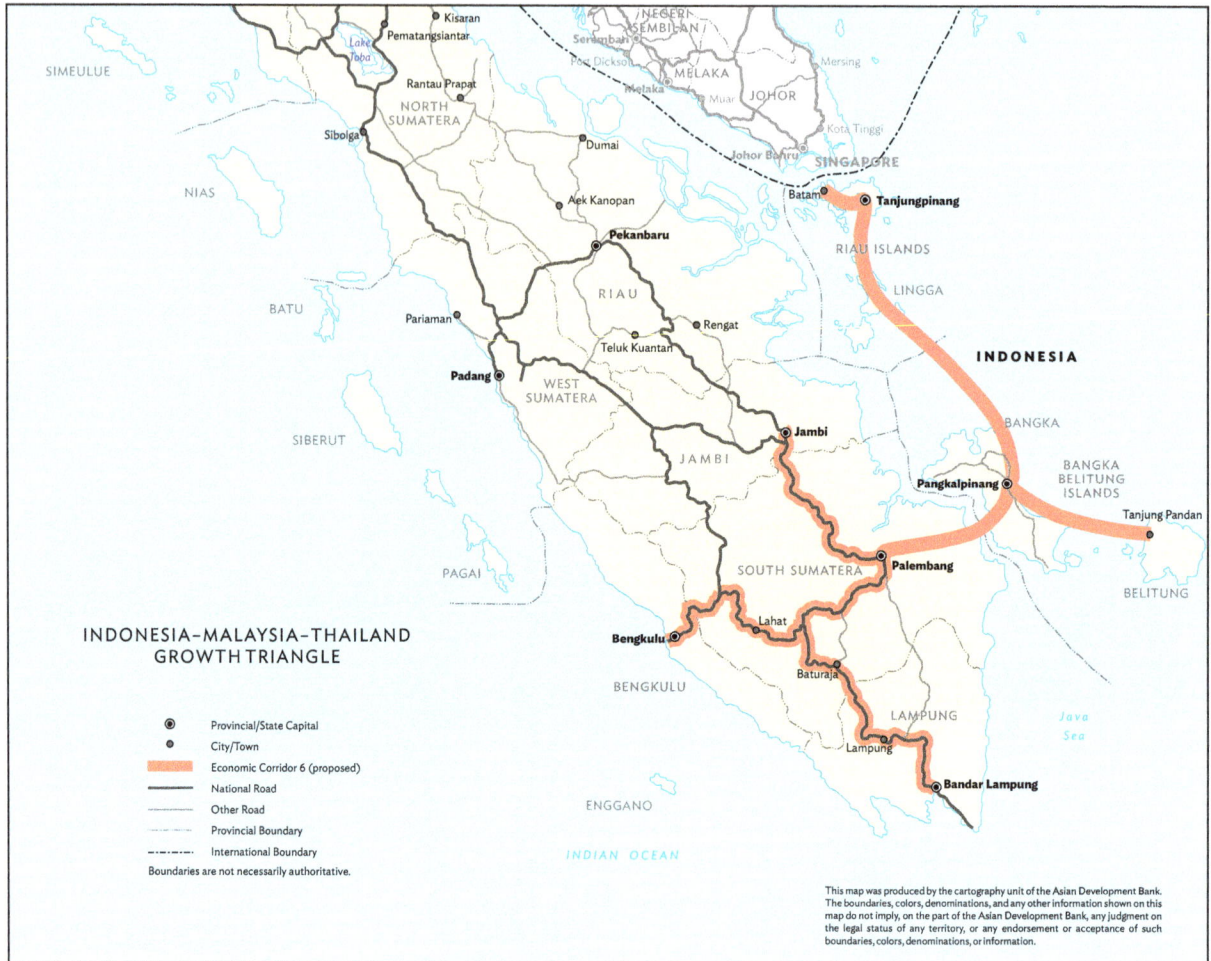

Source: Asian Development Bank

Batam is the largest city in Riau Islands Province, even though the administrative capital of the province is Tanjungpinang. It is strategically located adjacent to the Singapore Strait with a distance of about 20 km by sea, which can be reached by ferry for only 45 minutes. As such, Batam has established itself as a base for various industries such as shipbuilding, apparel, plastic-based products, tooling and stamping, and emergency lanterns, among others, geared toward the world market. Processing and manufacturing industries are supported by several industrial estates such as Kabil Integrated Industrial Park, Bintan Inti Industrial Estate, Batamindo Industrial Park, and West Point Batam Industrial Park. Raw materials (especially mineral fuels and CPO) are supplied from Sumatera and other regions in Indonesia as well as from other countries through Batu Ampar, Sekupang, Kabil, and Pulau Sambu ports. Batam is part of the growth corridor of Sumatera, connecting with Pekanbaru by plane, ferry, and bus. The Trans-Sumatera Toll Road will also run from Batu Ampar Port to Hang Nadim Airport. Batam–Bintan–Karimun has been designated as free trade zone and free port and is also part of the National Strategic Tourism Zone.

Tanjungpinang (Bintan) is the capital of Riau Islands Province, located in Bintan Island. Located on the same island is Galang Batang SEZ covering an area of 2,334 ha. Operating since December 2018, this SEZ focuses on bauxite as the main source of aluminum minerals. Among ten SEZs in Indonesia, Galang Batang has made the highest contribution to the Indonesian economy of Rp36.25 trillion (38.60%) as of November 2019. It plays an important role in the bauxite supply chain in Sumatera and other IMT-GT areas. Tanjungpinang also hosts the Bintan Aerospace Industrial Zone.

Bangka Belitung Islands Province is composed of two main islands—Bangka and Belitung—and several smaller ones. The province covers an area of 16,424 km^2 and has a population of 1.46 million in 2018 (Table 54). The province is part of the growth corridor in Sumatera, with Pangkalpinang as the major link to the mainland through Palembang. Bangka Belitung is also part of the National Strategic Tourism Zone.

Tin mining is the major economic driver in the province, taking place inland and offshore, including in protected forests and marine ecosystems. The effects of tin mining on the environment is a major policy issue that the government continues to address. The total production of tin ore in 2019 was 37,700 tons or 49.5% of tin production in Indonesia and 12.3% of global supply.[51] Tin is usually exported to India, Japan, the Netherlands, the Republic of Korea, and Singapore without any downstream processing. The main gateway ports for Bangka Island are Muntok, Pangkal Balam, and Belinyu.

Pangkalpinang, located in Bangka Island, is the capital and largest city of Bangka Belitung Islands Province.[52] South of Pangkalpinang is the Sadai Industrial Zone in South Bangka Regency, where a PRC-invested silica sand mining company will be located. Apart from mining, agriculture and fishery are also important sectors for Bangka Island, which is also famous for its high-quality white pepper. The major agriculture products in Bangka Island are captured fish (228,525 tons), palm oil (142,495 tons), cassava (73,696 tons), paddy rice (55,212 tons), rubber (35,625 tons), and pepper (32,811 tons). Palm oil is shipped to processing companies in Riau, Riau Islands, and North Sumatera, while fishery and other agricultural products are sent to Java.

Tanjung Pandan, located in Belitung Island, is the capital of Belitung Regency. Belitung has become a popular tourism destination in Indonesia since it was featured in a popular movie that showed the pristine beauty of the island. The products of Belitung Island are similar to the mining and agriculture products in Bangka Island, although lower in volume. These products are shipped to domestic and foreign destinations through Manggar and Tanjung Pandan ports. Belitung depends more on the tourism sector. The growing number of tourist arrivals is supported by the flight routes from Jakarta, Palembang, Singapore, and Kuala Lumpur. Tanjung Pandan provides accommodations and other services to the tourists visiting various sites in Belitung Island. Tanjung Kelayang SEZ is also located near Tanjung Pandan town.

South Sumatera Province has the largest rubber plantation in Indonesia (24% of the total national area planted to rubber) and the largest producer of dried natural rubber (28% of total national production) in 2018. The capital city of Palembang is the center of the rubber processing industry with raw materials coming from Muara Enim, Ogan Ilir, and other regencies. South Sumatera also has large CPO plantations. Rubber and CPO from this province can be further processed in some industrial estates in Batam, Riau Islands.

---

[51]   The data have been generated from three different sources: https://www.sebuahutas.com/2020/12/daftar-5-daerah-penghasil-timah.html, https://databoks.katadata.co.id/datapublishembed/117442/produksi-timah-nasional-lampaui-target-pemerintah-pada-2019, and https://www.internationaltin.org/wp-content/uploads/2020/02/Global-Resources-Reserves-2020-Update.pdf.

[52]   Bangka Belitung Islands Province was established in 2000. Previously, it was a part of South Sumatera Province.

Palembang is the commercial center in southern Sumatera and has strong domestic trade links with Bengkulu and Bangka Belitung. It is also a popular tourist destination. The main attractions include the province's authentic cuisine and the sophisticated Jaka Baring Sports Center, which was the venue of the Southeast Asian Games 2011 and Asian Games 2018. Under RPJMN 2020–2024, the city will be developed to become Metropolitan Palembang for southern Sumatera, just like Metropolitan Medan for northern Sumatera. Palembang will connect to Bengkulu, Jambi, and Lampung through the Trans-Sumatera Toll Road. It also connects to Bangka, Belitung, and Riau Islands through ferries and commercial flights.

Jambi Province has the third largest rubber plantation area in Indonesia after South Sumatera and North Sumatera. Jambi City, the capital, is a center for midstream rubber products for export to Japan, India, the PRC, Canada, Germany, Poland, and the US through Saicom Rubber, based in Singapore. Jambi's largest export gateway is Belakang Padang Port in Riau Islands, followed by Muara Sabak and Talang Duku Jambi in Jambi Province. Other export gateways include Belawan Port and Kualanamu Airport in North Sumatera, Teluk Bayur Port in West Sumatera, Musi River and Plaju in South Sumatera, and Panjang Port in Lampung. Together with South Sumatera, North Sumatera, and Riau, Jambi plays a significant role in developing Indonesia as the second-largest rubber exporter worldwide, after Thailand. Jambi City is part of the Sumatera growth corridor under RPJMN 2020–2024. The Kemingking Industrial Zone, 20 km from Jambi City, will be developed for the agriculture industry.

Bengkulu Province is located on the less-developed western coast of Sumatera. Bengkulu's main products include fish from the Indian Ocean, rubber, wood, and palm oil. Grouper and tuna are exported to Malaysia, while palm oil shells are exported to Thailand and the PRC. In addition to the existing national highway, Bengkulu will also connect to Palembang through the Trans-Sumatera Toll Road, under Lubuk Linggau–Curup-Bengkulu section with the length of 95.8 km. Before the COVID-19 pandemic, Bengkulu also connected to Batam in Riau Islands through regular direct flights.[53]

Lampung Province is the base of the sugar industry in Indonesia, contributing 38% of national sugar production (750,000–800,000 tons per year). Established or mature sugarcane plantations can be found in Lampung Tengah, Tulang Bawang, and Lampung Utara regencies, while developing plantations can be found in Mesuji and Lampung Timur regencies. Lampung sugar is then marketed domestically throughout Sumatera and other regions in Indonesia. Panjang Port in Bandar Lampung is the gateway for general commodities. Meanwhile, Tarahan Port is the biggest coal port in Sumatera. Coal from the mining sites of South Sumatera and West Sumatera is transported both by train and road to Tarahan, and then processed to serve the domestic (65%)[54] and foreign markets. Lampung is part of Sumatera's growth corridor where four industrial zones are planned to be developed: Tanggamus, Pesawaran, Way Pisang, and Katibung. In the proposed EC6 route, Lampung will connect to South Sumatera (Palembang) through the Trans-Sumatera National Highway, Trans-Sumatera Toll Road, and regular flights. South Sumatera has become one of the top five domestic trade partners for Lampung (23.32% of total sales and 13.56% of total purchases in 2018).[55] Lampung is also connected to Riau Islands via direct flights to Batam.[56] Lampung was the second top destination for

53   R. M. Aufar. 2016. *Jadwal Penerbangan Bandara Fatmawati Soekarno – Bengkulu Juli 2016*. 25 August. https://radityoaufar.blogspot.com/2016/08/jadwal-penerbangan-bandara-fatmawati.html.

54   Dian Hadiyatna. 2020. Bukit Asam segera bangun pelabuhan batu bara baru. *Antara News*. 18 February. https://www.antaranews.com/berita/1304702/bukit-asam-segera-bangun-pelabuhan-batu-bara-baru.

55   BPS-Statistics Indonesia. 2019. *Regional Trade in Indonesia 2019*. Jakarta: BPS-Statistics Indonesia.

56   Rini Isparwati. *Jadwal Penerbangan Bandara Lampung dan Rute Kota Tujuan*. Accessed on 4 September 2018. https://riniisparwati.com/jadwal-penerbangan-bandara-lampung-dan-rute/.

Riau Island's domestic trade in 2017 (7.77%).[57] It is also the second biggest destination for Bangka Belitung's domestic trade in 2017 (18.27%), especially for mining commodities.[58]

Table 53: Provinces, States, and Nodes in the Proposed Economic Corridor 6, by Type

Province/State	Node	Type				
		CAP	COM	BCP	MGP	TOUR
INDONESIA						
South Sumatera	Palembang	✓	✓			✓
Jambi	Jambi	✓	✓			
Lampung	Bandar Lampung	✓	✓		✓	
Bengkulu	Bengkulu	✓	✓		✓	
Riau Islands	Batam		✓		✓	
	Tanjungpinang	✓			✓	
Bangka Belitung Islands	Tanjung Pandan		✓			✓
	Pangkalpinang	✓				
MALAYSIA						
Kelantan	Rantau Panjang			✓		✓
	Bukit Bunga			✓		✓
	Pengkalan Kubor			✓		✓
	Kota Bharu	✓				
	Tok Bali Port		✓		✓	
Terengganu	Kuala Terengganu	✓				
	Kemaman Port		✓			
Pahang	Kuantan	✓	✓	✓		
	Kuantan Port		✓			
Perak	Ipoh	✓				
	Lumut Port				✓	
Selangor	Port Klang				✓	
Melaka	Melaka City	✓				
	Tanjung Bruas Port (Port of Melaka)				✓	
	Melaka International Ferry Terminal				✓	
Johor	Johor Bahru	✓				
	Tanjung Pelepas Port, Gelang Patah				✓	
	Johor Port, Pasir Gudang				✓	
Negeri Sembilan	Seremban	✓				
	Port Dickson				✓	✓
THAILAND						
Pattani	Pattani City	✓				
Yala	Yala City	✓				
	Betong			✓		✓
Narathiwat	Narathiwat City	✓	✓			
	Su-ngai Kolok		✓	✓		
	Buketa			✓		
	Tak Bai		✓	✓		

BCP = border crossing point, CAP = capital, COM = commercial, MGP = maritime gateway port, TOUR = tourism.
Source: Study team.

---

[57]   BPS-Statistics Indonesia. 2018. *Regional Trade in Indonesia 2018*. Jakarta: BPS-Statistics Indonesia.

[58]   Data on export and import by ports in Bangka Belitung Islands could be accessed in modified search through https://www.bps.go.id/exim.

Table 54: Economic Corridor 6: Socioeconomic Profile of the Provinces in Southern Sumatera

Province/ Node	Land Area (km²)	Population 2018 (thousand)	Share to Province (%)	Share to Sumatera (%)	Rank in Sumatera/ Indonesia	Population Density (2018)	GRDP (constant prices) ($ million)	Share to Province (%)	Share to Sumatera/ Indonesia (%)	Rank in Sumatera/ Indonesia	GRDP per Capita ($)	Rank in Sumatera/ Indonesia
Riau Islands	**8,202**	**2,136.5**	**100.00**	**3.70**	**8/26**	**260**	**11,994**	**100.00**	**7.79**	**5/12**	**5,614**	**1/3**
Batam	3,849	1,329.77	62.24	–	–	345	7,048	58.76	–	–	5,300	–
Tanjungpinang	151	209.28	9.80	–	–	1,385	965	8.05	–	–	4,614	–
Bangka Belitung Islands	**16,424**	**1,460**	**100.00**	**2.53**	**10/29**	**89**	**3,606**	**100.00**	**2.34**	**9/29**	**2,470**	**4/12**
Pangkalpinang	119	208.52	14.28	–	–	1,755	606	16.82	–	–	2,909	–
Tanjung Pandan (Belitung)*	378	103.594	7.10	–	–	274	434*	12.03*	–	–	2,334*	–
South Sumatera	**91,592**	**8,370**	**100.00**	**14.49**	**3/9**	**91**	**20,618**	**100.00**	**13.39**	**3/10**	**2,463**	**5/13**
Palembang	366	1,643	19.63	–	–	4,519	6,813	33.70	–	–	4,145	–
Jambi Province	**50,058**	**3,570**	**100.00**	**6.18**	**7/20**	**71**	**9,875**	**100.00**	**6.41**	**7/16**	**2,766**	**3/8**
Jambi	205	598	16.75	–	–	2911	1,291	13.08	–	–	2,159	–
Bengkulu Province	**19,919**	**1,963**	**100.00**	**3.40**	**9/27**	**99**	**3,050**	**100.00**	**1.98**	**10/30**	**1,554**	**10/30**
Bengkulu	152	376.5	19.18	–	–	2,482	1005	32.89	–	–	2,669	–
Lampung Province	**34,624**	**8,370**	**100.00**	**14.49**	**2/8**	**242**	**16,036**	**100.00**	**10.42**	**4/11**	**1,916**	**8/23**
Bandar Lampung	296	1,034	12.35	–	–	3,492	2,561	16.36	–	–	2,477	–

– = not available, GRDP = gross regional domestic product, km² = square kilometer.
* Since there is no available data for Tanjung Pandan for some indicators, the table used aggregate data of Belitung Regency where Tanjung Pandan is the capital.
Source: Compiled by the author from various publications of BPS–Statistics Indonesia.

Status of Physical Connectivity

Land connectivity. The four provinces in mainland Sumatera are connected by the existing national highway and the ongoing Trans-Sumatera Toll Road that traverses their capital cities.

(i)   Palembang connects with Jambi in the north, Bengkulu in the west, and Bandar Lampung in the South. Palembang is a node in both EC3 and EC6.

(ii)   Jambi city is located along the main eastern Trans-Sumatera National Highway, connecting to Palembang and is also covered by the Trans-Sumatera Toll Road under the section Jambi–Rengat (198 km) and Betung–Tempino–Jambi (190 km).

(iii) Bengkulu city is connected to Padang and Bandar Lampung through the western Trans-Sumatera National Highway. In the Trans-Sumatera Toll Road, the city will be connected to Palembang under the Lubuk Linggau–Curup–Bengkulu section (95.8 km).

(iv)   Bandar Lampung is connected to other cities in Sumatera via western Trans-Sumatera National highway, especially Bengkulu. It is also indirectly connected to Palembang via the Trans-Sumatera Toll Road under the sections of Bakauheni–Terbanggi Besar (140 km) and Terbanggi Besar–Pematang Panggang– Kayu Agung (185 km).

Maritime connectivity. Port-to-port transport connects the two archipelagic provinces (Riau Islands and Bangka Belitung Islands) to each other and to mainland Sumatera's provinces (Table 55). For intra-Sumatera connection, Riau Islands (Belakang Padang, Batu Ampar, Kabil ports) has strong port-to-port connection with Jambi (Muara Sabak and Talang Duku ports), Riau (Dumai Port), and Bangka Belitung Islands (Pangkal Balam, Belinyu, Muntok, Tanjung Pandan ports).[59] Meanwhile, Bangka Belitung Islands has strong port-to-port connectivity with Riau, Riau Islands, North Sumatera (Belawan Port), and South Sumatera (Boom Baru Port). For international and/or subregional connection, ports in Riau Islands and Bangka Belitung are linked primarily to Singapore and Johor (Malaysia). For passengers, Batam has ferry routes from Batam Center to Stulang Laut Jetty in Johor Bahru. In addition, Riau Islands also exports its products to Thailand, especially from Kabil, Batu Ampar, and Sekupang ports. Bangka Belitung Islands also exports zircon sand via Pangkal Balam port to Thailand, as well as white pepper and fish products via Pangkal Balam and Tanjung Pandan ports.

---

[59]   BPS-Statistics Indonesia. 2019. *Regional Trade in Indonesia 2019*. Jakarta: BPS-Statistics Indonesia.

Table 55: Economic Corridor 6: Port Links in Sumatera

City/Port	Type	Domestic	International
Riau Islands			
Batam/Batam Center	Passenger ferry	Harbour Bay	HarbourFront, Singapore Stulang Laut Jetty in Johor Bahru, Malaysia
Batam/Sekupang	Passenger ferry	Dumai Port	–
Tanjungpinang/Sri Bintang Pura Port	Ro-Ro ferry/ Express ferry	Batam Center	HarbourFront Singapore Stulang Laut jetty in Johor and
Bintan/Bintan Resort	Cruise ships		Port Klang, Malaysia
Batu Ampar	Ferry	Belawan port in Medan	
Bangka Belitung Islands			
Pangkalpinang/Muntok	Ro-Ro ferry	Tanjung Api-Api in Palembang	–
Pangkalpinang/Pangkal Balam	Bulk	Tanjung Priok	Thailand[a]
	Passenger ferry	Tanjung Pandan	
Tanjung Pandan	Ferry, container, and bulk	Pangkalpinang	Port Klang, Malaysia
Mainland Sumatera			
Palembang/Tanjung Api-Api	Ferry	Muntok Port in Bangka	–
Jambi/Muara Sabak and Kuala Tungkal	Bulk	Belakang Padang Port (Riau Islands)	Kuala Lumpur, Malaysia[b]
	Passenger ferry	Punggut Port in Batam, Tanjungpinang	
Bengkulu/Pulau Baai	Passenger ferry	Panjang Port in Lampung	Thailand,[c] Malaysia[d]
Bandar Lampung /Bakauheni Port	Ferry	Merak Port (Java)	–
Bandar Lampung/Panjang and Tarahan Ports	Passenger ferry, container, and bulk	Pulau Baai in Bengkulu, Padang Port in West Sumatera, Belawan Port	Thailand,[e] Tanjung Pelepas, Malaysia[f]

– = not applicable.
[a] R. Pratama. 2020. ESDM Babel Sebut Ekspor 350 Ton Pasir Zirkon ke Thailand Telah Memiliki Persyaratan Lengkap. *BANGKAPOS.com*. 24 September. https://bangka.tribunnews.com/2020/09/24/esdm-babel-sebut-ekspor-350-ton-pasir-zirkon-ke-thailand-telah-memiliki-persyaratan-lengkap.
[b] R. Burhani. 2007. Jambi Ekspor Kentang 100 Ton ke Malaysia. *Antara*. 6 January. https://www.antaranews.com/berita/50310/jambi-ekspor-kentang-100-ton-ke-malaysia.
[c] H. Marini. 2019. Bengkulu ekspor komoditi pertanian ke China dan Thailand. *Antara*. 19 March. https://www.antaranews.com/berita/812546/bengkulu-ekspor-komoditi-pertanian-ke-china-dan-thailand.
[d] G. Alkalis. 2021. Pemerintah Akan Bangun Infrastruktur Terintegrasi di Provinsi Bengkulu. *Ruang Energi*. 14 April. https://www.ruangenergi.com/pemerintah-akan-bangun-infrastruktur-terintegrasi-di-provinsi-bengkulu/.
[e] Y. Mursalin. 2018. Beras Impor Mulai Masuk Lampung 5.500 Ton. *REPUBLIKA.CO.ID*. 16 February. https://www.republika.co.id/berita/ekonomi/makro/18/02/16/p48os5382-beras-impor-mulai-masuk-lampung-5500-ton.
[f] S. M. Sari. 2019. Ini Perkembangan Transshipment di Pelabuhan Cabang Pelindo II. *EKONOMI*. 18 March. https://ekonomi.bisnis.com/read/20190318/98/901353/ini-perkembangan-transshipment-di-pelabuhan-cabang-pelindo-ii.
Source: Compiled by the author from various sources.

Air connectivity. Destinations served by airports in EC6 provinces are mostly the big cities in Sumatera and Java. International destinations are limited to Kuala Lumpur in Malaysia and Singapore. There are no flights to Thailand (Table 56).

Table 56: Economic Corridor 6: Domestic and International Destinations Served by Airports in Sumatera

Domestic Destinations	International Destinations
Hang Nadim International Airport, Batam, Riau Islands	
Most capitals in mainland Sumatera, except Banda Aceh; big cities in Java; Pontianak City in Kalimantan	Kuala Lumpur/Subang (passenger); Singapore (cargo)
Raja Haji Fisabilillah, Bintan, Tanjungpinang, Riau Islands	
Batam, Medan, Pekanbaru	
Depati Amir Airport Pangkalpinang, Bangka Belitung	
Batam, Palembang, Tanjung Pandan, and Jakarta	none
HAS Hanandjoeddin International Airport, Tanjung Pandan, Bangka Belitung	
Pangkalpinang, Pelambang, and Jakarta	Singapore and Kuala Lumpur
Sultan Mahmud Badaruddin II International Airport, Palembang	
Several cities in Indonesia and towns in South Sumatera such as Lubuklinggau and Pagaralam	Singapore and Kuala Lumpur
Sultan Thaha Airport, Jambi City	
Medan, Batam, Padang, Pekanbaru, Palembang, Bandar Lampung, and Jakarta	None
Fatmawati Soekarno Airport, Bengkulu City	
Medan, Pekanbaru, Padang, Palembang, Bandar Lampung in Sumatera Island; Jakarta and Yogyakarta in Java Island	None
Raden Inten II Airport, Bandar Lampung	
Bengkulu, Palembang, Jambi, and Batam in Sumatera; Jakarta, Bandung, and Yogyakarta in Java	Kuala Lumpur

Source: Compiled by the author from various sources.

Trade

Riau Islands

Foreign trade. Riau Islands' foreign trade in 2018 was the highest in Sumatera in terms of value (33.62%) and the second-highest (21.56%) in terms of volume. During 2014–2018, its foreign trade grew by 2.28% in volume but declined by (1.90%) in value. Riau Islands recorded a trade surplus for the same period, with its exports contributing almost 54% of its total trade in 2018. Singapore, the PRC, and the US are the top export destinations in 2018, with Malaysia ranking 4th, and Thailand ranking 13th. For imports, Singapore, the PRC, and Malaysia are the top countries of origin, with Thailand ranking 17th. Batam was the biggest contributor to Riau Island's foreign trade in 2018 (72.06%), while Tanjungpinang contributed less than 1%.

Batam imports iron and steel, salt, sulfur, lime, plastics, and other capital goods from Singapore (34.03% of total import volume), Malaysia (19.27%), the PRC (14.21%), and Japan (11.31%). The industrial products are exported to Singapore (62.92%), India (5.67%), the PRC (4.85%), Malaysia (2.38%), and Thailand (0.82%). The export gateway ports in Batam city are Belakang Padang, Kabil, Batu Ampar, Sekupang, Pulau Sambu, and Hang Nadim (Airport).

Trade with Malaysia. Riau Islands' exports to Malaysia declined by 8.29% during 2014–2018, while imports grew by 1.52% (Table 57). Exports contributed 4.89% to the province's total exports in 2018, while imports contributed 8%. From 2016 to 2018, Riau Islands was on a trade deficit with Malaysia, with the value of imports surpassing the value of exports. Mineral fuels are the top trade commodity with Malaysia. The average value of mineral fuels exported to Malaysia was about $0.37/kilogram (kg), while the value of mineral fuel products imported from Malaysia was higher at $0.68/kg. This difference in the value of imports and exports of mineral fuel products can be accounted for by the fact that exports to Malaysia are mainly upstream/midstream products, while imports from Malaysia consist mainly of downstream products. Batam's imports from Malaysia (especially Johor) are shipped mostly through Batu Ampar and Sekupang ports. Other important commodities traded with Malaysia are machinery and mechanical appliances, electrical machinery, chemical products, animal or vegetable fats and oils and cocoa/chocolate. The bulk of the exports (30%) from Riau Islands Province is shipped through Tanjung Uban port in Bintan followed by Tanjung Balai Karimun Port in Karimun Island and Batu Ampar Port in Batam.

Table 57: Economic Corridor 6: Trade between Riau Islands Province and Malaysia 2014–2018

($ million)

Year	Riau Islands' Exports to Malaysia	Total Exports of Riau Islands	Share (%)	Riau Islands' Imports from Malaysia	Total Imports of Riau Islands	Share (%)
2014	912.3	15,707.3	5.8	869.2	10,877.4	8.0
2015	623.3	11,949.0	5.2	589.6	8,462.0	7.0
2016	397.3	11,030.4	3.6	581.8	7,749.7	7.5
2017	564.9	12,182.0	4.6	725.4	8,790.6	8.2
2018	645.5	13,193.0	4.9	923.2	11,423.5	8.1

Sources: BPS-Statistics Indonesia, 2015–2019 (BPS-Statistics Indonesia. 2019. *Kepulauan Riau dalam Angka 2019*. Tanjungpinang: BPS Provinsi Kepulauan Riau. p. 386; BPS-Statistics Indonesia. 2019. *Indikator Ekonomi Provinsi Kepulauan Riau 2019*. Tanjungpinang: BPS Provinsi Kepulauan Riau p. 76; BPS-Statistics Indonesia. 2019. *Statistik Ekspor Provinsi Kepulauan Riau 2018*. Tanjungpinang: BPS Provinsi Kepulauan Riau. p. 12; BPS-Statistics Indonesia. 2018. *Statistik Ekspor Provinsi Kepulauan Riau 2017*. Tanjungpinang: BPS Provinsi Kepulauan Riau. p. 12; BPS-Statistics Indonesia. 2017. *Statistik Ekspor Provinsi Kepulauan Riau 2016*. Tanjungpinang: BPS Provinsi Kepulauan Riau. p. 12; BPS-Statistics Indonesia. 2016. *Statistik Ekspor Provinsi Kepulauan Riau 2015*. Tanjungpinang: BPS Provinsi Kepulauan Riau. p. 12; BPS-Statistics Indonesia. 2015. *Statistik Ekspor Provinsi Kepulauan Riau 2014*. Tanjungpinang: BPS Provinsi Kepulauan Riau. pp. 12–15. BPS-Statistics Indonesia. 2019. *Statistik Impor Provinsi Kepulauan Riau 2018*. Tanjungpinang: BPS Provinsi Kepulauan Riau. p. 12; BPS-Statistics Indonesia. 2018. *Statistik Impor Provinsi Kepulauan Riau 2017*. Tanjungpinang: BPS Provinsi Kepulauan Riau. p. 12; BPS-Statistics Indonesia. 2017. *Statistik Impor Provinsi Kepulauan Riau 2016*. Tanjungpinang: BPS Provinsi Kepulauan Riau. p. 12; BPS-Statistics Indonesia. 2016. *Statistik Impor Provinsi Kepulauan Riau 2015*. Tanjungpinang: BPS Provinsi Kepulauan Riau. pp. 14–17; BPS-Statistics Indonesia. 2016. *Statistik Impor Provinsi Kepulauan Riau 2015*. Tanjungpinang: BPS Provinsi Kepulauan Riau. pp. 10–13.

Table 58: Economic Corridor 6: Major Export–Import Commodities Traded by Riau Islands Province with Malaysia, 2018

No.	Export Commodity	Value ($ million)	Import Commodity	Value ($ million)
1	Mineral fuels	276.6	Mineral fuels	210.3
2	Machinery and mechanical appliances	148.2	Electrical machinery and equipment and parts thereof	189.3
3	Electrical machinery and equipment and parts thereof	80.2	Various chemical products	154.8
4	Animal or vegetable fats and oils	55.7	Cocoa/chocolate	81.0
5	Cocoa/chocolate	34.7	Machinery and mechanical appliances	43.2

Sources: BPS-Statistics Indonesia, 2019 (BPS-Statistics Indonesia. 2019. *Statistik Ekspor Provinsi Kepulauan Riau 2018. Tanjungpinang: BPS Provinsi Kepulauan Riau.* pp. 51–52; BPS-Statistics Indonesia. 2019. Statistik Impor Provinsi Kepulauan Riau 2018. Tanjungpinang: BPS Provinsi Kepulauan Riau. pp. 66–68).

Trade with Thailand. Riau Island's trade with Thailand is small: the share of exports to Thailand to the province's total trade averaged only 1.24% during 2014–2018, while the share of imports averaged less than 1% (Table 59). Iron and steel articles were Riau Island's top exports, while electrical machinery and equipment were the top imports (Table 60). Kabil, Batu Ampar, and Sekupang, Hang Nadim, Tanjung Balai Karimun, and Lobam are ports used in Riau Islands' trade with Thailand.[60]

Table 59: Economic Corridor 6: Trade between Riau Islands Province and Thailand 2014–2018
($ million)

Year	Exports to Thailand	Total Exports of Riau Islands	Share (%)	Imports from Thailand	Total Imports of Riau Islands	Share (%)
2014	181.0	15,707.3	1.2	79.0	10,877.4	0.7
2015	144.9	11,949.0	1.2	78.9	8,462.0	0.9
2016	164.7	11,030.4	1.5	71.1	7,749.7	0.9
2017	147.1	12,182.0	1.2	78.8	8,790.6	0.9
2018	151.3	13,193.0	1.1	110.6	11,423.5	1.0

Sources: BPS-Statistics Indonesia, 2015-2019 (BPS-Statistics Indonesia. 2019. *Indikator Ekonomi Provinsi Kepulauan Riau 2019*. Tanjungpinang: BPS Provinsi Kepulauan Riau. p. 76; BPS-Statistics Indonesia. 2019. *Statistik Ekspor Provinsi Kepulauan Riau 2018*. Tanjungpinang: BPS Provinsi Kepulauan Riau. p. 12. BPS-Statistics Indonesia. 2018. *Statistik Ekspor Provinsi Kepulauan Riau 2017*. Tanjungpinang: BPS Provinsi Kepulauan Riau. p. 12; BPS-Statistics Indonesia. 2017. *Statistik Ekspor Provinsi Kepulauan Riau 2016*. Tanjungpinang: BPS Provinsi Kepulauan Riau. p. 12; BPS-Statistics Indonesia. 2016. *Statistik Ekspor Provinsi Kepulauan Riau 2015*. Tanjungpinang: BPS Provinsi Kepulauan Riau. p. 12; BPS-Statistics Indonesia. 2015. *Statistik Ekspor Provinsi Kepulauan Riau 2014*. Tanjungpinang: BPS Provinsi Kepulauan Riau. pp. 12–15. BPS-Statistics Indonesia. 2019. *Statistik Impor Provinsi Kepulauan Riau 2018*. Tanjungpinang: BPS Provinsi Kepulauan Riau. p. 12; BPS-Statistics Indonesia. 2018. *Statistik Impor Provinsi Kepulauan Riau 2017*. Tanjungpinang: BPS Provinsi Kepulauan Riau. p. 12; BPS-Statistics Indonesia. 2017. *Statistik Impor Provinsi Kepulauan Riau 2016*. Tanjungpinang: BPS Provinsi Kepulauan Riau. p. 12; BPS-Statistics Indonesia. 2016. *Statistik Impor Provinsi Kepulauan Riau 2015*. Tanjungpinang: BPS Provinsi Kepulauan Riau. pp. 14–17; BPS-Statistics Indonesia. 2016. *Statistik Impor Provinsi Kepulauan Riau 2015*. Tanjungpinang: BPS Provinsi Kepulauan Riau. pp. 10–13).

Table 60: Economic Corridor 6: Major Export–Import Commodities of Riau Islands Province with Thailand, 2018

No.	Exports	Value ($ million)	Imports	Value ($ million)
1	Iron and steel articles	46.3	Electrical machinery and equipment and parts thereof	42.4
2	Mineral fuels	39.8	Machinery and mechanical appliances	22.2
3	Tobacco	22.0	Plastics and articles thereof	11.2
4	Electrical machinery and equipment and parts thereof	16.5	Ships, boats (and floating structures)	7.4
5	Tanning and dyeing extracts	7.4	Iron and steel articles	4.9

Sources: BPS-Statistics Indonesia, 2019 (BPS-Statistics Indonesia. 2019. *Statistik Ekspor Provinsi Kepulauan Riau 2018*. Tanjungpinang: BPS Provinsi Kepulauan Riau. pp. 66–67; BPS-Statistics Indonesia. 2019. *Statistik Impor Provinsi Kepulauan Riau 2018*. Tanjungpinang: BPS Provinsi Kepulauan Riau. pp. 87–89).

[60] The dynamic data could be checked by country and by port through https://www.bps.go.id/exim.

Bangka Belitung Islands

Foreign trade. The contribution of Bangka Belitung Islands' foreign trade in 2018 ranked seventh in Sumatera in terms of value (2.62%) and 10th (0.75%) in terms of volume. In 2014–2018, the value of foreign trade grew by 2.0%, while volume grew by 24.21%. Bangka Belitung Islands recorded a trade surplus for the same period, with exports comprising 92.5 % of its total trade in 2018. Singapore, Japan, and the Republic of Korea were the top export destinations in 2018. Malaysia and Thailand ranked in 9th and 12th place, respectively. Malaysia, Singapore, and the PRC were the top sources of imports, with Thailand at sixth place. Pangkalpinang was the biggest contributor for Bangka Belitung Island's foreign trade in 2018 by 43.42%, thanks to the Pangkal Balam port, while Tanjung Pandan contributed 0.27%.Tin was the dominant export commodity, while fuel oil and other fuels were the main import commodities.

Trade with Malaysia. Exports to Malaysia contributed 3.75% of the province's total export value. Kaolin is the primary commodity exported to Malaysia. Meanwhile, imports from Malaysia accounted for 77.4% of the province's imports in 2018, with mineral oils (petroleum oils and diesel fuels) as the major import commodities (footnote 55).

In Bangka Island, the Port of Pangkal Balam in Tanjungpinang City can accommodate only small ships under 3,000 GT. Export and import activities are transshipped through other ports, especially in Lampung (Panjang Port) and Jakarta (Sunda Kelapa and Tanjung Priok Ports).[61] In Belitung Island, the Port of Tanjung Pandan (Pelindo II) serves direct exports of kaolin to Malaysia and the PRC.[62] As of December 2019, 20 ships exported kaolin directly to Port Klang in Malaysia and two overseas ships to the PRC (Table 61).[63]

Table 61: Economic Corridor 6: Trade between Bangka Belitung Islands Province and Malaysia, 2015–2018

($ million)

Year	Exports to Malaysia	Total Exports of Bangka Belitung	Share (%)	Imports from Malaysia	Total Imports of Bangka Belitung	Share (%)
2014	21.8	1,653.1	1.3	21.7	59.0	36.8
2015	8.9	1,191.1	0.8	10.8	50.0	21.7
2016	29.4	1,290.7	2.3	10.0	132.0	7.6
2017	59.3	1,784.1	3.3	31.6	74.4	42.5
2018	66.5	1,774.9	3.8	11.0	144.7	77.4

Sources: BPS-Statistics Indonesia, 2015-2019 (BPS-Statistics Indonesia. 2019. *Statistik Ekspor – Impor Provinsi Kepulauan Bangka Belitung 2018*. Pangkalpinang: BPS Provinsi Kepulauan Bangka Belitung. pp. 27 and 50; BPS-Statistics Indonesia. 2018. *Statistik Ekspor – Impor Provinsi Kepulauan Bangka Belitung 2017*. Pangkalpinang: BPS Provinsi Kepulauan Bangka Belitung. pp. 27 and 48; BPS-Statistics Indonesia. 2017. *Statistik Ekspor – Impor Provinsi Kepulauan Bangka Belitung 2016*. Pangkalpinang: BPS Provinsi Kepulauan Bangka Belitung. pp. 27 and 46; BPS-Statistics Indonesia. 2016. *Statistik Ekspor – Impor Provinsi Kepulauan Bangka Belitung 2015*. Pangkalpinang: BPS Provinsi Kepulauan Bangka Belitung. pp. 26 and 41; BPS-Statistics Indonesia. 2015. *Statistik Ekspor – Impor Provinsi Kepulauan Bangka Belitung 2014*. Pangkalpinang: BPS Provinsi Kepulauan Bangka Belitung. pp. 21 and 40).

---

[61]   Aprionis. *Pemprov Babel kembangkan Pelabuhan Pangkal Balam bertaraf internasional*. Accessed on 13 May 2020. https://www.antaranews.com/berita/1489016/pemprov-babel-kembangkan-pelabuhan-pangkalbalam-bertaraf-internasional.

[62]   Bayu. 2018. Pelabuhan Tanjung Pandan Didominasi Pengapalan Komoditi Kaolin. *Maritimnews*. 17 August. http://maritimnews.com/2018/08/pelabuhan-tanjung-pandan-didominasi-pengapalan-komoditi-kaolin/.

[63]   Kasmono. 2019. IPC Tanjung Pandan catat ekspor kaolin sebanyak 34.808 ton. *Antara News*. 3 December. https://www.antaranews.com/berita/1191216/ipc-tanjung-pandan-catat-ekspor-kaolin-sebanyak-34808-ton.

Trade with Thailand. Exports to Thailand contributed 1.67% of the province's total export value (Table 62). Muntok and Pangkal Balam are the main export gateways to Thailand. Mineral oil condensate is the top commodity exported to Thailand. Meanwhile, imports from Thailand accounted for 0.20% of the province's imports in 2018. Pangkal Balam is the importing gateway from Thailand, that include lubricating/cooling medium pump as the imported product.[64]

Table 62: Economic Corridor 6: Trade between Bangka Belitung Islands Province and Thailand, 2014–2018 ($ million)

Year	Exports	Total Exports	Share (%)	Imports	Total Imports	Share (%)
2014	2.5	1,653.1	0.2	4.5	59.0	7.6
2015	0.0	1,191.1	0.0	5.7	49.9	11.5
2016	27.2	1,290.7	2.1	–	132.0	0.0
2017	25.9	1,784.1	1.4	0.2	74.4	0.3
2018	29.7	1,774.9	1.7	0.3	144.7	0.2

– = not available.
Sources: BPS-Statistics Indonesia, 2015–2019 (BPS-Statistics Indonesia. 2019. *Statistik Ekspor – Impor Provinsi Kepulauan Bangka Belitung 2018*. Pangkalpinang: BPS Provinsi Kepulauan Bangka Belitung. pp. 27 and 50; BPS-Statistics Indonesia. 2018. *Statistik Ekspor – Impor Provinsi Kepulauan Bangka Belitung 2017*. Pangkalpinang: BPS Provinsi Kepulauan Bangka Belitung. pp. 27 and 48; BPS-Statistics Indonesia. 2017. *Statistik Ekspor – Impor Provinsi Kepulauan Bangka Belitung 2016*. Pangkalpinang: BPS Provinsi Kepulauan Bangka Belitung. pp. 27 and 46; BPS-Statistics Indonesia. 2016. *Statistik Ekspor – Impor Provinsi Kepulauan Bangka Belitung 2015*. Pangkalpinang: BPS Provinsi Kepulauan Bangka Belitung. pp. 26 and 41; BPS-Statistics Indonesia. 2015. *Statistik Ekspor – Impor Provinsi Kepulauan Bangka Belitung 2014*. Pangkalpinang: BPS Provinsi Kepulauan Bangka Belitung. pp. 21 and 40).

Mainland Sumatera

Among the four provinces in the southern part of Sumatera, South Sumatera had the highest export trade value with Malaysia (Table 63). Boom Baru, Kertapati, and Plaju ports are the gateways for South Sumatera's products to Malaysia, particularly for residues of petroleum/bituminous mineral oils. Meanwhile, Lampung has the highest import trade value with Thailand. Panjang Port is the importing gateway for Thailand's products to Lampung, in particular, for different types of raw sugar. Some commodities from the southern Sumatera provinces, especially Jambi and Bangka Belitung Islands, are transshipped through ports in Batam (such as Belakang Padang) to be exported to other countries, including Malaysia through ports in Johor (Table 64). This means that the development of EC6 has the potential to increase the flow of trade from southern Sumatera provinces via Riau Islands (Batam) to Malaysia (Johor) and Thailand, especially for rubber (from Jambi) and pepper (from Bangka Belitung Islands).

---

[64]   Data on export and import by ports in Bangka Belitung Islands could be accessed in modified search through https://www.bps.go.id/exim.

**Table 63: Economic Corridor 6: Trade of Four Mainland Sumatera Provinces
with Malaysia and Thailand, 2018**

Item	Foreign Trade		Trade with Malaysia		Trade with Thailand	
	Value 2018 ($ million)	Share to Sumatera 2018 (%)	Value 2018 ($ million)	Share to Province 2018 (%)	Value 2018 ($ million)	Share to Province 2018 (%)
South Sumatera	**4,479.3**	**6.1**	**611.3**	**13.7**	**132.7**	**3.0**
Export	3,734.5	7.4	551.7	14.8	122.7	3.3
Import	744.7	3.2	59.7	8.0	10.0	1.3
Jambi	**1,290.6**	**1.8**	**194.9**	**15.1**	**166.3**	**12.9**
Export	1,204.6	2.4	181.8	15.1	165.1	13.7
Import	86.0	0.4	13.1	15.2	1.2	1.4
Bengkulu	**370.6**	**0.5**	**28.6**	**7.7**	**11.0**	**3.0**
Export	271.9	0.5	25.0	9.2	10.9	4.0
Import	98.7	0.4	3.6	3.7	0.2	0.2
Lampung	**6,309.0**	**8.6**	**197.5**	**3.1**	**292.3**	**4.6**
Export	3,440.1	6.9	125.8	3.7	54.8	1.6
Import	2,868.9	12.4	71.7	2.5	237.5	8.3

Source: Compiled by the author from various publications of BPS-Statistics Indonesia.

**Table 64: Economic Corridor 6: Major Commodities Traded between the Four Mainland Sumatera
Provinces and Malaysia and Thailand, 2018**

	Trade with Malaysia		Trade with Thailand	
	Exports*	Imports*	Exports*	Imports*
South Sumatera	Petroleum oils	Compressors, automotive AC and sealed unit for AC machine	Coal	Hydrogen peroxide
	Coal Pulp	Prefabricated structural components	Anhydrous ammonia	Personal computers in the form of systems excluding portable computers
	Solid fractions of refined palm oil Rubber	Petroleum bitumen Other lubricating oils	Urea	seed groundnuts, not roasted or otherwise cooked, shelled, whether or not broken
	Urea Rubber derivatives	Other (wood) treated with paint, stains, creosote or other preservatives, of beech	Coconuts in the inner shell	Motor vehicle for transport of good, diesel, not CKD
	Coal anthracite	Automotive diesel fuel 4,7		Combined harvester-threshers, machinery

continued on next page

Table 64 continued

	Trade with Malaysia		Trade with Thailand	
	Exports*	Imports*	Exports*	Imports*
Jambi	Vegetable oil (palm oil)	Parts of machinery plant	Pinang (betel nut)	Hydrogen peroxide in liquid form
	Mineral fuels	Soya beans	Mineral fuels	Quicklime
	Coal	Ethylene polymers Aseptic bags	coal	–
Bengkulu	Coal but not agglomerated, other coal	Petroleum bitumen	Coal but not agglomerated, other coal	Gypsum anhydrite
			Palm kernel shells	
Lampung	Coffee Arabica WIB or Robusta OIB, not roasted, not decaffeinated	Manufacture of fuel from oil refining and refining	Coal	Raw sugar
	Cocoa beans, whole or broken, raw or roasted	Methanol	Pulp	Purifying machinery and apparatus
	Vegetable cooking oil	Machinery used in the manufacture of wine, cider, fruit juices or similar beverages	Coffee Arabica WIB or Robusta OIB, not roasted, not decaffeinated	Rice
				Machinery used in the manufacture of wine, cider, fruit juices, or similar beverages
	Palm kernel olein, refined, bleached, and deodorized	Fish meal Filtering/ purifying machine and apparatus		Cassava residue machinery

AC = air conditioner, CKD = completely knocked down, OIB = Ost Indische Bereiding, WIB = West Indische Bereiding.
* Commodities are listed from highest to fifth highest.
Sources: Compiled by the author from various publications of BPS-Statistic Indonesia, 2019, and https://www.bps.go.id/exim.

Therefore, the inclusion of southern Sumatera provinces (Bangka Belitung Islands, South Sumatera, Jambi, Bengkulu, and Lampung), together with Riau Islands as transit point and center for industrial zones, has the potential to strengthen economic linkages with Malaysia and Thailand.

Malaysia and Thailand also have their own strategies to develop the proposed EC6. The EC6 route in Malaysia will start from the BCP in Kelantan (bordering Thailand), extending southward to Melaka (Tanjung Bruas Port) and Johor. Melaka will link to Dumai (Riau Province) under EC4. Johor will link with Batam (Riau Islands), which Indonesia has proposed to be part of EC6. For Thailand, The EC6 route will start from Pattani, continuing south to Yala and Narathiwat. Narathiwat will connect with Kelantan through BCPs of Su-ngai Kolok, Buketa, and Tak Bai. The rail link at Su-ngai Kolok–Rantau Panjang–Pasir Mas–Tumpat, which is currently dormant, will also be reactivated. Narathiwat is connected to Kota Bharu (Kelantan) through Asian Highway No. 17 (Thailand) and No. 7 (Malaysia) (footnote 1).

CHAPTER

5

THE NETWORK OF IMT-GT ECONOMIC CORRIDORS

Revisiting the Economic Corridor Concept

The concept of economic corridor. Economic corridors are developed along a major transport route to provide production units with access to markets through distribution centers and gateway ports. A transport corridor is a foundation for developing an economic corridor. As the corridor develops, the "narrow" transport corridor expands as urban infrastructure, industrial parks, and other agglomeration spaces emerge as part of development plans.

Economic corridor development in IMT-GT traverses national borders and, as such, requires collaboration between countries to ensure that goods and people move seamlessly across national boundaries. These require measures such as transport and trade facilitation to transform national corridors that are merely juxtaposed at the borders into fully functioning cross-border economic corridors. Deliberate and collaborative planning between countries is critical to optimize spatial use by taking advantage of new production, growth and logistics centers, expanded connectivity, and access to gateways. As discussed in the economic corridor chapters of this study, this approach to economic corridor development has not fully materialized in IMT-GT. For the most part, Indonesia, Malaysia, and Thailand have been pursuing strategies, programs, and projects in their respective "country segments" of the IMT-GT economic corridors rather than as a result of collaborative and deliberate planning at the subregional level.[65]

Corridor nodes. As part of the review, the study identified specific nodes in each corridor. For a given corridor, the relationship and continuity between the different nodes is important to help delineate core areas, i.e., the growth and catalytic centers from which spillovers are expected to radiate (peripheral areas). The nodes identified were the points or areas that perform catalytic roles in the corridor influence areas, with the potential to contribute to trade and economic growth by leveraging on infrastructure connectivity.

The nodes identified in this study were classified as follows:
(i)   **Capital city**: the main urban and administrative center in a province or state; the area is compact, transit-oriented, and densely populated, and where high concentrations of residential, employment, retail, and key services are located;

(ii) **Border crossing point (BCP)**: the point where border areas between two countries in the corridor converge and where customs, immigration, and quarantine facilities are provided to enable the entry and exit of goods across the borders;

(iii) **Commercial node**: an area where there is a high concentration of economic activity such as industrial parks, SEZs, distribution centers; usually accompanied by redevelopment around the area that includes residential, retail, and services facilities;

(iv) **Maritime gateway port**: an area for the transport of cargo and/or passengers to external markets and/or destinations comprising a land domain (the port's region and its locality) and the maritime domain which services ships for global trade;

(v)   **Tourism node**: an area with a medium to high density of tourists having the full range of facilities, services, and amenities, usually part of a cluster of destinations where tourists can engage in a variety of activities beyond visiting a single attraction or tourist site.

---

[65]   C. S. Guina. 2023. *Review and Assessment of the Indonesia–Malaysia–Thailand Growth Triangle Economic Corridors: Integrative Report.* Manila: Asian Development Bank. The contents of this section was based on the integrative report, which is published as a separate publication.

Interlink corridors. The new provinces and nodes proposed under the reconfigured corridors in Chapter 3 expanded the existing corridors significantly, resulting in interlink corridors. An interlink corridor is the "route that connects two or more points in different corridors." Interlink corridors enable corridors to function as a network, rather than as a single corridor. Corridors functioning as the network can change the pattern of mobility for both goods and people. They can facilitate access to a larger and more diverse base of inputs (raw materials, parts, energy, or labor) and broader markets for diverse outputs (intermediate and finished goods).

The concept of economic corridors as networks rather than as point-to-point connections implies that spatial development would need to be more deliberate and coordinated. At present, economic corridor projects are typically national projects located in a corridor; and the mere collation of these projects would be considered as the set of projects for the corridor. In a network perspective, this piecemeal approach may have to give way to a more comprehensive spatial planning aimed at reducing economic distance and overcoming trade barriers in the corridors to promote complementarities in production and trade and realize scale economies for enhanced competitiveness.

Interlink Corridors in Sumatera

Map 20 shows that there are three interlink corridors in Indonesia, which link one economic corridor to each other.

Interlink Corridor A connects Belawan (EC1) and Medan (EC3) by a 12-km toll road (Belawan–Medan–Tanjung Morowa section). This interlink corridor also connects provinces to the northern part of Sumatera (Aceh, North Sumatera, West Sumatera, and northern part of Riau)—which are the main sources of CPO, rubber, coffee, vegetables, cement, and other export commodities to Malaysia through the maritime link between Belawan Port and Penang Port. This interlink corridor is supported by the development of the overland route in EC3 (both the national highway and toll road) that facilitates transport of commodities from the source areas to Belawan Port, as well as tourism across Sumatera. Belawan is also connected to other areas in North Sumatera through rail transport.

Interlink Corridor B connects Pekanbaru in land-based EC3 and Dumai in maritime-based EC4. The interlink corridor connects with other cities in Sumatera that are part of EC3 (including the expanded EC3) (Medan, Padang, and Jambi). Dumai in EC4 connects to Malaysia through port-to-port maritime links. This interlink corridor supports the palm oil industry as Dumai has several industrial estates that focus on midstream and downstream processes that can have easy access to Dumai Port—biggest maritime gateway for Indonesia's palm oil and other export commodities (e.g., vegetable products, animal and/or vegetable fats and oils, wood and articles of wood and cement). It is especially beneficial for Riau, the southern part of North Sumatera, West Sumatera, Jambi, and Bangka Belitung Islands. Dumai is connected with these provinces in EC3 through the Trans-Sumatera Highway and the Trans-Sumatera Toll Road (Dumai–Pekanbaru section). Dumai Port, through its ferry services, also serves as the gateway for tourists' arrival and departure between EC3 and EC4, especially for the southern part of Sumatera.

Interlink Corridor C between Palembang and Pangkalpinang connects land-based EC3 with the proposed maritime-based EC6. Palembang is connected with Pangkalpinang in Bangka Island via Ro-Ro ferry from Tanjung Api-Api Port to Tanjung Kalian Port. This interlink corridor supports the rubber industry. Raw materials coming from Muara Enim, Ogan Ilir, and other areas in EC3 are transported to Palembang as the center of midstream rubber industry and processed to be SIR 20. This connectivity is supported by the

Map 20: Interlink Corridors in Indonesia

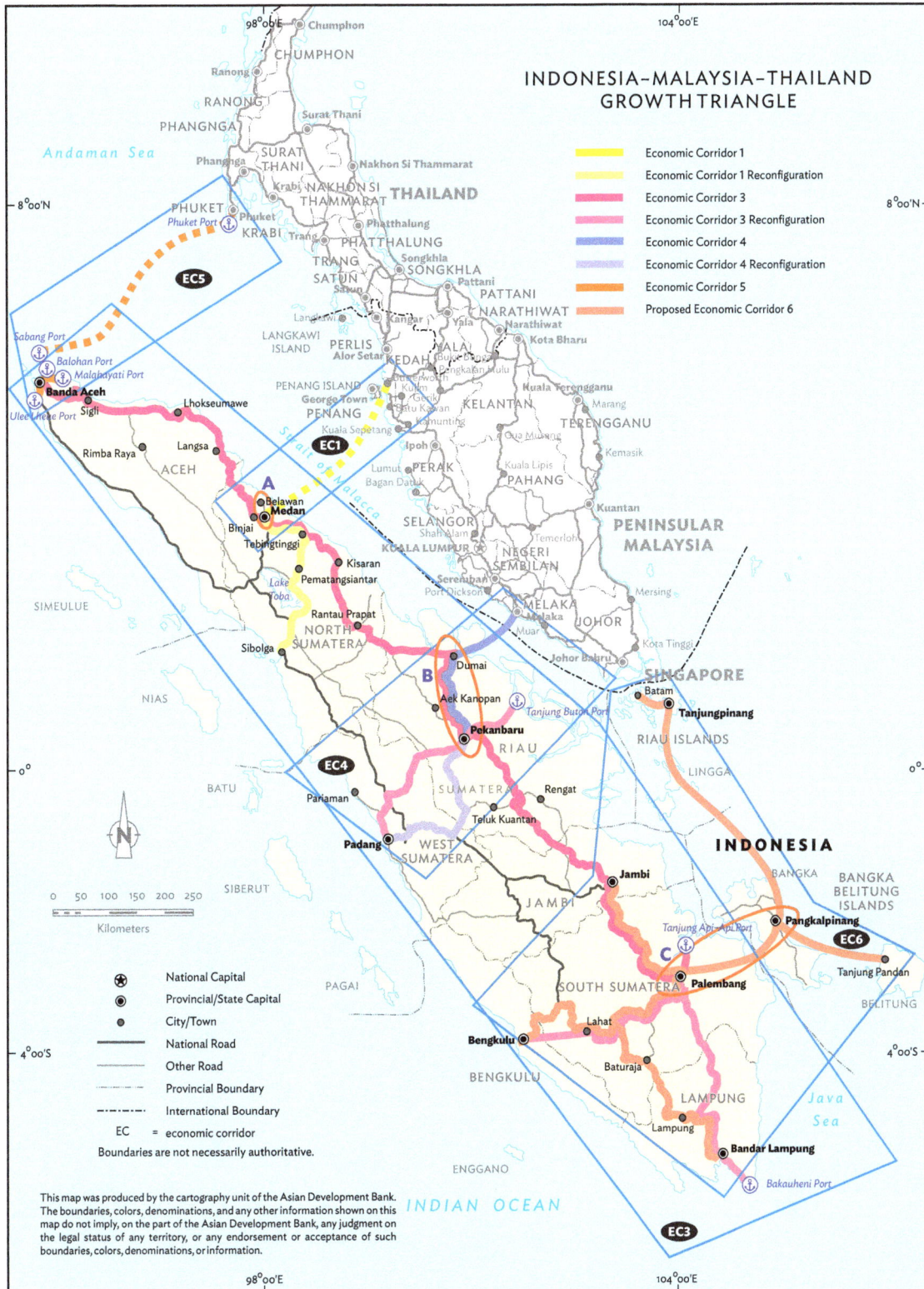

INDONESIA–MALAYSIA–THAILAND
GROWTH TRIANGLE

Economic Corridor 1
Economic Corridor 1 Reconfiguration
Economic Corridor 3
Economic Corridor 3 Reconfiguration
Economic Corridor 4
Economic Corridor 4 Reconfiguration
Economic Corridor 5
Proposed Economic Corridor 6

⊛ National Capital
◉ Provincial/State Capital
● City/Town
—— National Road
—— Other Road
—·—· Provincial Boundary
------ International Boundary
EC = economic corridor
Boundaries are not necessarily authoritative.

This map was produced by the cartography unit of the Asian Development Bank. The boundaries, colors, denominations, and any other information shown on this map do not imply, on the part of the Asian Development Bank, any judgment on the legal status of any territory, or any endorsement or acceptance of such boundaries, colors, denominations, or information.

Source: Asian Development Bank.

Trans-Sumatera Toll Road (Palembang–Kayu Agung–Pematang Panggang–Terbanggi Besar–Bakauheni section), which connects Palembang with Lampung, as well as national road and partial toll road (Palembang–Simpang Indralaya section), which connects Palembang with Bengkulu. The links facilitate the transport of export commodities from EC3 provinces to Boom Baru, Palembang–Kertapati, and Palembang–Plaju, ports in Palembang which are gateways to Malaysia and other destinations. For EC6, this interlink corridor also plays important role in trade. Ports in Pangkalpinang and its surrounding areas are major gateways of Bangka Belitung to Riau Islands.

ECONOMIC CORRIDORS FROM A VALUE CHAIN PERSPECTIVE

Economic Corridors and Value Chains

The development of value-chain linkages is a key motivation for economic corridor development. This chapter looks at the value chain[66] of three major products in IMT-GT—palm oil, rubber, and halal foods—to get a broad perspective on the geography of their production, processing, and distribution components. Value chains can be facilitated by efficient physical infrastructure to facilitate the movement of goods between their various stages. Value chains can also be impacted by the location of SEZs and industrial clusters, which are crucial for attracting investments and creating the density required to enable logistics services to operate efficiently.

The role of economic corridors can be better appreciated when seen as a part of the country's or the region's value chain. The study thus examined the value chain of three products of strategic importance to the IMT-GT countries: palm oil, rubber, and halal food.[67] The study looked at the spatial dimensions of the different stages of these value chains focusing on the role of economic corridors.

Provinces located in EC1, EC3, EC4, EC5 and the proposed EC6 are important locations in the value chain stages of major commodities traded for both the domestic and export markets.

- For EC3 and EC4 (as well as the proposed EC6), the top export commodities include (i) palm oil-based products for West Sumatera, Riau, Jambi, Lampung, and Bangka Belitung); (ii) seafoods for Aceh, North Sumatera, West Sumatera, and Bengkulu; (iii) fruits and vegetables for North Sumatera and Riau; and (iv) rubber for South Sumatera.

- For EC 5 and EC 1 (as well as the proposed EC6), the main commodities include (i) fruits and vegetables, including coffee for Aceh, North Sumatera, Riau, Jambi, and Lampung; (ii) mineral fuels and coal for Aceh, Jambi, and Riau Islands; and (iii) palm oil-based products for North Sumatera, Riau, and Bengkulu.

These provinces host plantations, palm oil mills, refineries, and also serve as consolidation and transit points toward international gateways (Table 65).

Table 65: Economic Corridors Involved in Major Commodities Traded in Sumatera

Industries	EC1	EC3*	EC4	EC5	EC6
Palm oil	✓	✓	✓		✓
Rubber		✓	✓		
Potential halal food (coffee, fruits, vegetables, and seafood)	✓	✓		✓	✓

EC = economic corridor.
*Based on domestic trade data.
Source: Based on analysis on domestic trade and export–import data from various publications of BPS-Statistics Indonesia, 2019.

---

[66] In this study, the distinction between the terms *value chain* and *supply chain* is not strictly applied. It is noted that a value chain is the process by which a company adds value to its raw materials to produce products eventually sold to consumers; while the supply chain represents all the steps required to get the product to the customer. E. Tarver. 2021. *Value Chain vs. Supply Chain: What's the Difference?* 2 August. https://www.investopedia.com/ask/answers/043015/what-difference-between-value-chain-and-supply-chain.asp.

[67] Unlike Malaysia, the Government of Indonesia (BPS-Statistics Indonesia) does not publish Halal statistics. Therefore, this report takes halal food products as the main trade commodities in Sumatera's IMT-GT area.

Palm Oil

Indonesia is the largest palm oil-producing country in the world, contributing around 51% of total global production (2019). Malaysia (34%) and Thailand (3%) are the second and third largest producers. Indonesia is also the largest palm oil exporter in the world. In 2018, Indonesia gained 57.1% of the global export market, followed by Malaysia (30.6%). Thailand accounted for only 0.3% of global exports as most of its palm oil production is consumed domestically. Figure 1 shows the palm oil supply chain.

Figure 1: Palm Oil Supply Chain

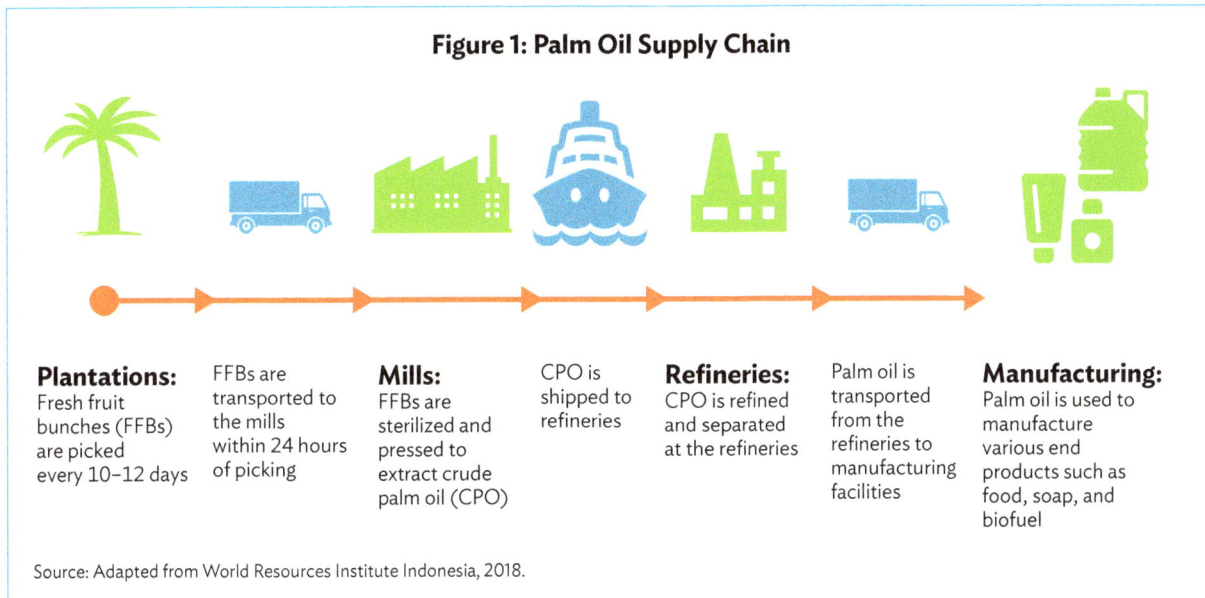

Plantations:
Fresh fruit bunches (FFBs) are picked every 10–12 days

FFBs are transported to the mills within 24 hours of picking

Mills:
FFBs are sterilized and pressed to extract crude palm oil (CPO)

CPO is shipped to refineries

Refineries:
CPO is refined and separated at the refineries

Palm oil is transported from the refineries to manufacturing facilities

Manufacturing:
Palm oil is used to manufacture various end products such as food, soap, and biofuel

Source: Adapted from World Resources Institute Indonesia, 2018.

Plantations. As the biggest palm oil producer globally, Indonesia's plantations are spread in 25 of its 34 provinces. The Sumatera region accounts for 57% of the total area planted to palm oil, followed by Kalimantan. The size of plantation areas in Riau, North Sumatera, and South Sumatera exceed 1 million ha. Smallholders manage around 60% of plantations in Sumatera (60%), followed by big private estates (34%), and government estates (6.63%) (Table 66).

Table 66: Palm Oil Plantations and Production in Sumatera, 2018

Province	Plantations			Production		
	Total Area (hectares)	Share to Sumatera (%)	Share to Indonesia (%)	Total Production (tons)	Share to Sumatera (%)	Share to Indonesia (%)
Aceh	450,810	6.17	3.53	889,379	4.03	2.43
North Sumatera	1,476,354	20.22	11.57	5,445,831	24.69	14.88
West Sumatera	398,784	5.46	3.12	1,254,875	5.69	3.43
Riau	2,323,831	31.82	18.21	7,136,648	32.35	19.50
Jambi	772,843	10.58	6.06	1,988,248	9.01	5.43
South Sumatera	1,073,840	14.71	8.41	3,042,132	13.79	8.31
Bengkulu	340,749	4.67	2.67	900,349	4.08	2.46
Lampung	225,896	3.09	1.77	489,551	2.22	1.34
Bangka Belitung Islands	228,452	3.13	1.79	882,506	4.00	2.41
Riau Islands	10,460	0.14	0.08	31,104	0.14	0.08
Sumatera	**7,302,019**	**100.00**	**57.22**	**22,060,623**	**100.00**	**60.28**
INDONESIA	**12,761,586**		**100.00**	**36,594,813**		**100.00**

Note: Totals may not sum precisely because of rounding.
Source: BPS-Statistics Indonesia. 2019. Indonesian Oil Palm Statistics 2018. Jakarta: BPS-Statistics Indonesia.

Fresh fruit bunches being picked every 10–12 days are transported to the palm oil mills in the same province, or to the mills in the neighboring provinces. Like the plantation pattern, palm oil production in Indonesia has also been dominated by the Sumatera region, which accounts for 60% of national production. The Sumatera region's productivity (3.02 ton/ha) is higher than the national average (2.87 ton/ha). Riau is the biggest palm oil producer in Sumatera with 7.13 million tons or 32.4% of Sumatera's total production, followed by North Sumatera (24.7%). Riau also has the largest number of mills and the highest processing capacity of 6,600 tons per hour.

Processing. After fresh fruit bunches are picked every 10–12 days, they are transported to the palm oil mills in the same province, or to the mills in the neighboring provinces. For example, North Sumatera has 92 palm oil mills that are capable of processing 22 million tons of fresh palm fruit bunches every year, while the plantation in North Sumatera produced only 5.4 million tons in 2018. Therefore, North Sumatera needs to buy fresh palm fruit bunches from other provinces. These mills only produce CPO and CPKO.

Table 67: Palm Oil Mills by Province in Sumatera, 2017

Province	Number of Mills	Production Capacity (ton/hour)
Aceh	25	980
North Sumatera	92	3,815
West Sumatera	26	1,645
Riau	140	6,600
Jambi	42	2,245
South Sumatera	58	3,555
Bengkulu	19	990
Lampung	10	375
Bangka Belitung Islands	16	1,235
Riau Islands	1	40
Sumatera	**429**	**21,480**
Indonesia	**608**	**34,280**

Source: Indonesia EximBank Institute. *Analisa Rantai Pasok (Supply Chain) Komoditas Unggulan Ekspor Indonesia: Minyak Sawit.* http://www.indonesiaeximbank.go.id/research/downloads/13. (accessed 1 September 2020).

After processing, the CPO and CPKO are transported to the refineries and transit points before being exported out of Sumatera. Provinces that serve as production bases or transit points are

(i)   North Sumatera, for Aceh, West Sumatera, Riau, and Bangka Belitung Islands;

(ii)   Riau, for North Sumatera West Sumatera, Jambi, and Bangka Belitung Islands;

(iii)   West Sumatera, for North Sumatera, Jambi, and Bengkulu; and

(iv)   South Sumatera, for Jambi and Bengkulu, as well as for Bangka Belitung Islands.

In North Sumatera, the Sei Mangkei SEZ is a center for palm oil refineries. Some of the big companies located in the SEZ include PT Unilever Oleochemical Indonesia, which produces detergent, soap, and other downstream products; and PT Industri Nabati Lestari which produces olein, refined bleached palm oil, stearin, and fatty acid. North Sumatera also serves as a transit point with Belawan Port being the second biggest maritime gateway port for palm oil exports.

In Riau, especially in Dumai, refineries are located in industrial estates focusing on the palm oil industry: Pelintung, Lubuk Gaung, and Pelindo Port Industrial Estates. Products manufactured in these industrial estates include palm kernel oil, cooking oil, biodiesel, and other palm oil-based products. Products can be conveniently transported to Dumai Port, which is the biggest maritime gateway port for palm oil exports in Indonesia. West Sumatera and South Sumatera serve as transit points for CPO from other provinces. Teluk Bayur Port in West Sumatera is the third largest maritime gateway for CPO and PKO that are processed in the province as well as in Jambi and Bengkulu. The Musi River in South Sumatera is also an important maritime gateway for palm oil exports.

Distribution. Based on 2018 data from GAPKI (Indonesian Palm Oil Association), 73.2% of Indonesia's total palm oil production was exported, 28.5% was sold to the domestic market, and 6.9% was managed for stocks. National Domestic distribution is mainly directed to Java Island (Jakarta and West Java), where most national industrial estates are located (Table 68).

In Sumatera Island, palm oil-based products are exported through seven maritime gateway ports: (i) Dumai in Riau; (ii) Belawan Port; and (iii) Kuala Tanjung Port, both in North Sumatera; (iv) Teluk Bayur in West Sumatera; (v) Tarahan Port in Lampung; (vi) Kabil in Riau Islands; and (vii) Musi River in South Sumatera (Table 69). Based on the value of exports, the largest loading ports are Dumai (43.3%) and Belawan (11.5%). Smaller export volumes are served by other ports such as Rengat, Su-ngai Gunung, and Tembilahan in Riau Province; Jambi and Muara Sabak in Jambi Province; Panjang in Lampung Province; Manggar and Tanjung Pandan in Bangka Belitung Islands Province, as well as Batu Ampar in Riau Islands Province. Only Aceh and Bengkulu Provinces have no internal ports. In total, more than 76.33% of Indonesia's palm oil export are coming out from Sumatera.

Table 68: Volume of Crude Palm Oil Exports by Port of Loading, 2018

No.	Port of Loading	Volume (million tons)					Share to Indonesia (%)
		CPO	Other Palm Oil	CPKO	Other Palm Oil Kernel	Total	
1	Dumai (Riau)	3.10	8.90	0.20	0.70	12.80	43.30
2	Belawan	0.13	3.20	0.01	0.12	3.40	11.50
3	Teluk Bayur (West Sumatera)	0.84	1.01	0.04	0.03	1.90	6.50
4	Tarahan (Lampung)	0.60	0.70	0.06	0.14	1.50	5.00
5	Kabil (Batam, Riau Islands)	0.20	1.20	–	0.10	1.30	4.80
6	Kuala Tanjung	0.02	1.10	0.00	0.10	1.20	4.00
7	Musi River	0.20	0.20	–	–	0.30	1.10
8	Others	–	–	–	–	–	23.80
	INDONESIA	**6.50**	**21,344.00**	**0.40**	**1.40**	**29.70**	**100.00**

– = not applicable, CPO = crude palm oil, CPKO = crude palm kernel oil.
Source: BPS-Statistics Indonesia, 2019.

Table 69: Value of Crude Palm Oil Exports by Port of Loading, 2018

No.	Port of Loading	Value ($ million)					Share to Indonesia (%)
		CPO	Other Palm Oil	CPKO	Other Palm Oil Kernel	Total	
1	Dumai (Riau)	1,705	5,336	171	626	7,838	43.0
2	Belawan	67	1,967	6	132	2,172	11.9
3	Teluk Bayur (West Sumatera)	464	616	33	27	1,140	6.3
4	Tarahan (Lampung)	335	418	58	141	952	5.2
5	Kabil (Batam, Riau Islands)	101	688	–	84	873	4.8
6	Kuala Tanjung	13	666	2	91	772	4.2
7	Musi River	80	90	–	–	170	1.9
8	Others	–	–	–	–	–	22.7
	INDONESIA	**3,576**	**12,954**	**333**	**1,369**	**18,232**	**100.0**

– = not applicable, CPO = crude palm oil, CPKO = crude palm kernel oil.
Source: BPS-Statistics Indonesia, 2019.

Export destinations. The major markets of palm oil-based exports from Sumatera and Indonesia in general are India, the PRC, Pakistan, Bangladesh, the Netherlands, and Malaysia. Exports to Malaysia and Thailand are small because they are also major palm oil producers. Products exported to Malaysia are stearin, and to Thailand, palm kernel expeller (Table 70).

Table 70: Top Destination Countries of Indonesia's Palm Oil Exports, 2018

No	Destination Country	Volume (million tons)					Share (%)
		CPO	Other Palm Oil	CPKO	Other Palm Oil Kernel	Total	
1	India	4.00	2.30	0.07	0.00	6.40	21.60
2	China, People's Republic of	0.00	3.60	0.02	0.60	4.20	14.10
3	Pakistan	0.10	2.40	–	0.01	2.50	8.30
4	Bangladesh	0.010	1.40	0.01	–	1.41	4.80
5	Netherlands, The	0.60	0.50	0.10	0.06	1.30	4.30
6	Malaysia	0.40	0.60	0.09	0.10	1.30	4.20
7	Spain	0.20	0.90	0.00	0.00	1.20	4.00
8	United States	–	0.91	–	0.20	1.10	3.80
	Total Export	**6.60**	**21.30**	**0.40**	**1.40**	**29.70**	**100.00**
	Share (%)	**22.10**	**72.00**	**1.20**	**4.70**	**100.00**	

– = not applicable, CPO = crude palm oil, CPKO = crude palm kernel oil.
Source: BPS-Statistics Indonesia, 2019.

Since 2018, there has been a significant increase in the export of oleochemicals and biodiesel. Oleochemicals exports increased by 15.7% in 2018 compared to the previous year, but increased dramatically to almost 200% in 2019. Biodiesel exports also rose drastically by 851.22% in 2018. On the other hand, exports of other forms of palm oil products (crude, refined, and lauric) have remained stagnant over the last 3 years. These trends imply increasing downstream industry activities for palm oil, while the growth of midstream industry activities tend to be sluggish. However, midstream industry-based products still dominate Indonesia's palm oil exports. In 2018, midstream industry-based products (crude, refined, and lauric) contributed 92.27% of total exports, while downstream industry-based products (biodiesel and oleochemicals) only accounted for 7.72% (Figure 2).[68] This may be explained by the fact that value-added at the plantation stage in Indonesia is higher than in the processing stage. Based on research conducted by Hidayati and Hasibuan (2019), a company's value-added in palm plantations is 72.42%, while value-added in the processing stage is only 10.13%.[69]

---

[68] GAPKI. 2020. *Kinerja Industri Sawit Indonesia 2019*. Jakarta: GAPKI. Retrieved from https://gapki.id/KINERJA_INDUSTRI_SAWIT_INDONESIA_2019.pdf.

[69] J. Hidayati and S. Hasibuan. 2019. Value Chain Analysis and Value Added Enhancement of Indonesia Crude Palm Oil Supply Chain. *International Journal of Advanced Science Engineering Information Technology*. 9(2). pp. 397–404.

Figure 2: Palm Oil Exports by Products, 2015–2019

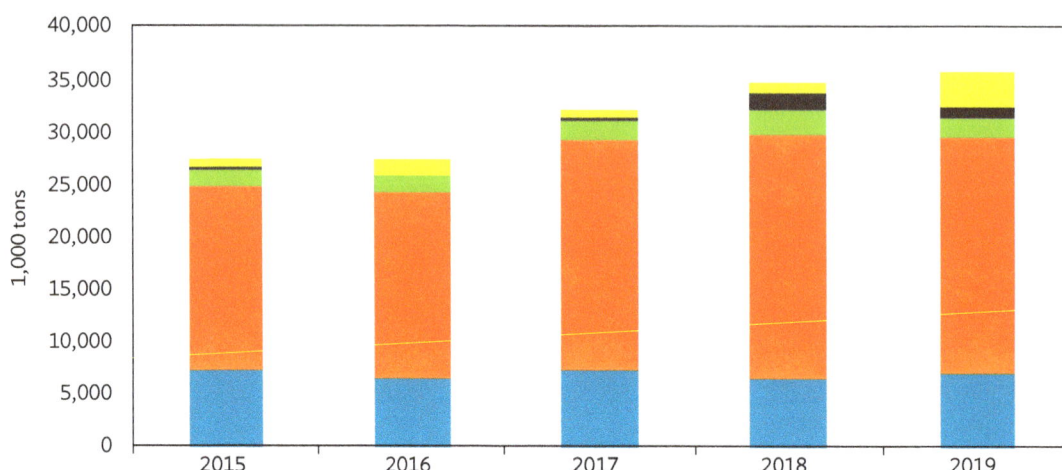

	2015	2016	2017	2018	2019
Oleochemicals	832	1,465	970	1,122	3,354
Biodiesel	206	4	164	1,560	1,148
Lauric	1,684	1,674	1,951	2,359	1,938
Refined	17,506	17,602	21,941	23,104	22,327
Crude	7,232	6,515	7,158	6,561	7,065

Source: GAPKI. 2020. *Kinerja Industri Sawit Indonesia 2019.* Jakarta: GAPKI.

Ecological Impacts of the Palm Oil Industry

The carbon footprint of the palm oil industry is high and results from two components: emissions from deforestation, and emissions from the processing of palm oil.[70] Since oil palm trees grow in tropical climates near the equator, palm oil has been and continues to be a major driver of deforestation in biodiverse forests. Burning down forests lead to a loss of biodiversity, an increase in air pollution and climate change. Many companies prefer to establish their plantations in peatlands and forestland because of the reduced likelihood of land conflicts and the potential to cover the cost of establishing a plantation by selling timber cleared for these plantations. Drained peatlands have been strongly linked to very high carbon emissions. Moreover, palm oil processing requires the use of fossil fuel inputs for mechanized plantation equipment, chemical fertilizer, transportation of goods, and industrial processing.

Indonesia is one of the world's top five greenhouse gas (GHG) emitters. Based on its updated nationally determined contribution (NDC)[71] in the lead up to the 26th Conference of the Parties under the Paris Agreement, Indonesia has set an unconditional reduction target of 29% and a conditional reduction target up to 41% of the business-as-usual scenario by 2030. These targets in emission reduction are considered as an ambitious step, taking into consideration its development challenges in eradicating poverty. Indonesia will continue to intensify the efforts to reduce emissions, of which 97.2% comes from forest-and-land and

---

[70] C. Petrenko, J. Paltseva, and S. Searle. 2016. Ecological Impacts of Palm Oil Expansion in Indonesia. *ICCT White Paper.* July. https://theicct.org/sites/default/files/publications/Indonesia-palm-oil-expansion_ICCT_july2016.pdf.

[71] The Government of Indonesia. 2021. The Updated Nationally Determined Contribution. July.

energy sectors. This is considered a huge challenge to Indonesia, as more than 75% of the country's carbon dioxide-equivalent emissions can be attributed to land-use change, including destruction of peatlands (Indonesian National Council on Climate Change, 2010).

Reducing carbon emissions in the oil palm sector has been hampered by current regulations that allow the use of forested or high carbon stock areas for plantations combined with poor use of degraded and less productive areas. In 2019, Indonesian President Joko Widodo signed a moratorium on new palm oil concession permits. During the 3-year freeze, the government will undertake a comprehensive nationwide review of palm oil licenses and develop efforts to enhance productivity—particularly for smallholders. This move is seen as a significant step forward to improving governance in this sector.

Recommendations

The Government of Indonesia has begun to shift its priorities to downstream industries for palm oil. In line with this policy, IMT-GT economic corridors in Sumatera could be developed to reinforce this policy shift. Some developments to be considered are as follows:

(i)   The ongoing development of SEZ Sei Mangkei should be assured and accelerated, including the completion of Tebingtinggi–Kisaran toll road segment, which will connect Sei Mangkei to all provinces in Sumatera via Trans-Sumatera Toll Road.

(ii)   As a complement to Trans-Sumatera Highway and toll road, Trans-Sumatera Railway project should also be considered to be reactivated, especially the development of Sei Mangkei–Kuala Tanjung segment, which will smoothen the transportation of palm oil downstream products to the designated International Hub Port of Kuala Tanjung.

(iii)   The development of toll road segment connecting Palembang–Jambi–Riau–North Sumatera should be prioritized to facilitate palm oil transportation from the four largest palm oil plantations in Sumatera (Riau, Riau, South Sumatera, and Jambi) to the midstream–downstream processing centers and transit points in Dumai and Belawan.

(iv)   The availability of good feeder roads from peripheral plantation areas to the toll roads and national highways should also be put on the agenda of the regional development plan of each related province, in collaboration with palm oil companies. If it is possible, feeder roads for palm oil should be separated from public roads.

(v)   The proposed EC6 could support palm oil downstream policy by using a business-friendly environment in Batam, Bintan, Karimun as the free trade zone and free port to support palm oil refinery and manufacturing industries. It is hoped to reduce the large portion of palm oil export in the form of CPO and CPKO.

(vi)   To accommodate big export markets across the Indian Ocean (Bangladesh, India, and Pakistan), refineries in the western part of Sumatera (Padang, West Sumatera Province) should start to be considered and the road-to-port infrastructure should be improved. The proposed expansion of EC3 and EC4 to include West Sumatera is an important step in this direction. Panjang Port in Padang is potential as it becomes export gateways for West Sumatera and Bengkulu provinces, even though this area is prone to earthquakes. To further explore this idea, a feasibility study may be needed.

Halal Food and Beverages

The Indonesia Islamic Economic Masterplan 2019–2024 adopted the definition of Islamic economy as covering all the core sectors of the economy together with the ecosystem, which is structurally influenced by consumers' lifestyles and business practices driven by Islamic values. Based on this definition, Indonesia has taken measures to strengthen its halal value chain for six halal-related industries: (i) halal food and beverages, (ii) halal tourism, (iii) Muslim fashion, (iv) halal media and recreation, (v) halal pharmaceutical and cosmetics, and (vi) renewable energy.

The study focused on the value chain for halal food and beverages. The coverage of halal food is not confined to only meat and poultry, but also includes other foods such as candies, canned and frozen foods, dairy products, bread, organic food, herbal products, and beverages. As palm oil and rubber (estate crops) are discussed separately in the study, the review of the halal food and beverages value chain focused on the fisheries and horticulture subsectors.[72]

The halal food and beverage industry is important in the IMT-GT context, given that approximately 70.14% of the combined population of the three countries are Muslims (2020).[73] Indonesia's Muslim population is the largest in the world—229 million or 13% of the world's total (2020).[74] Agriculture and fishery are also dominant sectors in the three countries, providing abundant raw materials that could be processed into halal products to meet the increasingly diverse needs of consumers in the region.[75]

As the largest consumer market for halal, Indonesia spent $170 billion in 2017 on halal food, the biggest level of spending globally in that year (Figure 3). Due to the COVID-19 pandemic, spending decreased to $144 billion in 2019, but is still the biggest spender.[76] About 88% ($150 billion) of market demand is supplied by domestic production, and 8% ($14.3 billion) is supplied by imports. Indonesia's domestic production is far greater than the import value of the biggest halal food importer, Saudi Arabia, which was $21.54 billion. Sumatera could potentially become a significant global producer for halal food products because of its geographical proximity to the halal consumer markets of (i) Malaysia and Thailand in Southeast Asia through the Strait of Malacca, and (ii) the Middle East area through the Indian Ocean.

A unique feature of the halal value chain is the requirement for products to undergo an official halal certification process to obtain the halal logo. For Muslims, halal logo means that the food and beverages are permitted to be consumed; for non-Muslims, it could represent a symbol of cleanliness, quality, purity, and security. The halal certification is based, among others, on the manner of preparing the various components of the food (e.g., the manner of slaughtering animals and the composition of the additives and other inputs used in processing) as well as the quality (cleanliness and purity) of the packaging and distribution process.

---

72   In Indonesia's statistics data, agriculture sector consists of food crops, estate crops, horticulture crops, forestry, livestock, and fisheries.

73   Based on the data of Cornell University. *Islam in Southeast Asia: Country, Area & Regional Profiles/Data 2020.* Accessed on 23 November 2020. https://guides.library.cornell.edu/c.php?g=141521&p=926391, compared with the UN Population Division. *World Population Prospects 2019.* https://population.un.org/wpp/Download/Files/1_Indicators%20(Standard)/EXCEL_FILES/1_Population/WPP2019_POP_F01_1_TOTAL_POPULATION_BOTH_SEXES.xlsx.

74   B. Radaksil. 2020. Data Populasi Penduduk Muslim 2020: Indonesia Terbesar di Dunia. *IB Times.* 8 April. https://ibtimes.id/data-populasi-penduduk-muslim-2020-indonesia-terbesar-di-dunia/.

75   Indonesian Ministry of National Development Planning. 2018. *Indonesia Islamic Economic Masterplan 2019–2024.* Jakarta: Indonesian Ministry of National Development Planning. p. 51.

76   DinarStandard. *2020/2021 State of the Global Islamic Economy Report.* https://cdn.salaamgateway.com/reports/pdf/2df5b5106072e6319d06888481e8faf3e3297e09.pdf.

Halal certification considers aspects of financing, research and development, and technology applications as inputs to prepare the final products.

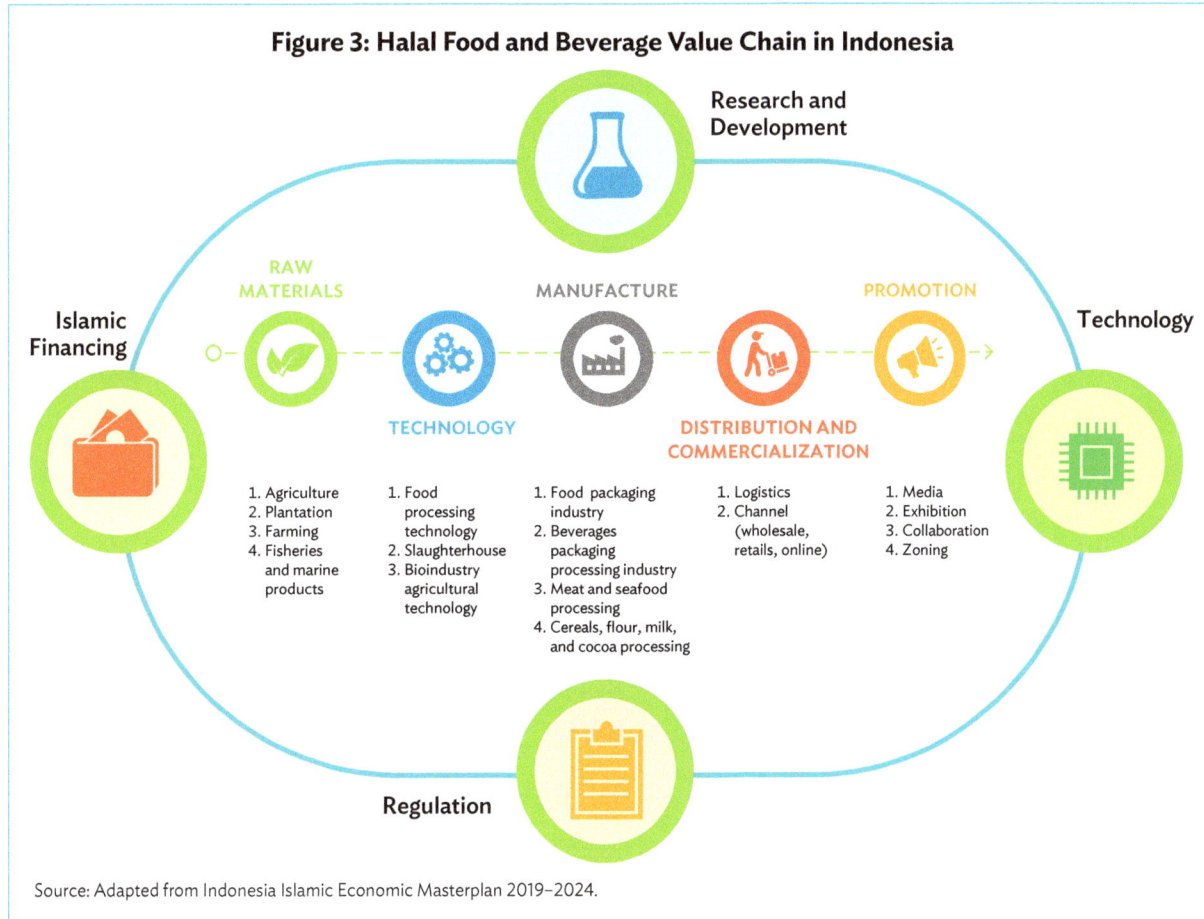

Figure 3: Halal Food and Beverage Value Chain in Indonesia

Research and Development

Islamic Financing

Technology

RAW MATERIALS

MANUFACTURE

PROMOTION

TECHNOLOGY

DISTRIBUTION AND COMMERCIALIZATION

1. Agriculture
2. Plantation
3. Farming
4. Fisheries and marine products

1. Food processing technology
2. Slaughterhouse
3. Bioindustry agricultural technology

1. Food packaging industry
2. Beverages packaging processing industry
3. Meat and seafood processing
4. Cereals, flour, milk, and cocoa processing

1. Logistics
2. Channel (wholesale, retails, online)

1. Media
2. Exhibition
3. Collaboration
4. Zoning

Regulation

Source: Adapted from Indonesia Islamic Economic Masterplan 2019–2024.

Production. The agriculture sector contributed 12.8% to Indonesia's GDP in 2018. Estate crops (which includes palm oil and rubber) was the largest contributor (3.30%), followed by food crops (3.03%), fisheries (2.60%), and livestock (1.56%).[77] The table of leading domestic and foreign trade commodities in Sumatera, 2018 showed that palm oil and rubber (estate crops subsector), seafood (fisheries subsector), as well as fruits and vegetables (horticulture subsector) are the strategic commodities both for domestic, inter-IMT-GT, and overall foreign trade for Sumatera's provinces.

---

[77]   BPS-Statistics Indonesia. *2019. Agricultural Indicators 2018*. Jakarta: BPS-Statistics Indonesia. p. xv.

Table 71: Production of Capture Fisheries and Horticulture in Sumatera, 2017
(million tons)

Province	Capture Fisheries	Main Commodities	Vegetables	Main Commodities	Fruits	Main Commodities
Aceh	0.24	Eastern little tuna (tongkol)	0.27	Chili	0.20	Banana
North Sumatera	0.80	Shrimp	1.00	Chili and cabbage	1.22	Tangerine, pineapple, salak
West Sumatera	0.22	Eastern little tuna (tongkol)	0.73	Tomato, red onion	0.57	Passion fruit, tangerine
Riau	0.13	Shrimp	0.12	Cucumber	0.26	Pineapple
Jambi	0.05	Shrimp	0.23	Potato	0.19	Pineapple
South Sumatera	0.13	Shrimp	0.16	Chili	0.43	Banana, pineapple
Bengkulu	0.07	Eastern little tuna (tongkol)	0.35	Cabbage	0.08	Banana
Lampung	0.18	Eastern little tuna (tongkol)	0.27	Chili	2.39	Banana, papaya
Bangka Belitung Islands	0.22	Eastern little tuna (tongkol)	0.02	Eggplant	0.03	Banana
Riau Islands	0.11	Eastern little tuna (tongkol)	0.03	Kale	0.02	Watermelon
Sumatera	**2.14**		**3.20**		**5.40**	
INDONESIA	**7.07**		**16.15**		**19.64**	
Share to Indonesia (%)	**30.27**		**19.81**		**27.49**	

Note: Some provinces had data in 2018, some others such as Aceh, have only the latest data in 2017. Therefore, this table used the data in 2017.
Source: Ministry of Marine and Fisheries-Republic of Indonesia. 2018. *Marine and Fisheries in Figures 2018*. Jakarta: The Center for Data, Statistics and Information. Data for vegetables is downloaded from https://www.bps.go.id/indikator/indikator/view_data/0000/data/61/website_55/1, while data for vegetables is downloaded from https://www.bps.go.id/indikator/indikator/view_data/0000/data/62/website_55/1.

Captured fisheries, vegetables, and fruits are the main subsectors in Sumatera involved in the halal food value chain (Table 71). These three subsectors combined contributed 77.6 % to total national production in 2017.

(i)   In captured fisheries, Sumatera contributed 30.34% of total national production in 2017. Eastern little tuna, known locally as "tongkol," and shrimp are the main commodities in this subsector. North Sumatera (37.3%) and Aceh (11%) are the largest producers in the Sumatera region.

(ii)   For vegetables, the Sumatera region contributed 19.8% to the national production in 2017. Big chilies, cabbage, tomato, potato, eggplant, tiny chilies (cayenne pepper), cucumber, carrot, and long beans are the main commodities in this subsector. North Sumatera (31.3%) and West Sumatera (23%) are the major producers.

(iii) For fruits, Sumatera's production accounted for 27.52% of total national production. Banana, pineapple, tangerine, and durian are the main commodities in this subsector. Lampung (44.2%) and North Sumatera (22.5%) are the largest producers.

The largest producers of the above commodities are in EC1 (North Sumatera), EC4 (West Sumatera), and EC5 (Aceh). Lampung has been proposed to be part of the extended EC3 which will eventually cover all eight provinces in mainland Sumatera.

Other important sectors in the upstream level of halal food and beverages are food crops and livestock. However, Sumatera region's contribution in these subsectors is far behind Java. Java Island contributed close to 50% to the national paddy rice production and 58.24% to the national beef meat production in 2017.[78]

Processing. Obtaining a halal certification from competent authorities is crucial in the halal value chain as it is a requirement to affix the halal logo in product packages. LPPOM-Indonesian Ulema Council (LPPOM-MUI), established in 1989, was the halal certification authority in Indonesia until 2014, when Law No. 33/2014 shifted the certification authority to the *Badan Penyelenggara Jaminan Produk Halal or BPJPH* (The Organizing Agency for Halal Product Assurance) under the Ministry of Religious Affairs. The BPJPH conducts inspection in all stages of halal product development—from purchasing, receiving, storage, processing, packaging, and distribution. Figure 4 illustrates the six steps in the certification process. The BPJPH also continuously coordinates with other halal authorities in Malaysia and Thailand through the Working Group on Halal Products and Services, especially in the issue of Halal product Assurance.

Figure 4: Procedure for Halal Product Certification in BPJPH

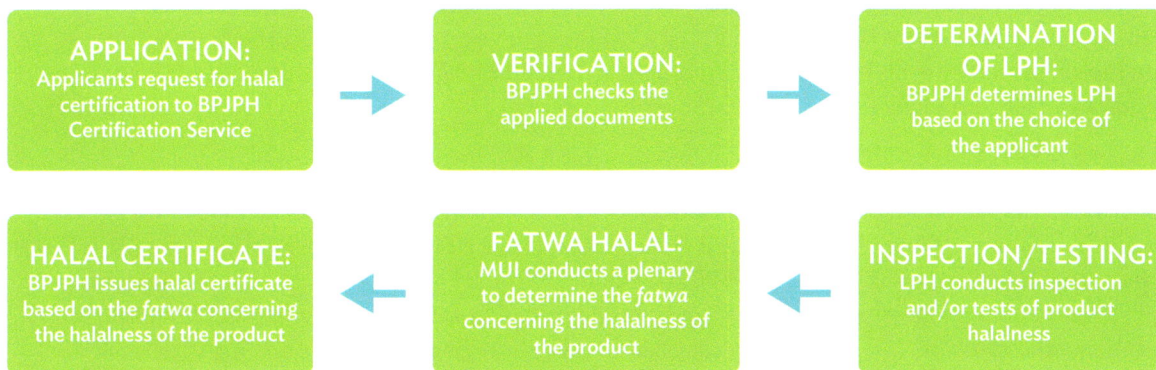

APPLICATION: Applicants request for halal certification to BPJPH Certification Service	→	VERIFICATION: BPJPH checks the applied documents	→	DETERMINATION OF LPH: BPJPH determines LPH based on the choice of the applicant
HALAL CERTIFICATE: BPJPH issues halal certificate based on the *fatwa* concerning the halalness of the product	←	FATWA HALAL: MUI conducts a plenary to determine the *fatwa* concerning the halalness of the product	←	INSPECTION/TESTING: LPH conducts inspection and/or tests of product halalness

BPJPH = Badan Penyelenggara Jaminan Produk Halal, LPH = Lembaga Pemeriksa Halal, MUI = Majelis Ulama Indonesia.
Note: *fatwa* is a ruling on a point of Islamic law given by a recognized authority.
Source: BPJPH. *Procedure of Halal Product Certification*. Accessed on 26 September 2020. http://www.halal.go.id/cms/assets/files/WhatsApp_Image_2020-04-06_at_3_38_08_PM.jpeg.

It is difficult to find the data on the number of manufacturers that have obtained halal certification for their products. In general, however, there has been an increasing trend in the number of products that get halal-certified from year to year.

---

[78] The detailed table of production for both subsectors issued by the Ministry of Agriculture could be downloaded from https://www.pertanian.go.id/home/?show=page&act=view&id=61.

Table 72: Number of LPPOM Halal-Certified Products, 2012–2017

Year	Total Entrepreneurs	Total Products
2012	626	19,830
2013	913	34,634
2014	960	40,684
2015	1,052	46,260
2016	1,335	65,594
Oct 2017	1,168	52,982

LPPOM = Lembaga Pengkajian Pangan, Obat-obatan, dan Kosmetika Majelis Ulama Indonesia (Assessment Institute for Foods, Drugs, and Cosmetics).
Source: LPPOM-MUI, quoted from Indonesia Islamic Economy Masterplan 2019–2024.

Data from the Ministry of Industry records 22 food factories and 25 beverage factories in Sumatera in (2020). There is no data on whether these factories are halal-certified. Some of these factories use agricultural raw materials in the manufacture of final products (e.g., chili for chili sauce, soya bean for soya bean milk drink, and coconut for nata de coco). The number of food and beverage factories in Sumatera is only about 10% of the total food and beverage factories in Indonesia. Considering the huge quantities of agricultural raw materials produced in Sumatera, there is a huge opportunity to further develop the halal food and beverage industries in the region, especially in EC1 (North Sumatera), the extended EC3 (Lampung), the extended EC4 (West Sumatera and Riau), and the proposed EC6 (South Sumatera).

To boost the halal food industry, the Government of Indonesia is developing three halal industrial zones in 2021: Modern Cikande Industrial Estate in Serang (capital of Banten), Safe n Lock Halal Industrial Park in Sidoarjo, East Java, and Bintan Inti Halal Hub in Riau Islands. The last one is located in IMT-GT area. The Bintan Inti Industrial Estate covers an area of 6.5–100 ha. Bintan Inti Halal Food Hub is in the Bintan Industrial Estate area. This halal industrial area is developing food processing with halal raw materials from agriculture, plantations, and livestock. In addition, they will also support packaging, cold chain, and logistics services. Moreover, Indonesia also plans to develop three other halal industrial zones, one of them is located in Batam, Riau Islands, called Batamindo Industrial Zone. It indicates the prospective strategic role of EC6 in developing the halal food industry in IMT-GT.

Distribution. As the country with the biggest Muslim population in the world, Indonesia is also the biggest halal food market. Based on the State of the Global Islamic Economy Report 2018/19, Indonesia has the highest Muslim food expenditure amounting to $170 billion in 2017 or 13.04% of total global halal food market spending ($1,303 billion). However, in terms of halal food development, including exports, Indonesia only placed 11th, together with Saudi Arabia. The United Arab Emirates and Malaysia ranked second in terms of halal food development.[79] Indonesia's weak position in the halal food industry could be explained by the fact that standardization and halal product certification is still not widely recognized in the global market.[80] With some strategic policies being taken, including the development of halal industrial zones, Indonesia's position continues to improve. Based on data from The State of The Global Islamic Economy Report, Indonesia's position has increased from 10th in 2018, 5th in 2019, and 4th in 2020.

---

[79]   Dubai International Financial Centre, Thomson Reuters, & DinarStandard. *State of the Islamic Economy Report 2018/19*. Retrieved from https://haladinar.io/hdn/doc/report2018.pdf.

[80]   Indonesian Ministry of National Development Planning. 2018. *Indonesia Islamic Economic Masterplan 2019–2024*. Jakarta: Indonesian Ministry of National Development Planning. p. 59.

To increase its role as a global halal food exporter, the development of halal industrial zones is not enough. Indonesia also needs to anticipate the challenges that are predicted to be faced. Research by Widiatuti et al. (2020) states that there are five big challenges for Indonesia in developing halal industry sequentially: human resource, infrastructure, production, policy, and socialization.[81] Another concern is on halal logistics and distribution, in which Sazali and Ligte (2019) found that there was no specific regulation yet in Indonesia in terms of halal logistics and distribution.[82] Halal logistics here refers to logistic activities that cover warehousing, distribution, and retailing aspects based on Islamic law (Sharia). The Islamic Chamber of Commerce and Industry – International Halal Integrity (ICCI-IHI) Alliance has developed a halal standard that covers warehouse treatment, distribution, transportation treatment, and terminal treatment. This requires improvements for ports that will become export gateways for halal food and beverage. There should be a special warehouse, cargo, transportation, and terminal which separate halal and non-halal products. Therefore, there is a need to rule and promote halal logistics certification, that many manufacturers foresee this process will increase their distribution cost. But with increasingly halal product demands, even in the time of the COVID-19 pandemic,[83] this opportunity should not be missed.

Recommendations

The Government of Indonesia has been seriously developing halal industries, especially in the last 2 years. To support this effort, there are some steps that could be exercised regarding the IMT-GT's economic corridors:

(i)   Some prominent ports along the IMT-GT economic corridors could be appointed as halal product gateways, both for export and import. It should be followed by all improvements needed to fulfill Halal Logistics Standard, which covers warehouse, distribution–transportation, and terminal treatments.

(ii)   As North Sumatera, West Sumatera, and Aceh are the main producers of fish, vegetables, and fruits in Sumatera, while the designated halal industrial zones are in Bintan and Batam of Riau Islands, there should be an efficient port-to-port connection between port of origin and destination port. Both ports should also implement Halal Logistics Standard.

(iii)   EC6 could play as the center for the downstream halal industry, as there will be two designated halal industrial zones in Riau Islands. This potential could be strengthened by combining various subsectors of the halal industry, especially food, modest fashion, as well as Muslim-friendly travel which was previously known as the leading sector for the proposed EC6.[84]

---

[81]   T. Widiastuti et al. 2020. Obstacles and Strategies in Developing Halal Industry: Evidence from Indonesia. *Humanities & Social Sciences Reviews*. 8(4). pp. 398–406. https://doi.org/10.18510/hssr.2020.8439.

[82]   A. M. Sazali and J. S. Light. 2019. The Importance of Halal Logistics Implementation in Indonesia in Compliance with Domestic and Global Halal Market Requirements. *Jurnal Transportasi Multimoda*. 17(2). pp. 17–26

[83]   Halal industry grew by 3.2% in 2020. For the details, please visit https://indonesia.go.id/kategori/feature/2794/indonesia-berpeluang-memimpin-industri-halal-dunia?lang=1.

[84]   Riau Islands places the third biggest tourist arrivals in Indonesia, after Bali and Jakarta.

Rubber and Rubber Products

There are two types of rubber—natural and synthetic. Natural rubber is made from the sap (latex) of the rubber tree, while synthetic rubber is made from raw materials derived from petroleum, coal, oil, natural gas, and acetylene petroleum.[85] In this study, the term rubber refers to natural rubber, unless specifically explained.

Indonesia was the world's second-largest rubber producer in 2018, accounting for 24.7% of global natural rubber production. Thailand was the largest producer (33.4%) while Malaysia was fifth (3.8%). The three countries combined produced more than 60% of the world's natural rubber. The major export markets for rubber are the PRC, the US, India, and Japan. Indonesia has the potential to boost its rubber production further because it has the largest rubber tree plantation areas worldwide, especially in the four provinces of South Sumatera, North Sumatera, Jambi, and Riau. Developing a rubber supply chain among the three IMT-GT countries could generate greater synergies and mutual benefits for the countries.

Production. The rubber plantation areas in Indonesia are spread over 26 out of its 34 provinces. In 2018, Sumatera region has the largest area planted to rubber (70.6%) followed by Kalimantan (25.2%). The top four provinces in Sumatera with the largest rubber plantations are South Sumatera (22.8%), North Sumatera (12.3%), Jambi (10.3%), and Riau (9.54%). Smallholders manage 86% of these plantations, followed by big private estates (8.35%), and government estates (5.27%).

Table 73: Rubber Plantations and Production in Sumatera, 2018

Province	Plantations			Production		
	Total Area (hectares)	Share to Sumatera (%)	Share to Indonesia (%)	Total Production (tons)	Share to Sumatera (%)	Share to Indonesia (%)
Aceh	97,951	3.8	2.7	98,380	3.6	2.7
North Sumatera	450,329	17.4	12.3	461,190	16.8	12.7
West Sumatera	130,331	5.0	3.6	152,508	5.5	4.2
Riau	350,205	13.5	9.5	368,904	13.4	10.2
Jambi	378,695	14.6	10.3	315,724	11.5	8.7
South Sumatera	838,636	32.3	22.8	982,423	35.7	27.1
Bengkulu	99,015	3.8	2.7	122,522	4.5	3.4
Lampung	157,682	6.1	4.3	160,022	5.8	4.4
Bangka Belitung Islands	47,286	1.8	1.3	59,478	2.2	1.6
Riau Islands	25,185	1.0	0.7	30,186	1.1	0.8
Sumatera	**2,593,561**	**100.0**	**70.6**	**2,751,337**	**100.0**	**75.8**
INDONESIA	**3,671,302**		**100.0**	**3,630,268**		**100.0**

Note: Totals may not sum precisely because of rounding.
Source: Ministry of Agriculture-Republic of Indonesia. 2018. *Tree Crops Estate Statistics of Indonesia 2017–2019*. Jakarta: Directorate General of Estate Crops-Ministry of Agriculture-Republic of Indonesia.

---

[85]   Indonesia Investment. *Rubber (Natural)*. Accessed on 12 September 2020. https://www.indonesia-investments.com/business/commodities/rubber/item185.

Similar to the plantation pattern, natural rubber production in Indonesia is also dominated by the Sumatera region (75.8%). The higher share of production compared to the share of plantation area implies that Sumatera region has higher productivity of 1.06 ton/ha compared to the national average productivity of 0.99 ton/ha. South Sumatera is the largest natural rubber producer in 2018 with 982,000 tons or 35.7% of Sumatera region's total production. Other major producers are North Sumatera (16.8%), Riau (13.4%), Jambi (11.5%), and Lampung (5.8%).

Indonesian rubber productivity is relatively low compared to other rubber producing countries (Table 75). While Indonesia's productivity averages around 1 ton/ha, Thailand's productivity could reach up to 1.80 ton/ha; Viet Nam, 1.72 ton/ha; and Malaysia, 1.52 ton/ha. The older age of rubber trees and low investment capability of smallholder farmers are among the major factors contributing to Indonesia's lower productivity.[86] It has been difficult to encourage smallholder farmers (86.4% of plantation owners) to regenerate their rubber trees due to the high cost and the potential loss of income during the replantation period.[87]

The Government of Indonesia needs to develop a strategy to change the behavioral tendency of smallholder farmers to increase productivity by clearing new forests. The government can encourage large companies, especially state-owned enterprises, to build partnerships with smallholder farmers in an effort to accelerate the regeneration of rubber trees, so that production levels can increase while promoting land-use practices that satisfy sustainable resource management. As part of its NDCs under the Paris Agreement, the government has set an unconditional reduction target of 29% and conditional reduction target up to 41% of the business-as-usual scenario by 2030. To reach these targets, Indonesia has taken significant steps to reduce emissions in land-use sector, including for the rubber industry, which includes instituting a moratorium on the clearing of primary forests and by prohibiting conversion of its remaining forests.

Processing. Rubber latex produced by farmers are accumulated by collectors, middlemen, and brokers in multiple levels of village or subdistrict, and transported to cities or urban areas where rubber factories are usually located. These factories could be classified into upstream and downstream industries. Factories in the upstream industry produce SIR, Technically Specified Rubber, commonly known as block rubber, ribbed smoked sheet (RSS) rubber, and concentrated latex. Factories in the downstream industry produce tires, gloves, rubber threads, footwear, retread tires, medical gloves, carpets and other rubber-based tools.[88] Upstream factories outnumber downstream factories in Sumatera.

[86]   Indonesia Investment. 2018. *Rubber (Natural)*. Accessed on 12 September 2020. https://www.indonesia-investments.com/business/commodities/rubber/item185.

[87]   Global Business Guide Indonesia. 2016. *Indonesia's Rubber Industry: Increased Competition and Falling Prices.* Accessed on 15 September 2020. http://www.gbgindonesia.com/en/agriculture/article/2016/indonesia_s_rubber_industry_increased_competition_and_falling_prices_11520.php.

[88]   Indonesia Investment. *Rubber (Natural)*. Accessed on 12 September 2020. https://www.indonesia-investments.com/business/commodities/rubber/item185.

Table 74: Natural Rubber Factories by Province in Sumatera, 2020

Province	Total Industrial Factories	Upstream Industry*		Downstream Industry*	
		Number of Factories	Products	Number of Factories	Products
Aceh	1	1	SIR (20)		
North Sumatera	29	10		19	Glove, footwear, tire for bicycle and motorcycle, bracelet, toys, etc.
West Sumatera	1	1	SIR (20)		
Riau	4	3	RSS, SIR (10, 20), rubberwood	1	Rubber blanket
Jambi	3	2	Crumb rubber, rubberwood	1	Rubberwood molding
South Sumatera	10	10	SIR (3CV,3L, 5, 10, 20), RSS 1, 2, 3), brown crepe		
Bengkulu	1	1	Crumb rubber		
Lampung	4	3	SIR, crumb rubber	1	Rubber tree veneer
Bangka Belitung Islands	1	1	SIR (20)		
Riau Islands	2	1	SIR	1	Rubber keypad
Sumatera	56	33		23	
Indonesia	**315**				

3CV = constant viscosity grade 3, 3L = light grade 3, RSS = ribbed smoked sheet, SIR = standard Indonesia rubber.
* The classification of downstream and upstream factories was determined by the author based on the type of the products produced.
Source: Ministry of Industry. *Direktori Perusahaan Industri*. Accessed on 18 October 2021. https://kemenperin.go.id/direktori-perusahaan?what=Karet&prov=0&hal=7.

Although South Sumatera has the largest number of plantations and the biggest producer of rubber in Sumatera region, the number of industrial rubber factories in that province is only 10—much smaller than North Sumatera, which has 29 factories. All 10 factories in South Sumatera are engaged in upstream activities, producing SIR, RSS, and brown crepe. Meanwhile, majority of the rubber factories in North Sumatera are engaged in downstream activities, producing consumer goods such as gloves, footwear, toys, and tires. Rubber latex produced in South Sumatera and other provinces such as Jambi and Riau (which have significant production volumes but small number of industrial factories) is transported to North Sumatera for further processing into downstream products because of the large number of factories there. For this reason, the Sei Mangkei SEZ in North Sumatera has been designated as one of the IMT-GT rubber cities that would focus on downstream rubber products.[89] The expanded EC3 that will include eight provinces in Sumatera island will play an important role in facilitating rubber transport from South Sumatera, Jambi, and Riau to North Sumatera.

---

[89]   Rubber Journal Asia. *Rubber City to be Developed by Indonesia, Malaysia, Thailand.* Accessed on 15 September 2020. http://rubberjournalasia.com/rubber-city-to-be-developed-by-indonesia-malaysia-thailand/.

Distribution. Based on the Indonesia investment data for 2018, around 15% of Indonesian rubber production was absorbed domestically, particularly by the automotive industry.[90] These rubber-based manufactures were concentrated in three provinces: North Sumatera, Banten, and West Java. The last two provinces are located on Java Island. The bulk (85%) of natural rubber production was exported (footnote 90). Indonesia's natural rubber exports consist of as many as 22 different products under HS code 40011000 for "natural, rubber, latex."

The biggest maritime gateway port for rubber-based products in Indonesia in 2018 was Tanjung Priok Port in Jakarta, contributing 38% in terms of volume or 46.5% in terms of value. Belawan Port in Sumatera is the second-largest, contributing around 19% both in terms of volume and value. Other prominent ports in Sumatera for rubber exports were Musi River (South Sumatera), Jambi, Teluk Bayur (West Sumatera), Panjang (Lampung), Batu Ampar (Riau Islands), and Palembang-Plaju (South Sumatera). Small-scale exports (less than 1,000 tons) are conducted through smaller ports in Sumatera such as Sekupang and Kabil in Riau Islands and Perawang in Riau. Aceh and Bengkulu are the only two provinces in Sumatera that do not have internal ports.

Table 75: Volume of Rubber Exports by Port of Loading, 2018

No.	Port of Loading	Rubber and articles thereof			
		Volume (million tons)	Share to Indonesia (%)	Value ($ million)	Share to Indonesia (%)
Sumatera					
1	Belawan	0.7	19.0	1,181.3	18.5
2	Musi River	0.7	19.0	949.1	14.9
3	Jambi	0.3	7.6	379.7	6.0
4	Teluk Bayur (West Sumatera)	0.2	5.7	290.4	4.6
5	Panjang	0.07	1.8	91.2	1.4
6	Batu Ampar (Batam)	0.00	0.07	22.8	0.4
7	Palembang-Plaju	0.00	0.06	3.3	0.05
Java					
1	Tanjung Priok	1.4	38.1	2,965.3	46.9
2	Tanjung Perak	0.22	6.2	320.3	5.0
3	Tanjung Emas	0.24	6.6	35.6	0.6
	Total Indonesia	**3.6**	**100.0**	**6,380.1**	**100.0**

Note: The export data include natural and synthetic rubber.
Source: BPS-Statistics Indonesia, 2020. Data of export and import by port could be modified searched through https://www.bps.go.id/exim/.

The major markets for Indonesia's natural rubber exports are the US (23%), Japan (14.8%), the PRC (11%), and India (8.64%) (Table 76). Most exports are in the form of Technically Natural Specified Rubber or Standard Indonesia Rubber 20 (85.4%) followed by mixtures of natural rubber (5.50%). In terms of the value chain, rubber exports consist basically of midstream products.

---

[90] Indonesia Investment. *Rubber (Natural)*. Accessed on 12 September 2020. https://www.indonesia-investments.com/business/commodities/rubber/item185.

Table 76: Top Destination Countries of Indonesia's Rubber Exports, 2018

Rank	Destination Country	Volume (tons)	Share (%)	Value ($ '000)	Share (%)
1	US	832,205	23.0	1,629,481.3	25.5
2	Japan	536,211	14.8	882,149.9	13.8
3	China, People's Republic of	396,881	11.0	581,579.6	9.1
4	India	312,716	8.6	460,066.1	7.2
5	Brazil	108,836	3.0	173,733.8	2.7
6	Türkiye	100,886	2.8	151,756.9	2.3
7	Canada	97,567	2.7	153,582.5	2.4
	Malaysia	34,989	1.0	94,698.3	1.5
	Thailand	17,563	0.5	64,118.9	1.0
	Total Export	**3,619,367**	**100.0**	**6,380,061.02**	**100.0**

US = United States.
Note: The export data include natural and synthetic rubber.
Source: BPS-Statistics Indonesia, 2020. Data of export and import by country could be modified searched through https://www.bps.go.id/exim/.

Rubber exports to Thailand or Malaysia contributed less than 2% in 2018 since these two countries are also major rubber producers. Indonesia imported rubber products from both countries in 2018. Indonesia's imports from Thailand (69,794 tons or 8.82% of total imports) are mostly in the form of natural rubber latex-centrifuge concentrate and synthetic rubber of other polybutadiene-styrene rubber and XSBR2. Imports from Malaysia (50,463 tons or 6.37% of total imports) mainly consisted of synthetic rubber of NBR in latex form and natural rubber latex-centrifuge concentrate. Most of these products entered Indonesia through Tanjung Priok and Belawan Ports. Belawan Port, a maritime gateway in EC1 and EC3, serves as an important node in the rubber value chain with Malaysia and Thailand both in terms of exports and imports.

Recommendations

Belawan Port, which is both in EC1 and EC3, currently serves as a strategic gateway for Sumatera's rubber exports and imports. With Sei Mangkei SEZ having been positioned to promote downstream activities for rubber and palm oil, the development of Kuala Tanjung Port closer to Sei Mangkei would further boost the rubber industry by easing logistics, infrastructure, and permit issuances needed for the SEZ to flourish. Considering that Sei Mangkei has been designated as a Rubber City under the IT-GT framework, the government will need to address the remaining issues in the development of the Sei Mangkei SEZ (e.g., land procurement, reliability of electricity, affordability of gas) to provide a conducive environment for investors, especially in downstream activities. Regarding Kuala Tanjung Port, it will give North Sumatera, which has the most number of rubber factories in Sumatera, direct access to world markets for the first time. Kuala Tanjung Port has already developed direct maritime links to several ports in Malaysia across the Strait of Malacca. The ongoing development of Kuala Tanjung Port will have to focus on its increasing role in global supply chain management and logistic networks, given the emerging competition among hub ports in the region.

The large quantity of rubber latex produced in South Sumatera—the biggest natural rubber producer in Sumatera region—is currently not supported by an adequate number of midstream and downstream manufacturers in the province. It is envisaged that Tanjung Api-Api SEZ in South Sumatera, which started operations in 2018, will address this gap through largescale investments in the rubber downstream industry as well as CPO and petrochemicals. At present, however, progress in the development of the Tanjung Api-Api

SEZ has met with several issues regarding land-use and the risk of land subsidence,[91] the safety of the port basin for big ships;[92] and the construction of the planned toll road from Palembang to Tanjung Api-Api, which has been held in abeyance pending the construction of the seaport in the SEZ.[93] The pressing resolution of these issues are critical to the further development of the rubber value chain considering that Tanjung Api-Api has also been designated as a Rubber City for Indonesia under the IMT-GT framework.

---

[91]   Andriani, E. Ibrahim, D. D. A. Putranto, A. K. Affandy, and H. G. Putra. 2019. Spatial Analysis of Land Subsidence Potential Due to Lowland Conversion (case study at Tanjung Api-Api). *IOP Conference Series: Materials Science and Engineering*, Volume 933, The 2nd Aceh International Symposium on Civil Engineering (AISCE) 18-19 September 2019, Banda Aceh, Aceh Province, Indonesia. https://iopscience.iop.org/article/10.1088/1757-899X/933/1/012054/meta. The conversion of lowland area into special economic zones at Tanjung Api-Api will trigger environmental degradations, one of which is land subsidence. Land subsidence potential is caused by several natural environmental factors, which are soil type, soft soil thickness, topography, geological conditions, and rainfall, and nonnatural factors, which are caused by land use or land cover, groundwater extraction, building density and others.

[92]   *Antara News*. 2017. Tanjung Api-Api Port to Start Operation in December. 20 May. https://en.antaranews.com/news/111017/tanjung-api-api-port-to-start-operation-in-december.

[93]   M. Parama. 2020. Ministry Proposes Five New Toll Road Projects in Strategic Project List. *Jakarta Post*. 21 October. https://www.thejakartapost.com/news/2020/10/21/ministry-proposes-five-new-toll-road-projects-in-strategic-project-list.html.

ADDRESSING GAPS IN
INSTITUTIONAL MECHANISMS
FOR ECONOMIC CORRIDOR
DEVELOPMENT

Studies on regional, subregional, and bilateral cooperation have emphasized that an effective institutional mechanism is essential for success (Thao 1999, Raharjo 2019).[94] The IMT-GT is a subregional cooperation program involving national or central government line ministries, subnational or provincial governments, and their relevant bureaus and/or departments. It, therefore, requires a well-established institutional coordinating mechanism at the national and subnational levels. Moreover, the institutional mechanism should also include coordination between the state and the private sector. This chapter will review the existing institutional mechanism for IMT-GT in Indonesia.

Coordination at the Subregional Level

The highest level of coordination at the subregional level involves the heads of government (referred to as "leaders") of the three member countries, meeting at an annual summit, which is held in conjunction with the ASEAN Summit. The IMT-GT Summit is attended by the president of Indonesia, the prime minister of Malaysia, and the prime minister of Thailand. Below the summit is the Ministerial Meeting, where the appointed IMT-GT signing ministers from the three countries discuss issues at the policy and strategic levels. Parallel to the Ministerial Meeting is the Chief Ministers and Governors Forum (CMGF), attended by governors or heads of the participating provinces or states in the three countries. A senior officials meeting (SOM) supports the Ministerial Meeting by conducting in-depth discussions of sectoral issues and monitoring the cooperation's overall progress. Below the SOM are working groups on IMT-GT's sectors of cooperation or focus areas. Working groups are composed of focal points from line ministries in the three countries who meet to consider joint initiatives and monitor the status of programs and projects. There are seven working groups at present (Figure 5).

The Centre for Indonesia–Malaysia–Thailand Growth Triangle (CIMT) based in Putrajaya, Malaysia, serves as the regional secretariat. The center is headed by a director whose position rotates among the three countries for a term of 3 years. Two deputy directors are designated by the countries that are not holding the position of director. The center is funded by contributions from the three countries. The mandates of the CIMT are to (i) strengthen coordination mechanisms and consultation processes among IMT-GT institutions in the subregion to support public and private sector activities; (ii) facilitate the implementation of priority projects, and monitor and evaluate projects and agreements; (iii) establish and enhance external relations with development partners and potential investors; and (iv) develop useful databases on IMT-GT activities and enhance information dissemination within and outside the subregion (Figure 5).

Coordination at the Country Level

Presidential Decree No. 13/2001 mandates the establishment of the Coordination Team for Subregional Economic Cooperation. The decree appointed the Coordinating Minister for Economic Affairs (CMEA) as the head of the team and the signing minister, CMEA's deputy minister of International Economic Cooperation as the secretary and the senior official, while line ministries, relevant governors, and chamber of commerce and industry representatives are team members. This decree also mandates the establishment of a national secretariat for Subregional Economic Cooperation, which was enabled by CMEA Decree No. 117/M.EKON/2012, appointing the deputy assistant for Regional and Subregional Economic Cooperation of CMEA as its head.

---

[94]   N. H. Thao. 2019. Joint Development in the Gulf of Thailand. *IBRU Boundary and Security Bulletin (Autumn)*, 1999: pp. 79–88; S. N. I. Raharjo, Ed *Membangun Konektivitas di Perbatasan: Kerja Sama Subregional Indonesia, Brunei Darussalam, Malaysia, dan Filipina.* Jakarta: LIPI Press.

Figure 5: IMT-GT Institutional Coordination Mechanism Structure

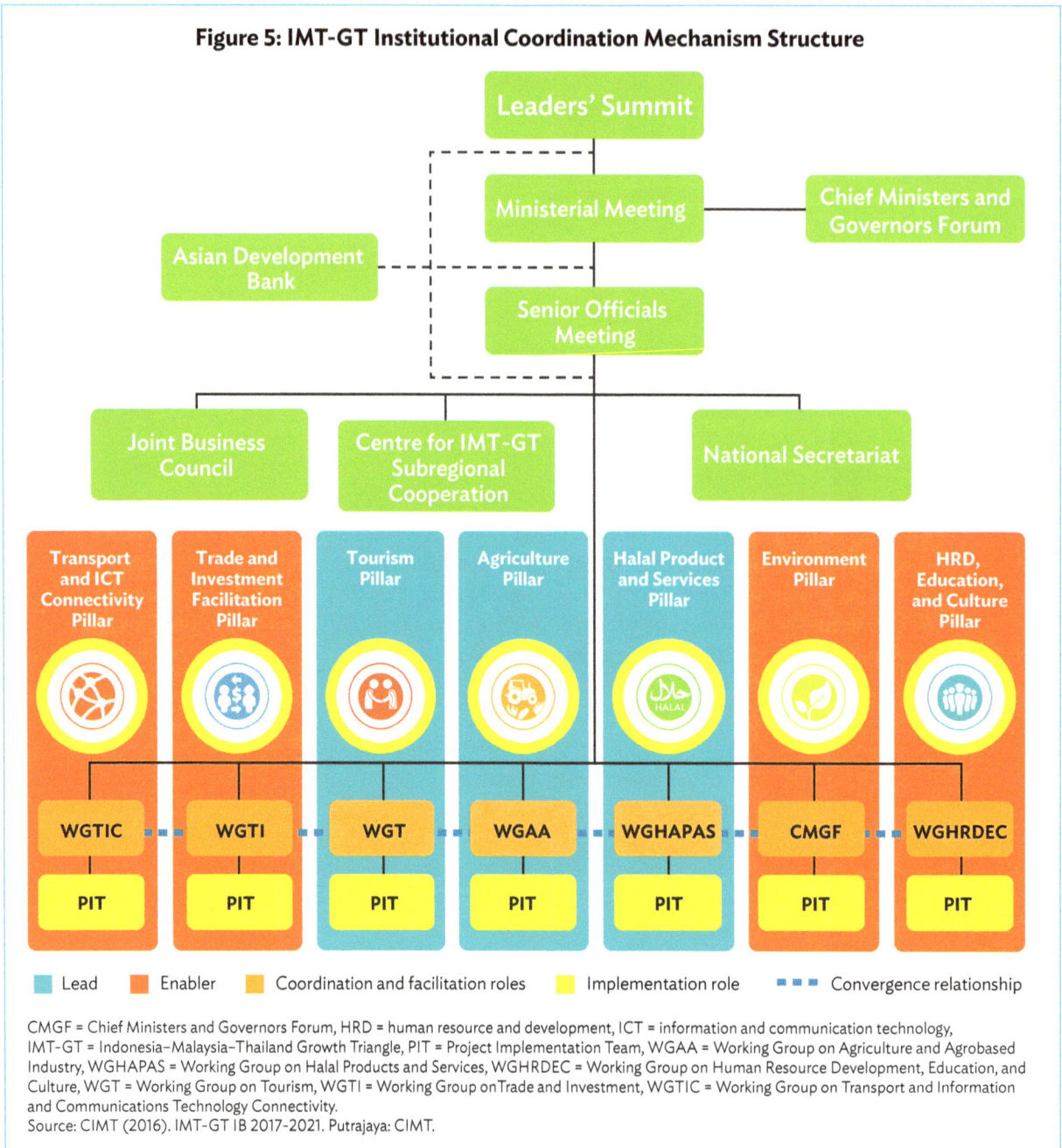

CMGF = Chief Ministers and Governors Forum, HRD = human resource and development, ICT = information and communication technology, IMT-GT = Indonesia–Malaysia–Thailand Growth Triangle, PIT = Project Implementation Team, WGAA = Working Group on Agriculture and Agrobased Industry, WGHAPAS = Working Group on Halal Products and Services, WGHRDEC = Working Group on Human Resource Development, Education, and Culture, WGT = Working Group on Tourism, WGTI = Working Group on Trade and Investment, WGTIC = Working Group on Transport and Information and Communications Technology Connectivity.
Source: CIMT (2016). IMT-GT IB 2017-2021. Putrajaya: CIMT.

The senior official is responsible to the signing minister and reports on the results and progress of agreements reached based on the minister's instructions or guidance. The signing minister reports matters that will be discussed at the summit to the president of Indonesia.

For the CMGF, the elected governor is automatically involved in the forum without a formal appointment. The establishment of the CMGF secretariat is in progress, spearheaded by the governor of Bangka Belitung Islands.

Coordination with Line Ministries

CMEA has appointed the focal ministry or agency for each working group as follows:

(i)   Working Group on Trade and Investment: Ministry of Trade and Coordinating Agency for Investment (*Badan Koordinasi Penanaman Modal-BKPM*),

(ii)   Working Group on Transport and ICT: Ministry of Transport and Ministry of Communication and Information,

(iii)   Working Group on Agriculture: Ministry of Agriculture,

(iv)   Working Group on Human Resource Development: Ministry of Manpower,

(v)   Working Group on Tourism: Ministry of Tourism and Creative Economy,

(vi)   Working Group on Halal product and Services: *Badan Penyelenggara Jaminan Produk Halal* or The Organizing Agency for Halal Product Assurance (BPJPH) at the Ministry of Religious Affairs, and

(vii) Working Group on Environment: Ministry of Environment and Forestry.

Interagency coordination meetings are held at the beginning of the year to formulate the work plan for each working group and at the end of the year to evaluate progress. Interagency meetings may be convened at any time during the year to discuss specific issues requiring an immediate decision or action (e.g., review of draft Implementation Blueprint and discussion on the Melaka–Dumai Ro-Ro Project issue.)

Information flow. All reports and documentation of Ministerial Meetings, SOMs, and meetings of the national secretariat are shared with line ministries and/or agencies as well as the participating provincial governments. Line ministry focal points to working groups also send written reports to the national secretariat on their attended subregional meetings. If an issue reported requires a follow-up action, the national secretariat may convene a coordination meeting. Presently, the national secretariat is developing an official website of the IMT-GT and the BIMP-EAGA programs (https://subregional.ekon.go.id/) to facilitate information sharing among stakeholders and the public.

Projects. At the early part of each year, the national secretariat holds a regular coordination meeting with all line ministries, provincial governments, and other relevant agencies to share ideas, discuss proposed projects and other vital issues, as well as get feedback and updates. The outcomes of the meeting are then presented to relevant working group meetings. Every project proposed by the working group is evaluated by the national secretariat, especially with regard to spatial planning to ensure consistency between Indonesia's National Development Plan and the IMT-GT Vision document and Implementation Blueprint (Appendix 1).

Although the participating entities in IMT-GT are at the level of provinces and states, central government agencies in the capitals play the dominant role in the program. CMEA's designated signing minister, senior official, and national secretariat head represent the country at all levels of the regional institutional mechanism. The line ministry representatives to the working groups are all based in Jakarta. Therefore, effective coordination between the central agencies and/or line ministries and the participating provinces has been a continuing challenge.

Coordination at the Provincial Level

Sumatera Governors Forum. Coordination among the leaders and officials from the 10 provincial governments is conducted annually through the Sumatera Governors Coordination Meeting (*Rapat Koordinasi Gubernur se-Wilayah Sumatera*). Each governor takes a turn to host and chair the meeting. The forum allows the provincial leaders to articulate their views, concerns, and project proposals to the national secretariat. The forum meetings are usually held in preparation for IMT-GT Ministers and the CMGF meetings. At times, the forum's meetings are held in conjunction with other meetings organized by the national secretariat or working groups to maximize the time and minimize the cost of travel to Jakarta.

Secretariat support. Each participating province has appointed a bureau, department, or agency to serve as the provincial secretariat (*Sekretariat Daerah*). For example, the Department of One-Stop Investment and Integrated Services is the secretariat in Aceh, while the Regional Development Planning Agency is the secretariat in South Sumatera.

It has been agreed among the participating IMT-GT provinces and states to establish a regional CMGF secretariat to enhance coordination among them. The regional secretariat would have national counterparts (i.e., CMGF Indonesia) that would correspond to the national secretariats. CMGF Indonesia is in the process of being established.

Projects. Prior to every subregional meeting, the national secretariat convenes a preparatory coordination meeting with relevant line ministries and participating provincial governments. Provincial governments will consult regarding projects and other activities that will affect, or be implemented in, their respective territories. This is also the venue where the provinces present new project proposals.

Most projects proposed at the national coordination meetings are endorsed at the subregional level. In some cases, some of these projects have not been listed in the national development plan and therefore have no planned budget. For example, not all segments of the Trans-Sumatera Railway Project listed in the Implementation Blueprint 2017–2021 have been included in the list of national strategic projects (e.g., the railway segment from Pekanbaru to Jambi). As a result, no budget allocation has been made to implement this railway segment.

Participation by provincial officials in national coordination meetings are often handicapped by the lack of sufficient budget for accommodation and travel to Jakarta. In lieu of face-to-face meetings, social media and digital platforms have been increasingly used since the onset of the COVID-19 pandemic.

Coordination between Government and the Private Sector

IMT-GT was envisaged to be a private sector-led growth area. The importance of private sector involvement in IMT-GT is reflected through the Joint Business Council (JBC), which is an integral part of the IMT-GT institutional mechanism. The JBC is the official voice of the private sector in the IMT-GT subregion. Its role includes (i) fostering closer relationships among business and business organizations in the IMT-GT subregion; (ii) advocating policies, programs, and projects supportive of increasing private sector participation in the development of the region; (iii) identifying IMT-GT commercial projects and key IMT-GT infrastructure requirements; and (iv) promoting linkages with the private sector bodies outside the subregion. The council is invited to participate in meetings of working groups, senior officials, ministers, and the national secretariats to give their views and perspectives on various initiatives. They can also propose and participate in IMT-GT projects.

In terms of economic corridor development, the JBC provides inputs by identifying key commodities with growth potentials, the strategic location for economic centers, and opportunities for business cooperation. The JBC has viewed that IMT-GT's focus on infrastructure should be accompanied by special privileges for businesses operating in the IMT-GT area to encourage more investments. The IMT-GT has agreed to take measures to provide JBC with legal status to strengthen the organization as a regional coordinating body, enhance its policy advocacy role, and enable it to raise funds independently and enter into formal contracts.

Coordination for Economic Corridor Development

There is no regional mechanism or forum to coordinate the development of IMT-GT economic corridors. Economic corridor development is discussed at national coordination meetings convened by the national secretariat. The discussion is limited to national perspectives and is usually focused on specific projects rather than on the broader perspective of cross-border spatial strategies. The fact that only four provinces are part of existing corridors has also limited the scope of discussions. Since the reconfigured economic corridors have included all the provinces in Sumatera, it is envisaged that more strategic and holistic discussions can take place, thus resulting in better coordinated economic corridor initiatives within Sumatera.

Coordination on economic corridor projects can also happen at the bilateral level between a province in Sumatera and a state or province in Malaysia or Thailand. A case in point is when the provincial government of North Sumatera welcomed the visit of the provincial government of Songkhla in September 2019 to discuss the possibility of a direct flight route from Medan to Hat Yai to improve air connectivity in EC1.[95]

Recommendations. To strengthen coordination among the provincial governments, the establishment of CMGF secretariat in Indonesia should be expedited and provided with an operating budget. It is crucial for the CMGF secretariat to have the capacity to perform analytical work, in addition to coordination functions. Analytical work by the secretariat should be the basis for conceptualizing projects with clear and targeted outcomes.

The vetting process should ensure that projects proposed in IMT-GT are aligned with the list of national strategic priorities to ensure the availability of a budget for its implementation.

The national secretariat, working closely with the provincial governments, should organize initiatives outside of the regular coordination meetings to promote greater awareness of economic corridor development in Sumatera among various stakeholders in the provinces. These initiatives should be able to gain momentum once the CMGF secretariat has been formed. Corridor-specific meetings can also be organized to deepen the spatial dimensions of the planning process for corridor development.

---

[95] Communication Office of North Sumatera Province. 2019. *Terima Deputi Gubernur Songkhla Thailand, Wagub Akan Tindaklanjuti Tawaran Kerja Sama Pariwisata.* 5 September. https://biroadpim.sumutprov.go.id/terima-deputi-gubernur-songkhla-thailand-wagub-akan-tindaklanjuti-tawaran-kerja-sama-pariwisata/.

The capacity of the national secretariat for coordinating subregional programs should be enhanced with additional human resources and operating budget. At present, the national secretariat for IMT-GT is also performing the same function for BIMP-EAGA. Both subregional programs require complex coordination work because they involve various stakeholders (line ministries, provincial governments, big investors, small and medium-sized enterprises, state-owned enterprises)—with different and sometimes competing interests. Additional staff for the national secretariat would allow it to have greater focus and effective reach to stakeholders at various levels. While the head of the national secretariat could be the same for both IMT-GT and BIMP-EAGA, each program could have its own dedicated staff support. At present, there are only five staff members serving both programs.

CHAPTER

8

SUMMARY OF FINDINGS
AND RECOMMENDATIONS

This chapter summarizes the key findings and recommendations relevant to Indonesia based on the review conducted in the preceding sections. Map 21 shows the full six IMT-GT economic corridors.

Physical Connectivity

EC1: Maritime connectivity will need to be further developed. Since 2018, there has been no direct maritime connectivity between Belawan and Penang (Malaysia), which indicates that the original objective of the corridor has not been met. However, Belawan has strong port-to-port connections with Port Klang (Selangor in EC2) and Tanjung Pelepas (Johor, in the reconfigured EC4). Moreover, the development of Kuala Tanjung Port as an international hub port with increased capacity to handle bigger cargo volume is envisaged to boost trade with Penang and improve overall maritime connectivity.

EC3: The completion of the Trans-Sumatera Toll Road will need to be accelerated to improve the flow of goods as well as access to ports in EC3, which has been reconfigured to include all eight provinces in Sumatera. Road transport along the eastern Trans-Sumatera Highway and the ongoing Trans-Sumatera Toll Road is currently the dominant transport mode for trade activities between commercial nodes in EC3. Although connectivity among the four EC3 provinces (Aceh, Riau, North Sumatera, and South Sumatera) is adequate, the quality of roads is uneven and there is heavy congestion that can be addressed with the full implementation of the Trans-Sumatera Toll Road.

As external trade expands and value chains develop in Sumatera, railways as an alternative and more efficient mode of transport will become increasingly important and should be given priority. There is no single railway line that connects the provinces in Sumatera, although there is a plan to construct a Trans-Sumatera Railway. There are only partial railway links that facilitate the transport of goods from production centers to the ports.

EC4: The Ro-Ro Ferry Services Project between Sri Junjungan Port and Tanjung Bruas Port needs to be expedited to provide low-cost and faster mode of transporting goods that could benefit small and medium-sized enterprises. This project will significantly reduce transport costs and travel time since lorries from Sumatera will reach Malaysian traders directly through the Ro-Ro service. Regarding land connectivity, there are good roads between Dumai and Pekanbaru with the recent completion of this road segment as part of the Trans-Sumatera Toll Road. There is currently no active railway line in Riau but there are railway projects in the pipeline that would connect Pekanbaru to key points in Sumatera.

EC5: The role of Meulaboh Port on the west coast of Aceh should be further developed as it is the port that trades actively with Thailand. This would address the present gap where no commercial links between Malahayati Port and Ulee Lheue Port with counterpart facilities in Ranong or Phuket. Maritime connectivity is primarily through cruise ships and yachts that call in Sabang and Phuket. Air connectivity between Sumatera and Thailand in EC5 is limited.

EC6: Maritime trade links between Riau Islands and Bangka Belitung Islands with Malaysia are limited and should be developed further, although port-to-port connectivity exists between Riau Islands and Bangka Belitung Islands, as well as between them and the provinces in mainland Sumatera. The maritime links between the two archipelagic island groups and Malaysia will allow Sumatera to benefit from extensive connectivity of the EC6 route, which connects all the IMT-GT corridors into a network. This will be further enabled by the completion of the Trans-Sumatera Toll Road that will traverse all capital cities (Map 21).

Map 21: Six Indonesia–Malaysia–Thailand Growth Triangle Economic Corridors

Southwestern Thailand–Northern Sumatera–Northwestern Malaysia Economic Corridor (Reconfigured EC5)

INDONESIA–MALAYSIA–THAILAND GROWTH TRIANGLE

Southern Thailand–Northern Malaysia–North Sumatera Economic Corridor (Reconfigured EC1)

Andaman Sea–Strait of Malacca Economic Corridor (Reconfigured EC2)

Central Sumatera–Southern Malaysia Economic Corridor (Reconfigured EC4)

Southeastern Thailand–Eastern Malaysia–Southern Sumatera Economic Corridor (EC6)

Trans-Sumatera Economic Corridor (Reconfigured EC3)

Economic Corridor 1 Reconfiguration
Economic Corridor 2 Reconfiguration
Economic Corridor 3 Reconfiguration
Economic Corridor 4 Reconfiguration
Economic Corridor 5 Reconfiguration
Proposed Economic Corridor 6

National Capital
Provincial/State Capital
City/Town
Airport
National Road
Other Road
Provincial Boundary
International Boundary
EC = economic corridor
Boundaries are not necessarily authoritative.

This map was produced by the cartography unit of the Asian Development Bank. The boundaries, colors, denominations, and any other information shown on this map do not imply, on the part of the Asian Development Bank, any judgment on the legal status of any territory, or any endorsement or acceptance of such boundaries, colors, denominations, or information.

Source: Asian Development Bank.

Considering the remote location of the Riau Islands and Bangka Belitung Islands, air connectivity will also need to be further developed. South Sumatera and Lampung have regular direct flights to Malaysia but no direct flights to Southern Thailand.

Resilient Infrastructure

In expanding physical connectivity of economic corridors, the critical nature of infrastructure systems and services would need to be given more emphasis as countries strive for a more resilient and sustainable recovery. Increasingly, infrastructure is being threatened by heavy downpours, extreme heat, and damages are projected to escalate with continued climate change. The IMT-GT would need to take more deliberate steps in climate proofing infrastructure through measures such as elevating road embankments to safeguard against flooding, relocating water intake and treatment facilities away from vulnerable areas, and improving design and maintenance of all infrastructure. Vulnerability is especially critical in the case of cross-border infrastructure where policies and processes can differ widely between two or more countries. Dimensions of resilience runs across the project life-cycle stages, from planning and designing, to construction, operations, and decommissioning. Elements of resilience include the physical aspects, operations, data protection and safety, governance structures, financing, and measures to mitigate risks of failures. Resilience as a process includes measures to anticipate and prevent risks, monitor performance, and mitigate the effects of failures when something goes wrong, allowing rapid recovery. Regional cooperation in infrastructure connectivity for economic corridors can be deepened by taking these dimensions into account.

Trade

EC1: **North Sumatera's declining trade with Malaysia suggests the need for diversification of traded products aligned with the planned development of new ports in Sumatera**. Although Malaysia is an important trading partner of Sumatera, its share of North Sumatera's total trade is relatively small. This trend could be explained by the similarity in the major commodities produced by North Sumatera and Malaysia, rubber and palm oil. The development of Kuala Tanjung Port as the main international hub will provide an opportunity to diversify North Sumatera's exports to Malaysia to include mineral fuel, oil products, chemicals, and fertilizers.

EC3: The development of EC3 should focus not only on land connectivity between provinces in Sumatera, but also in developing transportation systems and links between industrial zones and ports. Since most provinces in Sumatera produce similar products, mainly rubber and palm oil, commodities transported across these provinces either undergo further processing as part of value chains or are directed to gateway ports. A number of provinces in EC3 have their own international ports located in the vicinity of the capital city and SEZs or industrial zones. Land and port bottlenecks in these areas should be addressed as a priority to reduce logistics costs.

EC4: The trade value between Riau and Malaysia has been increasing by an average of 14.6% from 2014–2018, with exports consistently topping imports resulting in a trade balance in favor of Riau. Although export volume is more than twice import levels, its increase has been more moderate at 5.4% compared to imports which grew at an average of 35.9%. Trade with Thailand is less than 1%. **Presently, the provincial government plans to establish an SEZ to boost declining export levels, compared to rapidly increasing imports**. Although Dumai Port is the largest exporter of CPO in Indonesia, there is no SEZ in the province related to the palm oil industry. Under the National Logistics System Blueprint 2012, Dumai Port will be developed as the main port for CPO-based commodities.

EC5: Trade links have not developed in this corridor as originally intended. There are no commercial shipping routes for cargo from Malahayati Port to Phuket and Ranong ports, although Malahayati Port services routes to other international destinations. **Malahayati Port's potential to become a loading port for coffee, processed tuna, halal foods, and other exports to Thailand should be developed because of its proximity to Arun Lhokseumawe SEZ,** which hosts a consortium of companies participating in global value chains. Lhokseumawe Port can be developed in EC3 and linked with EC5. **The potential of the fish industry could also be developed to further promote trade with Thailand** through Meulaboh Port in Aceh which presently trades with provinces in Thailand that are not part of EC5.

EC6: The development of EC6 could further improve the flow of trade from southern Sumatera provinces via Riau Islands as a transit point to Malaysia (through Johor) and Thailand. Southern Sumatera's provinces have stronger trade relations with Malaysia than with Thailand, except for Lampung. Rubber from Jambi and pepper from Bangka Belitung Islands are transshipped through ports in Riau Islands for exports to other countries, including Malaysia, through ports in Johor.

Value Chains

EC1 and EC3 play an important role in the domestic value chain of palm oil, rubber, and coffee in the whole northern Sumatera region, both for the eastern and western coasts. Agriculture and seafood products are the main commodities traded between North Sumatera and Malaysia. However, most activities are still concentrated on the upstream and midstream industries. **Further development of downstream industries, especially palm oil, rubber, mineral fuels, and coffee, should be promoted by optimizing special economic zones and industrial zones in EC3**. This effort needs to be accompanied by measures to incentivize investors in the zone to use energy sources that are more environmentally friendly, as has been started in SEZ Sei Mangkei, North Sumatera.

In EC4, Dumai Port plays a vital role as Indonesia's biggest port for exporting CPO. Some commodities from West Sumatera are also being exported through ports in EC4. Dumai City has a developed oil refinery and palm oil processing industries in the industrial estate areas to produce higher value-added exports for CPO. Although Dumai Port is the largest exporter of CPO in Indonesia, there is no SEZ in the province related to the palm oil industry. **The establishment of SEZ for this purpose, as planned by the provincial government, will be an important catalyst to boost Riau Province's declining export levels, compared to rapidly increasing imports from Malaysia**.

The proposed route for EC6 offers an opportunity to further develop value chain linkages among the EC6 provinces in Sumatera, given the diversity in their product base and comparative advantage. South Sumatera, Bengkulu, Jambi, and Lampung are engaged in upstream activities for rubber, palm oil, and coffee, while Bangka Belitung Islands and Riau Islands are engaged in mineral-based commodities such as mineral fuel, tin, and kaolin. There are plans to develop SEZs (e.g., Galang Batang) and some industrial zones in Riau Islands to become international logistic hubs for Indonesia.

To support the development of value chains in Sumatera for palm oil, rubber and halal foods, the following infrastructure improvements would be needed:

Palm Oil

The ongoing development of SEZ Sei Mangkei in EC1 should be accelerated, including the completion of Tebingtinggi–Kisaran toll road segment, which will connect Sei Mangkei with all provinces in Sumatera via Trans-Sumatera Toll Road. The Sei Mangkei–Kuala Tanjung segment of the Trans-Sumatera Toll Road is crucial as it will facilitate the transport of palm oil downstream products to the designated international hub port of Kuala Tanjung.

The development of toll road segment connecting Palembang–Jambi–Riau–North Sumatera should be prioritized to facilitate palm oil transportation from the four largest palm oil plantations in Sumatera (Riau, North Sumatera, South Sumatera, and Jambi) to the midstream-downstream processing centers and transit points in Dumai and Belawan. The availability of good feeder roads that would connect plantation areas in the hinterlands to toll roads and national highways should be included and prioritized in the regional development plans of concerned provinces in collaboration with palm oil companies. Refineries in the western part of Sumatera (Padang, West Sumatera Province) should consider targeting big export markets across the Indian Ocean (Bangladesh, India, and Pakistan), and road-to-port infrastructure should be improved to make this happen.

Rubber

The remaining issues in the development of the Sei Mangkei SEZ (e.g., land procurement, reliability of electricity, affordability of gas) **would need to be addressed** to realize its full potential in providing a conducive environment for investors in the rubber industry. Tanjung Api-Api SEZ would play an important role in developing midstream and downstream rubber industries to support the production of large quantities of natural rubber in South Sumatera. **Issues pertaining to land use and the risks of land subsidence, as well as the pending construction of the seaport and the planned road from Palembang would need to be resolved expeditiously.** Tanjung Api-Api has been designated as a Rubber City for Indonesia under the IMT-GT framework.

Halal Food

(i) **Some prominent ports along the IMT-GT economic corridors could be designated as halal product gateways, both for export and import.** This will involve improvements required to comply with halal logistics standards which cover warehousing, distribution–transportation, and terminal treatments.

(ii) North Sumatera, West Sumatera, and Aceh are the main producers of fish, vegetables, and fruits but the designated halal industrial zones for halal food processing are in Bintan and Batam in Riau Islands. **Efficient connectivity between the ports of origin and destination ports would need to be considered in planning the development of halal supply chain and logistics services.**

(iii) **EC6 has the potential to serve as the center for downstream halal activities since there will be two designated halal industrial zones in Riau Islands.** This potential could be further strengthened by catering to various halal subsectors—not only food but also modest fashion, cosmetics, and Muslim-friendly travel.

Tourism

There are several opportunities for further developing tourism in economic corridors, which include the following:

In EC1, **air connectivity can be further expanded to enhance robust tourist flows between Medan and Penang**, with popular tourist spots such as Lake Toba that is attracting many tourists from Malaysia.

In EC3, strong reciprocal relations between Sumatera provinces and Malaysia in **leisure, medical, and education tourism should be further expanded**.

In EC4, tourism flows between Riau and Melaka, as well as other states in Malaysia, has been facilitated by both passenger ferry and regular commercial flights. **Riau can take advantage of the special tourism economic zone being planned in Rupat Island, which would link with tourism opportunities in Melaka**. The inclusion of Rupat Island as a new node in EC4 will also help change the direction of Rupat Island's development from being based on extractive and mining industries that damage the ecosystem to a nature-based tourism industry that maintains environmental sustainability.

In EC5, although Thailand's visitors to Aceh were relatively small, there is a growing number of yachts and cruises coming to Sabang from other areas in IMT-GT such as Phuket and Laem Chabang (Thailand), and Langkawi (Malaysia). **Collaboration in cruise tourism being developed between SAPULA should be pursued** to increase the demand for maritime services in the corridor as well as stimulate ancillary economic activities in the three provinces.

In EC6, direct flights (e.g., from Jambi and Bengkulu to Malaysia) and ferry routes along the EC6 routes in Sumatera to Malaysia could further stimulate people's mobility for the purpose of vacation, medical treatment, and education.

Addressing Institutional Gaps in Economic Corridor Development

There are no specific and regular forums at the national and subregional levels dedicated to economic corridor development. Discussions are limited to national perspectives and are usually focused on sector projects rather than on the wider perspective of cross-border spatial strategies. To address this gap, the following practical steps are recommended:

(i) **The national secretariat should organize additional activities outside of regular meetings to promote greater awareness of economic corridor development** in Sumatera involving various stakeholders in the provinces.

(ii) **The establishment of the CMGF secretariat for Indonesia should be expedited and provided with an operating budget**. The CMGF secretariat should be capable of conducting analytical work as a basis for conceptualizing projects with clear and targeted outcomes.

(iii) **Projects proposed at the national level and carried forward for endorsement at the subregional level should be included in the national development plan or the public investment program with a firm budget allocation to ensure that they can be implemented**.

(iv) **Regular meetings of clusters of provinces in a given corridor should be promoted as a venue for planning cross-border initiatives.** These initiatives need not necessarily be in the form of large projects but can focus on improvements in administrative process (trade facilitation) at the border or gateway ports.

(v) **The capacity of the national secretariats should be strengthened** through additional human and financial resources to enable it to effectively manage the coordination of subregional cooperation programs, including subregional economic corridor development.

REFERENCES

Alkalis, G. 2021. *Pemerintah Akan Bangun Infrastruktur Terintegrasi di Provinsi Bengkulu*. https://www.ruangenergi.com/pemerintah-akan-bangun-infrastruktur-terintegrasi-di-provinsi-bengkulu/.

Andriani, E. Ibrahim, D. D. A. Putranto, A. K. Affandy, and H. G. Putra. 2019. Spatial Analysis of Land Subsidence Potential Due to Lowland Conversion (case study at Tanjung Api-Api). *IOP Conference Series: Materials Science and Engineering*. (933). https://iopscience.iop.org/article/10.1088/1757-899X/933/1/012054/pdf.

Antara. 2015. Pelabuhan Bakal Berubah, Investor didatangkan Menhub. 14 October. https://redaksiindonesia.com/read/pelabuhan-bakal-berubah-investor-didatangkan-menhub.html.

Antara News. 2017. Tanjung Api-Api Port to Start Operation in December. 20 May. https://en.antaranews.com/news/111017/tanjung-api-api-port-to-start-operation-in-december.

Aprionis. 2020. Pemprov Babel kembangkan PelabuhanPangkal Balam Bertaraf Internasional. *Antara News*. 13 May. https://www.antaranews.com/berita/1489016/pemprov-babel-kembangkan-pelabuhan-pangkalbalam-bertaraf-internasional.

Aufar, R. M. 2016. *Jadwal Penerbangan Bandara Fatmawati Soekarno -- Bengkulu Juli 2016*. 25 August. https://radityoaufar.blogspot.com/2016/08/jadwal-penerbangan-bandara-fatmawati.html.

Bakri. 2019. Terminal Baru Balohan Mulai Dioperasikan. *Serambinews*. 16 April. https://aceh.tribunnews.com/2019/04/16/terminal-baru-balohan-mulai-dioperasikan.

Bayu. 2018. Pelabuhan Tanjung Pandan Didominasi Pengapalan Komoditi Kaolin. *Maritimnews*. 17 August. http://maritimnews.com/2018/08/pelabuhan-tanjung-pandan-didominasi-pengapalan-komoditi-kaolin/.

BPJPH. *Procedure of Halal Product Certification*. Accessed on 26 September 2020. http://www.halal.go.id/cms/assets/files/WhatsApp_Image_2020-04-06_at_3_38_08_PM.jpeg.

BPS-Statistics Indonesia. 2015a. Statistik Ekspor – Impor Provinsi Kepulauan Bangka Belitung 2014. Pangkalpinang: BPS Provinsi Kepulauan Bangka Belitung.

_____. 2015b. *Statistik Ekspor Provinsi Kepulauan Riau 2014*. Tanjungpinang: BPS Provinsi Kepulauan Riau.

_____. 2015c. *Statistik Perdagangan Luar Negeri Aceh 2014*. Banda Aceh: BPS-Statistics Indonesia.

_____. 2016e. *Statistik Ekspor – Impor Provinsi Kepulauan Bangka Belitung 2015*. Pangkalpinang: BPS Provinsi Kepulauan Bangka Belitung.

_____. 2016f. *Statistik Ekspor Provinsi Kepulauan Riau 2015*. Tanjungpinang: BPS Provinsi Kepulauan Riau.

_____. 2016g. *Statistik Impor Provinsi Kepulauan Riau 2015*. Tanjungpinang: BPS Provinsi Kepulauan Riau.

_____. 2016h. *Statistik Perdagangan Luar Negeri Aceh 2015*. Banda Aceh: BPS-Statistics Indonesia.

_____. 2017a. *Statistik Ekspor – Impor Provinsi Kepulauan Bangka Belitung 2016*. Pangkalpinang: BPS Provinsi Kepulauan Bangka Belitung.

_____. 2017b. *Statistik Ekspor Provinsi Kepulauan Riau 2016*. Tanjungpinang: BPS Provinsi Kepulauan Riau.

_____. 2017c. *Statistik Impor Provinsi Kepulauan Riau 2016*. Tanjungpinang: BPS Provinsi Kepulauan Riau.

_____. 2017d. *Statistik Perdagangan Luar Negeri Aceh 2016*. Banda Aceh: BPS-Statistics Indonesia.

_____. 2018a. *Statistik Ekspor – Impor Provinsi Kepulauan Bangka Belitung 2017*. Pangkalpinang: BPS Provinsi Kepulauan Bangka Belitung.

_____. 2018b. *Statistik Ekspor Provinsi Kepulauan Riau 2017*. Tanjungpinang: BPS Provinsi Kepulauan Riau.

_____. 2018c. *Statistik Impor Provinsi Kepulauan Riau 2017*. Tanjungpinang: BPS Provinsi Kepulauan Riau.

_____. 2018d. *Statistik Kunjungan Wisatawan Mancanegara Provinsi Aceh 2017*. Banda Aceh: BPS-Statistics Indonesia of Aceh Province.

_____. 2018e. *Statistik Perdagangan Luar Negeri Aceh 2017*. Banda Aceh: BPS-Statistics Indonesia.

_____. 2019a. *Agricultural Indicators 2018*. Jakarta: BPS-Statistics Indonesia.

_____. 2019b. *Indikator Ekonomi Provinsi Kepulauan Riau 2019*. Tanjungpinang: BPS Provinsi Kepulauan Riau.

_____. 2019c. *Indonesian Oil Palm Statistics 2018*. Jakarta: BPS-Statistics Indonesia, 2019.

_____. 2019d. *Kepulauan Riau dalam Angka 2019*. Tanjungpinang: BPS Provinsi Kepulauan Riau.

_____. 2019e. *Provinsi Riau dalam Angka 2019*. Pekanbaru: BPS Provinsi Riau.

_____. 2019f. *Statistik Ekspor – Impor Provinsi Kepulauan Bangka Belitung 2018*. Pangkalpinang: BPS Provinsi Kepulauan Bangka Belitung.

_____. 2019g. *Statistik Ekspor Provinsi Kepulauan Riau 2018*. Tanjungpinang: BPS Provinsi Kepulauan Riau.

_____. 2019h. *Statistik Ekspor Provinsi Kepulauan Riau 2018*. Tanjungpinang: BPS Provinsi Kepulauan Riau.

_____. 2019i. *Statistik Impor Provinsi Kepulauan Riau 2018*. Tanjungpinang: BPS Provinsi Kepulauan Riau.

_____. 2019j. *Statistik Kunjungan Wisatawan Mancanegara Provinsi Aceh 2018*. Banda Aceh: BPS-Statistics Indonesia of Aceh Province.

_____. 2019k. *Statistik Perdagangan Luar Negeri Aceh 2018*. Banda Aceh: BPS-Statistics Indonesia.

Burhani. 2007. Jambi Ekspor Kentang 100 Ton ke Malaysia. *Antara News*. 6 January. https://www.antaranews.com/berita/50310/jambi-ekspor-kentang-100-ton-ke-malaysia.

Communication Office of North Sumatera Province. *Terima Deputi Gubernur Songkhla Thailand, Wagub Akan Tindaklanjuti Tawaran Kerja Sama Pariwisata*. Accessed on 30 September 2020. https://www.sumutprov.go.id/artikel/artikel/terima-deputi-gubernur-songkhla-thailand-wagub-akan-tindaklanjuti-tawaran-kerja-sama-pariwisata.

Cornell University. *Islam in Southeast Asia: Country, Area & Regional Profiles/Data 2020*. Accessed on 23 November 2020. https://guides.library.cornell.edu/c.php?g=141521&p=926391.

DinarStandard. 2020. *2020/2021 State of the Global Islamic Economy Report*. https://cdn.salaamgateway.com/reports/pdf/2df5b5106072e6319d06888481e8faf3e3297e09.pdf.

Dinas Penanaman Modal dan Pelayanan Terpadu Satu Pintu Kabupaten Siak. *Kawasan Industri Tanjung Buton*. Accessed on 3 July 2020. https://web.siakkab.go.id/peluang-investasi/.

Dubai International Financial Centre, Thomson Reuters, & DinarStandard. *An Inclusive Ethical Economy: State of the Global Islamic Economy Report 2018/19*. 2018. https://ded.ae/DED_Files/StudiesAndResearch/SGIE-Report-2018-19_Eng_1540649428.pdf.

EU-Indonesia Business Networks. *North Sumatera*. Accessed on 18 October 2021. https://industrialestateindonesia.com/data-province.

Fred, C. 2017. *How do you evaluate a mental revolution? Wicked problems and economic development in Indonesia*. KSI Knowledge Sharing Session. 25 January. https://www.ksi-indonesia.org/file_upload/KSI-Knowledge-Sharing-Session-How-do-you-Evalu-01Feb2017112147.pdf.

GAPKI. 2020. *Kinerja Industri Sawit Indonesia 2019*. Jakarta: GAPKI.

Global Business Guide Indonesia. *Indonesia's Rubber Industry: Increased Competition and Falling Prices*. http://www.gbgindonesia.com/en/agriculture/article/2016/indonesia_s_rubber_industry_increased_competition_and_falling_prices_11520.php.

Government of Siak Regency, Riau. *Pelabuhan Tg. Buton-Siak*. Accessed on 3 July 2020. https://siakkab.go.id/pelabuhan-tg-buton-siak/.

Guina, C. S. 2023. *Integrative Report on the Review and Assessment of the Indonesia–Malaysia–Thailand Growth Triangle Economic Corridors*. Mandaluyong City: Asian Development Bank.

Gunawan, A., 2019. *Perbaikan Jalan Longsor di Pekanbaru-Dumai Diperkirakan 2 Bulan*. 1 October. https://sumatra.bisnis.com/read/20191001/533/1154242/perbaikan-jalan-longsor-di-pekanbaru-dumai-diperkirakan-2-bulan.

Gunawan, A. and M. A. Iswara. 2020. Pelindo to Upgrade Dumai, Belawan Ports to Accommodate Growing CPO Exports. *The Jakarta Post*. 7 February. https://www.thejakartapost.com/news/2020/02/06/pelindo-to-upgrade-dumai-belawan-ports-to-accommodate-growing-cpo-exports.html.

Hadiyatna, D. 2020. Bukit Asam Segera Bangun Pelabuhan Batu Bara Baru. *Antara News*. 18 February. https://www.antaranews.com/berita/1304702/bukit-asam-segera-bangun-pelabuhan-batu-bara-baru.

Haryanti, R. *Ini Tampilan Pelabuhan Sibolga yang Diklaim Terbaik se-Asia Pasifik*. Accessed on 17 December 2019. https://properti.kompas.com/read/2019/03/18/130000421/ini-tampilan-pelabuhan-sibolga-yang-diklaim-terbaik-se-asia-pasifik-.

Hidayati, J. and Hasibuan, S. 2019. Value Chain Analysis and Value Added Enhancement of Indonesia Crude Palm Oil Supply Chain. *International Journal of Advanced Science Engineering Information Technology*. 9(2). pp. 397–404.

Ihsan, M. 2019. *ASDP Tambah Jadwal Penyeberangan Banda Aceh-Sabang*. 6 June. Accessed on 9 October 2019. https://ekonomi.bisnis.com/read/20190606/98/931214/asdp-tambah-jadwal-penyeberangan-banda-aceh-sabang.

Indonesia–Malaysia–Thailand Growth Triangle (IMT-GT). *About IMT-GT*. https://imtgt.org/about-imt-gt/.

_____. *Implementation Blueprint 2012–2016*. Accessed on 11 October 2019. http://imtgt.org/Documents/IMT-GT_Implementation_Blueprint_2012-2016.pdf.

_____. *IMT-GT Vision 2036*. Adopted in Manila. 29 April 2017.

_____. 2018. *Joint Statement of the 24th Ministerial Meeting of Indonesia–Malaysia–Thailand Growth Triangle (IMT-GT)*. 1 October. Melaka, Malaysia. https://subregional.ekon.go.id/wp-content/uploads/2018/12/Joint-Statement-24th-IMT-GT-Ministerial-Meeting.pdf.

Indonesia EximBank Institute. *Analisa Rantai Pasok (Supply Chain) Komoditas Unggulan Ekspor Indonesia: Minyak Sawit*. Accessed on 1 September 2020. http://www.indonesiaeximbank.go.id/research/downloads/13.

_____. *Rubber (Natural)*. https://www.indonesia-investments.com/business/commodities/rubber/item185.

Indonesian Law No.17, 2007 on 2005-2025 National Long-Term Development Plan.

Indonesian Ministry of National Development Planning. 2018. *Indonesia Islamic Economic Masterplan 2019–2024*. Jakarta: Indonesian Ministry of National Development Planning.

Indonesian National Shipowner's Association. 2019. *Pelabuhan Malahayati Layani Angkutan Petikemas Domestik*. 31 January. http://insa.or.id/pelabuhan-malahayati-layani-angkutan-petikemas-domestik/.

International Tin Association. *Global Resources & Reserves: Security of long-term tin supply 2020 Update*. https://www.internationaltin.org/wp-content/uploads/2020/02/Global-Resources-Reserves-2020-Update.pdf.

Isparwati, R. *Jadwal Penerbangan Bandara Lampung dan Rute Kota Tujuan*. https://riniisparwati.com/jadwal-penerbangan-bandara-lampung-dan-rute/.

Karinov. *Daftar 5 Daerah Penghasil Timah Terbesar di Indonesia*. Accessed on 16 December 2020. https://www.sebuahutas.com/2020/12/daftar-5-daerah-penghasil-timah.html.

Kasmono. 2019. *IPC Tanjung Pandan catat ekspor kaolin sebanyak 34.808 ton*. Antara News. 3 December. https://www.antaranews.com/berita/1191216/ipc-tanjung-pandan-catat-ekspor-kaolin-sebanyak-34808-ton.

Komite Percepatan Penyediaan Infrastruktur Prioritas. 2019. *Laporan KPPIP Semester I 2019*. Jakarta: KPPIP.

Lingga, M. Ali. 2019. Hutama Karya Targetkan Tol Pekanbaru-Dumai Beroperasi Awal 2020. *kompas.com*. 5 September. https://money.kompas.com/read/2019/09/05/142900426/hutama-karya-targetkan-tol-pekanbaru-dumai-beroperasi-awal-2020.

Many, N. 2018. Developing the Port of Belawan as a Modern and International Port. *IOP Conference Series Earth and Environmental Science*. 126(1). 012182. March. https://iopscience.iop.org/article/10.1088/1755-1315/126/1/012182, accessed March 2021.

Marini, H. 2019. Bengkulu ekspor komoditi pertanian ke China dan Thailand. *Antara News*. 19 March. https://www.antaranews.com/berita/812546/bengkulu-ekspor-komoditi-pertanian-ke-china-dan-thailand.

Ministry of Agrarian Affairs and Spatial Planning-Republic of Indonesia. 2012. *Empat Kementerian Dorong DPRD Percepat Perda RTRW*. https://tataruang.atrbpn.go.id/Berita/Detail/2752.

Ministry of Agriculture-Republic of Indonesia. 2018. *Tree Crops Estate Statistics of Indonesia 2017-2019*. Jakarta: Directorate General of Estate Crops-Ministry of Agriculture-Republic of Indonesia.

Ministry of Industry. *Direktori Perusahaan Industri*. https://kemenperin.go.id/direktoriperusahaan?what=Karet&prov=0&hal=7.

Ministry of Marine Affairs and Fisheries, Republic of Indonesia. 2017. *Laut Masa Depan Bangsa: Kedaulatan, Keberlanjutan, Kesejahteraan*. Jakarta: Ministry of Marine Affairs and Fisheries, Republic of Indonesia.

_____. 2018. *Marine and Fisheries in Figures 2018*. Jakarta: The Center for Data, Statistics and Information.

Ministry of Public Works and Housing, Republic of Indonesia. 2015. *Konsep dan Arahan Kebijakan Daerah Provinsi dalam Pengembangan Infrastruktur Wilayah Pulau Sumatera*. Jakarta: Ministry of Public Works and Housing, Republic of Indonesia.

Ministry of Tourism and Creative Economy. *Data Kunjungan Wisatawan Mancanegara Bulan Desember Tahun 2018*. https://s3-kemenparekraf.s3.ap-southeast-1.amazonaws.com/media_1564113468_Laporan_Wisman_Bulan_Desember_2018_V_2_-_Klasik_12.pdf.

Mursalin, Y. 2018. Beras Impor Mulai Masuk Lampung 5.500 Ton. *Republika.id*. 16 February. https://www.republika.co.id/berita/ekonomi/makro/18/02/16/p48os5382-beras-impor-mulai-masuk-lampung-5500-ton.

Omed. 2019. Dari Dumai ke Malaka via Laut, Bisa! ini Rute dan Jadwal Kapalnya. *kataomed*. 15 May. https://kataomed.com/jadwal-kapal/dari-dumai-ke-malaka-via-laut-bisa-ini-rute-dan-jadwal-kapalnya.

Parama, M. 2020. Ministry Proposes Five New Toll Road Projects in Strategic Project List. *The Jakarta Post*. 21 October. https://www.thejakartapost.com/news/2020/10/21/ministry-proposes-five-new-toll-road-projects-in-strategic-project-list.html.

Pelindo 1 Cabang Dumai. *Map of CPO Distribution in Riau Province through Dumai Port*. Map.

_____. 2017. *2018, Pelindo I Akan Tingkatkan Kapasitas Pelabuhan Dumai.* https://www.wartaekonomi.co.id/read158458/2018-pelindo-i-akan-tingkatkan-kapasitas-pelabuhan-dumai.

_____. *Pelabuhan Pusat dan Pelabuhan Feedernya di Riau.* Accessed on 5 October 2019. https://pelindo.co.id/port/pelabuhan-dumai.

Pelindo 1 Dumai. *Segmen Usaha / Jasa PT Pelabuhan Indonesia I (Persero) Cabang Dumai.* Accessed on 5 October 2019. https://pelindo.co.id/page/kegiatan-utama.

Pesona Indonesia. *Pelabuhan Sabang, Raksasa Industri Bahari yang Ramah Wisatawan.* https://pesona.travel/keajaiban/2542/pelabuhan-sabang-raksasa-industri-bahari-yang-ramah-wisatawan.

_____. *Pelabuhan Ulee Lheue, Gerbang Laut Keluar Masuk Aceh.* https://pesona.travel/keajaiban/2347/pelabuhan-ulee-lheue-gerbang-laut-keluar-masuk-aceh.

Pratama, R. *ESDM Babel Sebut Ekspor 350 Ton Pasir Zirkon ke Thailand Telah Memiliki Persyaratan Lengkap.* 24 September 2020. https://bangka.tribunnews.com/2020/09/24/esdm-babel-sebut-ekspor-350-ton-pasir-zirkon-ke-thailand-telah-memiliki-persyaratan-lengkap.

Presidential Regulation No. 26/2012 about the Blueprint of Indonesian National Logistic System Development.

PT Semen Andalas Indonesia. 2006. *Summary Environmental Impact Assessment Project Number: 39932-01 Indonesia: Reconstruction of Cement Production Facility in Aceh Project.* Manila: Asian Development Bank. July 2020. https://www.adb.org/sites/default/files/project-document/66600/39932-ino-seia.pdf.

Pusparisa, Y. Produksi Timah Nasional Lampaui Target Pemerintah pada 2019.*Databoks.* https://databoks.katadata.co.id/datapublish/2020/10/20/produksi-timah-nasional-lampaui-target-pemerintah-pada-2019.

Regulation of Riau Province No.9/2018 on the Industrial Development Plan of Riau Province 2018–2038. https://ppid.riau.go.id/download/19/1543366590rpip-gabungan-fix.pdf.

Rubber Journal Asia. *Rubber City to be Developed by Indonesia, Malaysia, Thailand.* http://rubberjournalasia.com/rubber-city-to-be-developed-by-indonesia-malaysia-thailand/.

Sari, Sri Mas. 2019. Ini Perkembangan Transshipment di Pelabuhan Cabang Pelindo II. *Ekonomi.* 18 March. https://ekonomi.bisnis.com/read/20190318/98/901353/ini-perkembangan-transshipment-di-pelabuhan-cabang-pelindo-ii.

_____. 2019. Ini Profil Pelabuhan Penumpang & Kargo Tanjung Balai Asahan. *Ekonomi.* 20 February. https://ekonomi.bisnis.com/read/20190220/98/891335/ini-profil-pelabuhan-penumpang-kargo-tanjung-balai-asahan.

Sazali, A. M., and J. S. Ligte. 2019. The Importance of Halal Logistics Implementation in Indonesia in Compliance with Domestics and Global Halal Market Requirements. *Jurnal Transportasi Multimoda.* 17(2). pp. 17–26.

Sinaga, R., W. P. Humang, and A. Kurniawan. 2018. Potential Cargo Demand of Kuala Tanjung Port as International Hub Port in Western Indonesia. *MATEC Web of Conferences 181.* 09001. https://doi.org/10.1051/matecconf/201818109001 ISTSDC 2017. https://www.matec-conferences.org/articles/matecconf/pdf/2018/40/matecconf_istsdc2017_09001.pdf.

Siregar, S. 2018. Ikan Teri Sibolga tembus pasar Hongkong. *Medan Bisnis Daily.* 3 February. https://www.medanbisnisdaily.com/news/read/2018/02/03/336213/ikan_teri_sibolga_tembus_pasar_hongkong/.

Southern Group. *Loading Port.* https://www.southerngroup-thai.com/loading-port.

Tarver, E. 2021. Value Chain vs. Supply Chain: What's the Difference? *Investopedia.* 2 August. https://www.investopedia.com/ask/answers/043015/what-difference-between-value-chain-and-supply-chain.asp.

Tri, R. 2019. Libur Natal dan Tahun Baru, 2 Lintas Penyeberangan Paling Padat. *Tempo.* 1 December. https://bisnis.tempo.co/read/1278757/libur-natal-dan-tahun-baru-2-lintas-penyeberangan-paling-padat/full&view=ok.

United Nations. Population Division. *World Population Prospects 2019.* https://population.un.org/wpp/Download/Files/1_Indicators%20(Standard)/EXCEL_FILES/1_Population/WPP2019_POP_F01_1_TOTAL_POPULATION_BOTH_SEXES.xlsx.

Utami, T. K. 2020. Kajian Evaluasi Lintas Penyeberangan Merak –Bakauheni. *Warta Penelitian Perhubungan.* 32(1). pp. 43–52. http://dx.doi.org/10.25104/warlit.v32i1.1543.

Widiastuti, T., et al. 2020. Obstacles and Strategies in Developing Halal Industry: Evidence from Indonesia. *Humanities & Social Sciences Reviews.* 8(4). pp. 398–406. https://doi.org/10.18510/hssr.2020.8439.

Widyapratami, H., and B. Bagia. 2018. Achieving Palm Oil Traceability in Indonesia's Complex Supply Chain. *WRI Indonesia.* 6 March. https://wri-indonesia.org/en/blog/achieving-palm-oil-traceability-indonesia%E2%80%99s-complex-supply-chain.

Yahya. 2020. *Data Populasi Penduduk Muslim 2020: Indonesia Terbesar di Dunia. IB Times.* 8 April. https://ibtimes.id/data-populasi-penduduk-muslim-2020-indonesia-terbesar-di-dunia/.

7Saudara. *Inilah Jadwal dan Harga Tiket Kapal Cepat dan Kapal Lambat Banda Aceh – Sabang.* https://www.7saudara.com/inilah-jadwal-dan-harga-tiket-kapal-cepat-dan-kapal-lambat-banda-aceh-sabang/.

APPENDIXES

Appendix 1

Physical Connectivity Projects of the IMT-GT Implementation Blueprint 2017–2021

Table A1.1: Economic Corridor 1

No.	Project Name	Description	Estimated Cost ($ million)	Source of Funding	Progress
1	Tebingtinggi–Prapat–Kuala Tanjung Toll Road (2017)	The project is part of the proposed road improvement to support the Kuala Tanjung special economic zone and promote Toba Lake as a tourism destination in South Sumatera. Length: 143 km	451.12	National government and/or public–private partnership (PPP)	Expected year of operation: extended (from 2017) to 2020.

As of end-November 2019, the construction has started in two sections: (i) Tebingtinggi–Indrapura (land acquisition 76%, construction 37%); and (ii) Kuala Tanjung Indrapura (land acquisition 9%, construction 6%). |
| 2 | Kuala Tanjung Development Port, South Sumatera (2020) | Part of national strategic projects in South Sumatera to support the special industry zone of the Kuala Tanjung project | 33.76 | National government | Multipurpose terminal has been operational since February 2019.

Government of Batu Bara Regency has proposed the next master plan to develop an industrial zone in Kuala Tanjung. |
| 3 | Belawan Port (2019) | Part of Sumatera port development project carried over from IB 2012–2016 | 104.75 | National government | Completed in 2019, expanding capacity of container terminal up to 2 million TEUs a year. |
| 4 | Sei Mangkei Special Economic Zone (2020) | Part of national strategic projects in South Sumatera. The main purpose is to support the palm oil and rubber industries, increase tourism, and develop logistics services | 383.45 | National government | As of the end of 2019, investment commitment reached Rp11.2 trillion (equivalent to $800 million) from 11 industries. |

IB = Implementation Blueprint, km = kilometer, No. = number, TEU = twenty-foot equivalent unit.
Source: Study team.

Table A1.2: Economic Corridor 3

No.	Project Name	Description	Estimated Cost ($ million)	Source of Funding	Progress
1	Sumatera Toll Road Project (eight corridors Trans-Sumatera projects) (2021)	Trans-Sumatera toll road improvement and construction projects. There are eight sections from Aceh to Lampung Province.	6,273.00	National government	Completed and operationalized the following sections in October 2020: (i) Medan–Binjai (sections 2 and 3) (ii) Bakauheni–Terbanggi Besar (iv) Pekanbaru–Dumai (v) Terbanggi Besar–Pematang Panggang (vi) Pematang panggang–Kayu Agung (vii) Sigli–Banda Aceh (section 4)
2	Trans-Sumatera Railway Project (2021)	The project involves new sections along Aceh to Lampung.	819.54	National government	Based on *Peraturan Presiden No. 56/2018*, the sections listed in the revised national strategic projects are: (i) Prabumulih–Kertapati (South Sumatera) (ii) Tebingtinggi–Kuala Tanjung (North Sumatera) (iii) Rantau Prapat– Duri–Pekanbaru (North Sumatera–Riau)
3	Balinka–Matur–Ngarai Sianok Tunnel Construction (2019)	The project is listed in Indonesia's Blue Book 2015–2019;[a] The output of the project includes tunnels, bridges, and roads that will connect Balinka–Matur–Ngarai Sianok along approximately 5 kilometers (km). The project is located in West Sumatera.	183.75	National government	The project is not listed as a national strategic project because of difficulties in land acquisition.
4	Light Rail Transit (LRT)–South Sumatera (2018)	The project involves connecting the airport of Sultan Mahmud Badaruddin II Metro City Palembang and Jakabaring sport center. The project aims to support the Asian Games 2018, held in South Sumatera.	937.73	National government	Completed and operationalized in 2018.

continued on next page

Table A1.2 continued

No.	Project Name	Description	Estimated Cost ($ million)	Source of Funding	Progress
5	Develop of HAS Hanandjoedin, Tanjung Pandan	Part of national strategic projects in Bangka Belitung. The project aims to support tourism destinations in Bangka Belitung. The airport is proposed to be the international airport in Bangka Belitung province.	58.73	National government	This project has been excluded from the revised list of national strategic projects in 2018.
6	National Urban Development Project (2019)	The project is listed in Indonesia's Bluebook 2015–2019. The project aims to support and develop urban infrastructure in order to realize livable, green and smart cities. The project is basically planned for nationwide implementation but the base is located in South Sumatera and North Sumatera.	250.00	National government	Information on status is not available.
7	Tanjung Api-Api Special Economic Zone	Part of national strategic projects in South Sumatera. The project will support the palm oil and rubber industries.	946.15	National government	In August 2019, the special economic zone (SEZ) National Council approved the proposal from the Governor of South Sumatera to integrate 67 hectares of Tanjung Api-Api SEZ land and 2,170 hectares of PT Tri Patria Abadi land. The SEZ has not been operational.
8	Tanjung Kelayang Special Economic Zone, Bangka Belitung Province	Listed in the national strategic projects in Bangka Belitung Province. The main purpose is to support tourism in Bangka Belitung.	112.78	National government	Two investors have committed to invest the total amount of Rp839 billion ($59.93 million). The Sheraton Belitung Resort was completed in September 2020.

HAS = Haji Ahmad Sanusi, No. = number.
[a] The Blue Book is a medium-term (five-year) plan document containing the list of projects planned for external loans published by the Government of Indonesia.
Source: Study team.

Table A1.3: Economic Corridor 4

No.	Project Name	Description	Estimated Cost ($ million)	Source of Funding	Progress
1	Pekanbaru - Padang Toll Road construction (2024)	The project is part of the toll road improvement projects in Sumatera with a length of 240 km. Target completion year is 2024.	3,609.00	National government	As of October 2020: (i) Padang–Sicincin section —26% in construction and 8% in land acquisition. (ii) Pekanbaru–Bangkinang: 46% in construction and 3% in land acquisition.
2	Melaka–Dumai Economic Corridor Multimodal Transport Project (2020)	The project was carried over from Implementation Blueprint 2012–2016 to develop and reconstruct Dumai Port and Pekanbaru–Dumai Road	875.2	National government	Pekanbaru–Dumai toll road has been operational since September 2020. The development of the Ro-Ro ferry from Sri Junjungan Port in Dumai to Tanjung Bruas Port in Melaka has not yet been operationalized as of year-end 2020.

km = kilometer; No. = number; Ro-Ro = roll on, roll off.
Source: Study team.

Table A1.4: Economic Corridor 5

No.	Project Name	Description	Estimated Cost ($ million)	Source of Funding	Progress
1	Sumatera Toll Road Project	Trans-Sumatera Toll Road improvement project has eight sections along Aceh to Lampung Province	6,273.00	National government	As of October 2020, the Sigli–Banda Aceh section has been completed and operationalized.

Note: All projects (except projects no 3 and 6) above have been listed as national strategic project based on *Peraturan Presiden No. 3 Tahun 2016 tentang Percepatan pelaksanaan Proyek Strategies Nasional* (Presidential Decree No. 3/2016 on the Acceleration of National Strategic Projects).
Source: Study team.

Appendix 2

Ministries and Agencies Involved During the Country Consultations

A. Ministries and Agencies Met During the Fieldwork Conducted by the Study Team on 21–26 October 2019 and 3–7 December 2019

- Coordinating Ministry of Economic Affairs, Republic of Indonesia
- Regional Development Planning Agency of Riau Islands Province
- Transport Office of Riau Islands Province
- Trade Office of Riau Islands Province
- Tourism Office of Riau Islands Province
- Chamber of Commerce in Riau Islands
- Regional Development Planning Agency of South Sumatera Province
- Transport Office of South Sumatera Province
- Trade Office of South Sumatera Province
- Tourism Office of South Sumatera Province
- Chamber of Commerce in South Sumatera
- Economic Development Bureau of Bangka Belitung Islands Province
- Transport Office of Bangka Belitung Islands Province
- Trade Office of Bangka Belitung Islands Province
- Tourism Office of Bangka Belitung Islands Province
- Chamber of Commerce in Bangka Belitung Islands
- Management Agency of Tanjung Kelayang Special Economic Zone
- Regional Development Planning Agency of Riau Province
- Transport Office of Riau Province
- Trade Office of Riau Province
- Tourism Office of Riau Province
- Chamber of Commerce in Riau
- PT Pelindo 1 at Dumai Port
- Economic Bureau of North Sumatera Province
- Transport Office of North Sumatera Province
- Trade Office of North Sumatera Province

- Tourism Office of North Sumatera Province
- Chamber of Commerce in North Sumatera
- PT Pelindo 1 at Belawan Port
- PT ASDP Indonesia Ferry at Ulee Lheue Port
- Regional Development Planning Agency of Aceh Province
- Transport Office of Aceh Province
- Trade Office of Aceh Province
- Tourism Office of Aceh Province
- Chamber of Commerce in Aceh
- PT Pelindo 1 at Malahayati Port.
- Sabang Management and Development Agency (*Badan Pengusahaan Kawasan Sabang*-BPKS)

B. Ministries and Agencies that Participated During Various Consultation Meetings by the National Consultant with the National Secretariat

- Ministry of Transportation
- Ministry of Trade
- Ministry of Foreign Affairs
- Ministry of Tourism and Creative Economy
- National Border Management Agency
- National Council for Special Economic Zones
- Government of Aceh Province
- Government of North Sumatera Province
- Government of West Sumatera Province
- Government of Riau Province
- Government of Jambi Province
- Government of South Sumatera Province
- Government of Bengkulu Province
- Government of Lampung Province
- Government of Riau Islands Province
- Government of Bangka Belitung Islands Province